Hawthorne's Influence on Dickens and George Eliot

**THE UNIVERSITY OF QUEENSLAND PRESS
SCHOLARS' LIBRARY**

Hawthorne's Influence on Dickens and George Eliot

EDWARD STOKES

University of Queensland Press

ST LUCIA • LONDON • NEW YORK

First published 1985 by University of Queensland Press
Box 42, St Lucia, Queensland, Australia

Typeset by University of Queensland Press
Printed in Australia by Dominion Press—Hedges & Bell

Distributed in the USA and Canada by University of Queensland Press,
5 South Union Street, Lawrence, Mass. 01843 USA

Cataloguing in Publication Data

National Library of Australia

Stokes, Edward, 1922-   .
   Hawthorne's influence on Dickens and George Eliot.

   Bibliography.
   Includes index.

   1. Hawthorne, Nathaniel, 1804–1864 — Influence —
Dickens. 2. Hawthorne, Nathaniel, 1804–1864 —
Influence — Eliot. 3. Dickens, Charles, 1812–1870 —
Criticism and interpretation. 4. Eliot, George,
1819–1880 — Criticism and interpretation. I. Title.
(Series: University of Queensland Press scholars'
library).

823'.8

Library of Congress

Stokes, Edward, M.A.
   Hawthorne's influence on Dickens and George Eliot.

   (University of Queensland Press scholars' library)
   Bibliography: p.
   Includes index.

   1. English fiction — 19th century — History and criticism.
2. English fiction — American influences.
3 Hawthorne, Nathaniel, 1804–1864 — Influence.
4. Dickens, Charles, 1812–1870 — Criticism and interpretation.
5. Eliot, George, 1819–1880 — Criticism and interpretation.
I. Title. II. Series.
PR875.S7   1985   823'.8   84-3509

ISBN 0 7022 1689 5

Contents

Publisher's Note

This book is in a series designed by the University of Queensland Press to make reference and specialist works available. Titles in the series normally will not be stocked by booksellers and may be obtained by writing directly to the publisher.

Acknowledgments

Acknowledgments are due to the following publishers for permission to quote copyright material from the books named:

Chatto and Windus Ltd for *Dickens the Novelist*, by F.R. and Q.D. Leavis; Chatto and Windus Ltd and the Author's Literary Estate for *The Great Tradition* and *Anna Karenina and Other Essays*, by F.R. Leavis; Routledge and Kegan Paul for *Essays of George Eliot*, edited by Thomas Pinney; Cambridge University Press for *George Eliot*, by R.T. Jones; Oxford University Press for *The Hero in Eclipse*, by Mario Praz, translated by Angus Davidson; University of California Press for *The Metaphysical Novel in England and America*, by Edwin M. Eigner; Harvard University Press for *Hawthorne: A Critical Study*, by H.H. Waggoner; Princeton University Press for *Anatomy of Criticism: Four Essays*, by Northrop Frye; Yale University Press for *The George Eliot Letters*, Volumes II, III, IV and V, edited by Gordon S. Haight.

I gratefully record my indebtedness to the following authors and journals: Ghulam Ali Chaudhry, "Dickens and Hawthorne", *Essex Institute Historical Collections* (1964); Edward M. Passerini, "Hawthornesque Dickens", *Dickens Studies* (1966); William Axton, "Esther's Nicknames: a Study in Relevance", *The Dickensian* (1966); Curtis Dahl, "When the Deity Returns: *The Marble Faun* and *Romola*", *Papers on Language and Literature*, Southern Illinois University (1969); Jonathan R. Quick, "*Silas Marner* as Romance: The Example of Hawthorne", *Nineteenth Century Fiction* (1974).

Two unpublished theses were, for different reasons, of special interest and value to me. Ellin Jane Ringler's "The Problem of Evil: a Correlative Study in the Novels of Nathaniel Hawthorne and George Eliot" (University of Illinois, 1967), though not concerned with questions of influence, is the most thorough comparative treatment of the work of Hawthorne and George Eliot; I have quoted extensively from it in the second part of this book. I have quoted only one passage from Harry Lionel Knight's "Dickens and American Literature" (Brown University, 1974); that passage, from a chapter on Dickens and Hawthorne, raises a question which no one had previously asked, and to which the first part of this book gives a convinced (and, hopefully, convincing) positive answer: "Could not Hawthorne's work have had some role in the transition from early to late Dickens?"

General Introduction

The study of literary influence is at once one of the least-regarded and one of the most hazardously speculative varieties of literary scholarship. That it is a totally out-dated and thoroughly futile activity is assumed, for example, by one of the finest of American critics of the novel, Albert Guerard, in the opening paragraph of the monumental study of Dickens, Dostoevsky and Faulkner, which he added to his earlier separate studies of Hardy, Conrad and Gide. Guerard, in stating that his primary aim is "to throw some new light on three great novelists whose continuing 'presence' has affected . . . innumerable other writers" insists that "the new light should come from discerning kinships and affinities among writers from radically different cultures and . . . moments in the history of the novel. Kinship not influence. . . . American scholarship has not so long since freed itself from the good part of a century's obsessions with influence, and I have no desire to revive the academic dead. . . . The fact of influence teaches us almost nothing."[1]

That it is a highly risky business is suggested, for example, by the eminent Dickens scholar, George H. Ford, who remarked in *Dickens and his Readers*: "It has been said that the real danger in research is that unless we are very careful we always find what we are seeking."[2] With specific reference to the novel Ford commented that "with a novel (unlike a poem) the study of influence seems to be an elaborate exercise in walking upon eggs";[3] with a change of metaphor, Ford refrained from attempting to assess the indebtedness of various twentieth-century novelists to Dickens, because "it would take a critical Geiger counter of infinite delicacy to detect the Dickens element and to isolate it from other compounds under the surface of their writings."[4]

Why, then, devote a substantial part of one's life to such a difficult, dangerous, old-fashioned and pointless activity as trying to demonstrate the influence of Hawthorne on Dickens and George Eliot?

First, as to the difficulty of this particular enterprise: fortunately, an instrument of "infinite delicacy" is not needed in investigating the influence of a writer on his contemporaries, even his trans-Atlantic contemporaries, especially if, outside their novels, they expressed their admiration of his work (as both Dickens and George Eliot did of Hawthorne's). What is needed is patience, attentiveness and a reasonably retentive memory.

Secondly, as to the danger: to whatever degree I may have become guilty of the charge of finding what I was seeking, I can at least plead original innocence. I was not looking for anything, when one day in 1967, I happened to be re-reading part of *Bleak House* (for about the sixth time) the day after I had re-read *The Scarlet Letter* (for at least the tenth), and was startled by certain similarities never noticed by anyone before, but which, once noticed, seemed too striking to be mere coincidence — especially as Dickens' novel had been written so soon after Hawthorne's. I was not aware, at the time, of any external evidence that Dickens had indeed read *The Scarlet Letter*: it was with more than relief that I found the relevant letter in Forster's biography.

Third, as to the point or pointlessness of the investigation which I then undertook. I mention the date of my first shock of recognition because at the time there was still a strong tendency, especially among American critics, to regard English and American fiction as two distinct and separate genres — the novel and the romance. For some critics this division had become almost an article of faith. Most notably, Richard Chase's brilliant and influential book, *The American Novel and Its Tradition*,[5] was virtually based on two main assumptions. As re-stated by a later critic, Nicolaus Mills, these were:

First, American writers, in contrast to English writers, have not used social observation to achieve their profoundest effects but have sought a reality tangential to society. Second, in subject matter and presentation the American romance, unlike the English novel, is not bound by the ordinary and veers towards myth, allegory and symbolism.[6]

In making the distinction between novel and romance, Chase was, of course, drawing on a tradition that goes back at least as far as Clara Reeve's book *The Progress of Romance*, published in 1785 (four years before the first American novel). The difference between the two genres had recently been given one of its most authoritative statements by Northrop Frye.

> The essential difference between novel and romance lies in the conception of character. The romancer does not attempt to create 'real people' so much as stylized figures which expand into psychological archetypes. It is in the romance that we find Jung's libido, anima and shadow reflected in the hero, heroine and villain respectively. That is why the romance so often radiates a glow of subjective intensity that the novel lacks, and why a suggestion of allegory is constantly creeping in around its fringes. Certain elements of character are released in the romance which make it naturally a more revolutionary form than the novel. The novelist deals with personality, with characters wearing their *personae* or social masks . . . The romancer deals with individuality, with characters *in vacuo* idealized by revery. . . .

Frye, however, made an important qualification: " 'Pure' examples of either form are never found; there is hardly any modern romance that could not be made out to be a novel, and vice versa. The forms of prose fiction are mixed, like racial strains in human beings, not separable like the sexes."[7]

This warning (neatly restated by Gillian Beer in her little book, *The Romance*: "All fiction contains two primary impulses: the impulse to imitate daily life, and the impulse to transcend it")[8] Chase virtually ignored in setting up his dichotomy of English novel and American romance. One may have been ready to agree that American writers like Hawthorne and Melville did not use social observation to achieve their *profoundest* effects, while still maintaining that at least in Hawthorne's "romances" of contemporary American life, *The House of the Seven Gables* and *The Blithedale Romance*, social observation is an important element. One had to agree that nineteenth-century American fiction did veer towards myth, allegory and symbolism, but one also had to protest that it veered in this direction *more than*, rather than *unlike* nineteenth-century English fiction. Perhaps Thackeray and Trollope and Elizabeth Gaskell were "bound by the ordinary", but surely hardly anyone else? Leaving aside a novel like *Wuthering Heights*, which F.R. Leavis had to regard as a "sport", a kind of freak, because it did not conform to the requirements of his "great tradition";[9] leaving aside the later Hardy, who has been claimed as a displaced American by at least one critic[10] — at least the later novels of the two greatest Victorian novelists, Dickens and George Eliot, one demurred, also "veered towards myth, allegory and symbolism."

I must admit, however, that until I made the chance discovery of Dickens' (probably quite unconscious) reliance on Hawthorne in the Lady Dedlock — Esther Summerson strand of *Bleak House*, I did not suspect that one important reason that English novelists from 1850 on did not commit themselves more fully that they did to realism, to social documentation, to the ordinary and the probable, to the imitation of daily life, was simply the example and influence of Hawthorne. That, however, is what I came more and more strongly to believe as I read and re-read Dickens and George Eliot — particularly the latter. In the case of Dickens, who was never much attracted by realism, I became more and more convinced that the generally recognized developments in his work from *Break House* onward (the more disciplined form articulating dominant themes, the use of symbolism to amplify and qualify the narrative level, the preoccupation with solitude and alienation) owed at least a little to Hawthorne.

If these two essays, in establishing the *fact* of Hawthorne's influence on Dickens and George Eliot, cause anyone to share these convictions, I hope they will be judged as "teaching" a little more than "almost nothing".

Part I

Hawthorne and Dickens

It is my belief, and my contention, that the tales and romances of Hawthorne had some influence on the later work of Dickens. Since, given the obvious differences between the two writers, the proposition may appear startling or even absurd, it seems desirable first to review their careers, if only to demonstrate that a Hawthorne influence on Dickens is chronologically possible.

Introduction

Hawthorne, born in July 1804, was almost eight years older than Dickens, born in February 1812. Hawthorne's first novel, *Fanshawe*, was privately published in 1828 (and immediately withdrawn by the author, and not republished until after his death), when Dickens was still an office-boy in a legal office in London, teaching himself shorthand to qualify for newspaper reporting. But by the time Hawthorne's next, and his first acknowledged, volume, *Twice Told Tales* (which collected eighteen of the stories and sketches published during the previous decade) appeared in 1837, Dickens had published *Sketches by Boz* in 1836, and most instalments of *The Posthumous Papers of the Pickwick Club* had appeared, rocketing their young author to fame. Before the second, augmented edition of *Twice Told Tales* (containing thirty-nine stories) appeared in 1842, Dickens had published *Pickwick Papers* (1837), *Oliver Twist* (1838), *Nicholas Nickleby* (1839), *The Old Curiosity Shop* (1841) and *Barnaby Rudge* (1841); and before Hawthorne's next collection, *Mosses from an Old Manse*, appeared in 1846, Dickens had added *Martin Chuzzlewit* (1844), and the first three Christmas books, *A Christmas Carol* (1843), *The Chimes* (1844), and *The Cricket on the Hearth* (1845). The last two Christmas books, *The Battle of Life* and *The Haunted Man*, appeared in 1846 and 1848; and also in the latter year, after the longest gap so far between full-length novels, *Dombey and Son*.

By the middle of the century, then, Hawthorne, in his mid-forties, had produced only three volumes of short stories (a total of sixty-two), and a suppressed romance, while Dickens, not yet forty, had produced seven full-length novels and a volume of sketches, and the five Christmas books.

It was only during the next few years that Hawthorne exceeded Dickens in productiveness. Three of Hawthorne's four novels, or romances, followed one another in successive years — *The Scarlet Letter* in 1850, *The House of the Seven Gables* in 1851, and *The Blithedale Romance* in 1852. During this period Dickens published only *David Copperfield* in 1850.

But in the eight years between *The Blithedale Romance* and Hawthorne's final completed work of fiction, *The Marble Faun* (1860), Dickens wrote four novels — *Bleak House* (1853), *Hard Times* (1854), *Little Dorrit* (1857) and *A Tale of Two Cities* (1859). *Great Expectations* followed in 1861, and the first number of Dickens' last completed novel, *Our Mutual Friend*, in the month of Hawthorne's death, May 1864.

Evidence of Hawthorne's Knowledge of Dickens' Work

Hawthorne's output of only four completed novels (and *Fanshawe*, which he disowned) and the various unfinished, posthumously published romances — *Septimius Felton*, *The Ancestral Footstep*, *The Dolliver Romance* and *Dr Grimshawe's Secret* — is meagre beside Dickens' fourteen (and the unfinished *Edwin Drood*). On the face of it, it would seem more likely that Dickens, who achieved world renown during the years when Hawthorne, according to his famous assertion in 1851 (in the preface to the revised edition of *Twice Told Tales*), was "the obscurest man of letters in America", should have influenced Hawthorne than vice versa. Dickens may indeed have influenced Hawthorne; there is, at least, no question that Hawthorne knew and admired Dickens' work, at least up to and including *David Copperfield*.

The earliest evidence of Hawthorne's knowledge of Dickens' work is found in "A Virtuoso's Collection", originally published in the *Boston Miscellany of Literature and Fashion* (and collected in *Mosses from an Old Manse*, vol. 2). The narrator in this sketch asks his conductor, the Virtuoso, whether the raven displayed in his museum is " 'the same that fed Elijah in the wilderness' " and is informed that " 'it is a bird of modern date. He belonged to Barnaby Rudge; and many people fancied that the devil himself was distinguished under his sable plumage. But poor Grip has drawn his last cork, and has been forced to "say die" at last.' " Later, when the Virtuoso has displayed many articles associated with royalty, the narrator tells him: " 'If you could show me the straw hat of sweet little Nell I would far rather see it than a King's golden crown.' " Ghulam Ali Chaudhry, in his essay, "Dickens and Hawthorne", has pointed out that "Hawthorne made [this] complimentary reference to Dickens's latest books at a time when he was in America. Perhaps it was a gesture of good will to a visiting author."[1]

The only other reference to Dickens' work in Hawthorne's fiction that I have found (and the only one mentioned by Ghulam Ali Chaudhry) is in "P's Correspondence", (and also included in *Mosses from an Old Manse*, vol. 2). In this odd sketch, Dickens is described as a writer "very rich in humour, and not without symptoms of genuine pathos", who unfortunately died, after publishing only a few instalments of *The Pickwick Papers*.

While Hawthorne was working as surveyor in the Salem custom house from 1846 to 1849, and (according to "The Custom House", which serves as introduction to *The Scarlet Letter*) unable to write, he read a good deal of contemporary fiction, and Dickens was one of his favourite authors for reading aloud to the family circle. *David Copperfield*, soon after it was published, was among the books read. Later, in England, he read *Dombey and Son*.[2]

There are several references in Hawthorne's *English Notebooks* (1941), not to Dickens as writer, but to Dickens the man, who obviously fascinated Hawthorne.[3] But, even though his last comment, on July 10 1856, read: "There is a great variety of testimony, various and variant, as to the character of Dickens. I must see him before I finally leave England",[4] there is no evidence that the two novelists ever did meet.[5] Nor does there seem to be any recorded comment by Hawthorne on any of Dickens' work after *David Copperfield*.

In 1851 Hawthorne made a comparison between his own work and that of Dickens and other English novelists. When he was asked to contribute a serial to the Boston *Museum*, he replied:

In all my stories, I think, there is one idea running through them like an iron rod, and to which all other ideas are referred and subordinate; and the circumstance gives the narrative a character of monotony; which, possibly, may strengthen the impression which it makes, if read off at once, but would become intolerably wearisome, if dragged slowly before the reader, through a term of weeks or months. The serial productions of Dickens, Thackeray and others, are distinguished by a great variety of scenes and multiplicity of character[s], and the story is carried on through many threads of interest; and it appears to me that these characteristics are essential to the success of works so published. In short I am afraid to comply with your proposition.[6]

Fifty years later, it is worth mentioning, William Dean Howells referred, in very different terms, to this contrast between the unity and "monotony" of Hawthorne's work, and the "variety" and "multiplicity" of Dickens':

But when it came, the American fiction which owed nothing to English models differed from English fiction in nothing so much as its greater refinement, and its delicate perfection of form. While Dickens was writing in England, Hawthorne was writing in America; and for all the ostensible reasons the romances of Hawthorne ought to have been rude, shapeless, provisional, the novels of Dickens ought to have been fastidiously elect in method and material and of the last scrupulosity in literary finish. . . . But there were some facts which such hasty conclusions must have ignored; chiefly the fact that the first impulse of a new artistic life is to escape from crude conditions.[7]

A few years later again, W.R. Thayer made a similar comment: "Among all the master novelists of the nineteenth century [Hawthorne] and Turgeneff alone can be compared to the Greeks for the beauty, symmetry, compactness and finish of their work. *The Scarlet Letter* is a small volume — how small when you put it beside *Les Miserables* or *David Copperfield* or *Vanity Fair* — but it is complete. It has nothing superfluous; it lacks nothing."[8]

It is worth emphasizing, however, that, when Hawthorne made this comparison, he had himself written only the tales and *The Scarlet Letter*, and that he was referring to Dickens' novels up to *David Copperfield*. In his later romances he deliberately aimed at greater variety and expansiveness, while Dickens, conversely, sought for greater unity and shapeliness. One wonders whether Hawthorne found (if he read Dickens' later novels) such a complete structural contrast between *The House of the Seven Gables* and *Hard Times* as between *The Scarlet Letter* and *Martin Chuzzlewit*. Be that as it may, Hawthorne's recorded comments on Dickens show an admiring interest, coupled with an awareness of their differences in concerns and methods which seems to make any substantial indebtedness on Hawthorne's part unlikely. But even if some indebtedness on Hawthorne's part was established (and I do not discount the possibility of some connection, for example, between *Dombey and Son* and *The House of the Seven Gables*, even though there is no definite evidence that Hawthorne read Dickens' novel until five years after his own was published), I would at least maintain that there was a two-way trans-Atlantic traffic between them.[9]

Evidence of Dickens' Knowledge of Hawthorne's Work

If Hawthorne knew and admired Dickens' work, the interest and admiration were reciprocated. Dickens' recorded references to Hawthorne's work are more scanty than Hawthorne's to his, but one of them suggests at least an equal enthusiasm. John Forster records that: "In Mr Hawthorne's earlier books he had taken especial pleasure; his *Mosses from an Old Manse* having been the first book he placed in my hands on his return from America, with reiterated injunctions to read it."[10] As Ghulam Ali Chaudhry remarks, "Forster seems to have erred here and confused *Mosses*, first published in 1846, with *Twice Told Tales*, appearing in a second enlarged edition in 1842."[11] (Dickens was in Boston just after the book was published there.) It is tempting to speculate that Forster made this mistake because Dickens importuned him to read the two collections on different occasions some years apart.

But if this is only speculation, a passage from a letter to (and quoted by) Forster, apparently written in July 1851, shows that Dickens certainly did read *The Scarlet Letter* within a year or so of its publication. His verdict, however, was almost entirely unfavourable: "I finished the Scarlet Letter yesterday. It falls off sadly after that fine opening scene. The psychological part of the story is very much overdone, and not truly done I think. Their suddenness of meeting and agreeing to go away together, after all these years is very poor. Mr Chillingworth ditto. The child out of nature altogether. And Mr Dimmisdale [sic] certainly never could have begotten her."[12] There is no further mention of

Hawthorne or his work in Forster's *Life*. But Forster, in quoting the comment on *The Scarlet Letter*, remarks that there was never much notice of his reading in Dickens' letters; and in view of Dickens' interest in Hawthorne's earlier work, it seems extremely likely that he would have read at least *The House of the Seven Gables*, which appeared about the time he was reading *The Scarlet Letter*.

Nothing that Dickens wrote about *The Scarlet Letter*, and nothing that Forster reports him as saying about *Mosses* (or *Twice Told Tales*?) can be construed as any kind of admission of indebtedness on Dickens' part. But for the moment I want to underline one point. Everyone agrees that there was a distinct change in Dickens' work about the middle of the century; *Bleak House*, which is usually regarded as marking the beginning of Dickens' "major phase" was begun in March 1852. In the two preceding years Hawthorne published *The Scarlet Letter* and *The House of the Seven Gables*, of which at least the first was certainly read by Dickens. All sorts of reasons have been advanced for the changes in Dickens' work; I don't think that anyone has previously suggested that the example of Hawthorne may have played a modest part.[13]

Critical Comparisons of Hawthorne and Dickens, 1842–1910

When I became convinced of connections between the work of Dickens and Hawthorne, I was curious to find whether any critics during the lifetime of the two novelists, and in the following decades, had preceded me in this belief. In quest of allies I have examined almost every item (reviews, articles, chapters, books on Hawthorne) listed by Nina E. Browne[14] and by Bertha Faust,[15] as well as most of the books and many of the articles on Dickens written in the nineteenth century. It was something of a disappointment to find no cross-references in the work of prominent critics (like E.P. Whipple and W.C. Brownell in America, R.H. Hutton and Leslie Stephen in England) who wrote at length on both novelists; and, indeed, to find only one single brief suggestion of a possible Hawthorne influence on Dickens. On the other hand it was something of a surprise to discover how often the name of Dickens was introduced into criticism of Hawthorne — sometimes to point out similarities between them; sometimes to emphasize differences; sometimes to assert the superiority of one or the other.

Comparisons began at least as early as the publication of the second edition of *Twice Told Tales* in 1842. The very earliest of them, indeed, is the only nineteenth-century comment I have found which suggests the possibility of Dickens' indebtedness to Hawthorne. Evert Augustus Duyckinck, one of Hawthorne's earliest and most faithful admirers, commented in a brief review: "It would seem to us at times, in the sad and fanciful passages, (for H. unites these,) that Mr Dickens must have seen them, so great is the resemblance, in such parts, of the two authors. The little Nell of the latter is greatly and deservedly admired, but we hazard nothing in saying, that in the finer portions of sentiment, Hawthorne is fully equal to the author of the Old Curiosity Shop."[16] Almost simultaneously, though without suggesting any influence of Hawthorne on Dickens, Orestes Augustus Brownson, in his review, made a similar comparison, maintaining that Hawthorne

> may be, if he tries, with several improvements, to the literature of his country, all that Boz is to that of England. He possesses a higher order of intellect and genius than Boz, stronger, and purer. He has more earnestness. The creator of 'The Gentle Boy' compares advantageously with the creator of 'Little Nell'. The Gentle Boy is indeed but a sketch; yet a sketch that betrays in every stroke the hand of the master; and we think, it requires a much higher order of genius to conceive it, so gentle, so sweet, so calm, so full of life, of love, than it did to conceive the character of Little Nell, confessedly the most beautiful of Dickens's creations.[17]

After *The Scarlet Letter* was published Little Nell was again sometimes invoked for comparison with Pearl. A.D. Mayo, in one of the earliest general essays on Hawthorne, said of Pearl: "As a poetical creation, we know not where to look for her equal in modern literature. She is the companion of Mignon and Little Nell, more original in conception than either, if not as strong in her hold upon our affections."[18] And Henry Giles remarked: "Nothing, perhaps, has more tested genius than to give the ideal of childhood. We have now before our minds the Mignone of Goethe, the Fenella of Scott, the Little Nell of Dickens; but we think that Pearl takes hold of our last, almost strongest affection by a wildness, a delicacy, an enchantment which none of them possess."[19]

There were occasional comparisons of other pairs of characters — notably of Clifford Pyncheon in *The House of the Seven Gables* and Harold Skimpole in *Bleak House*. I shall return to these comments, by a *Blackwood*'s critic,[20] and by Andrew Lang.[21]

Most comparisons were of a fairly general and cursory kind. Perhaps the earliest was a comment by Anne W. Abbott in a review of *The Scarlet Letter*: "The delineations of wharf scenery, and of the Custom House, with their appropriate figures and personages, are worthy of the pen of Dickens, and really, so far as mere style is concerned, Mr Hawthorne has no reason to thank us for the compliment; he has the finer touch, if not the more genial feeling, of the two."[22] In the following year, Henry C. Tuckerman, in an essay which won Hawthorne's gratitude, declared *The Scarlet Letter* "in truth to costume, local manners, and scenic features . . . as reliable as the best of Scott's novels . . . while in developing bravely and justly the sentiments of the life it depicts, it is as true to humanity as Dickens."[23] No doubt it was to such comments that E.P. Whipple referred in his review of *The House of the Seven Gables*: "We have seen Hawthorne likened for this quality to Goldsmith, and for that to Irving, and for still another to Dickens, and some critics have given him the preference over all whom he seems to resemble."[24]

A more extended early comment, by Paul Siogvolk, in 1852, attempted to place Hawthorne in relation to both Dickens and Thackeray.

> Hawthorne seems to me to combine much of the magic creative power that so pre-eminently distinguishes Dickens' *genius*, with not a little of the critical acumen of Thackeray's *talent*. He cannot be ranked with Dickens, who is, beyond dispute, the greatest literary talent of our time. Nor can he cope with the brilliant Thackeray in his deep and thorough knowledge of conventional human nature. Still I claim for him that neither Dickens nor Thackeray could have written Hawthorne's later books. There runs through them a limpid stream of sentimentalism that would have been unsafe for Thackeray, and there is a literalness, sometimes a clean cutting, like an etching or the scratch of a diamond on glass, and sometimes a "hard finish" to some of his scenes and characters, that would have illsuited the warm and gushing power of that arch-magician of creative art, Dickens."[25]

In the course of a long general essay a few months earlier, an anonymous critic (in the journal *To-Day*) found Hawthorne

Dickens' superior in at least one respect — his use of the device of animation. He claimed that "Hawthorne must be a German" because "No Yankee or Englishman could ever invest with so complete a fog of mystery the commonest objects of our daily experience . . . Dickens has a very happy way, unless he has given us too much of it, of making the chairs wink at each other, and the tongs ogle the shovel round the chimney-corner. . . . But . . . in this faculty Dickens is far inferior to our author."[26]

A few years later, another anonymous critic considered that "Mr Hawthorne falls far short of the rich variety and comic power of [Dickens], but he may occasionally compete with him in the intensity wherewith certain strong emotions or situations are kneaded into the reader's mind, so as to leave an indelible impression."[27]

Shortly after Hawthorne's death C.A. Cummings made a much larger claim: "Hawthorne is to be measured by the side of the great examples of *imaginative* literature; and in such a comparison, who will not say that the most brilliant of these writers, that Addison or Goldsmith, Dickens or Thackeray, does not pale before the grace, the power, the color, the perfect ease of Hawthorne."[28]

A couple of years later again, however, Eugene Benson's view was very different: "Compared with hearty writers like Dickens or Irving, or with impassioned writers like de Quincey or George Sand [Hawthorne] is the chilliest, the most elusive of spirits, and his only merit seems to be that of a graceful habit of thinking, and of a temperate illustration and expression of his subject. His delicate humor oftenest is like the fantasy of an invalid; the merriment is pathetically contrasted with a sad and time-stricken face."[29]

The posthumous publication in 1872 of the first chapter of Hawthorne's last projected work, *The Dolliver Romance*, reminded Keningale Cook that Dickens had also left behind an unfinished work, and prompted him to suggest that "in several points the works of these two writers are susceptible of comparison. Dickens' wonderful faculty of accumulating and giving life to a rich fullness of descriptive detail Hawthorne certainly shares; and the quaint manner, half-humorous, half-sad, of painting the forlorn aspects of life, the individuals isolated and drooping, the neglected waifs and strays of humanity, they both have in common." He found in one paragraph "a touch of delicate and artistic fancy excelled by nothing of Dickens' in the same way", and maintained that

> besides their common faculty of sombre painting in the forlorn colour gray, there are many points of resemblance between Hawthorne and Dickens. The latter may have a wider scope of experience and a greater power of stamping his pictures upon the reader; but wherever we come upon a subject the treatment of which calls forth real pathos, we find the American drawing us into a higher and clearer light than his English brother. We have always thought some of Dickens's touching scenes rather forced and made up for effect; but then Dickens was a man of the world, who wrote as his knowledge of the world told him would be most taking, while Hawthorne seems to have inhabited a sort of spiritual fairyland, the greetings of whose denizens were always tender and touching.[30]

Hawthorne was commonly considered inferior to Dickens in one important respect — the individuality and vitality of his characters. So, for example, the critic in *To-Day*, quoted above, also commented: "Mr Hawthorne wants dramatic power, or that mimic faculty . . . which enables an author to represent successfully the colloquial peculiarity of different classes of persons. . . . We never could say of remarks in any of his books, that they were the peculiar property of any of his characters, but they might apply nearly as well perhaps to all. Whereas we can recognize at once an old acquaintance in the most trivial remark of the Wellers or Dick Swiveller or Miss Sally Brass."[31]

Dorville Libby, writing in 1869, went further in denying Hawthorne's characters not only distinctive modes of utterance, but human reality. It is, he claimed,

> an unquestionable fact that [Hawthorne] never presents what we commonly call a natural character. The characters of Dickens, with all their grotesque exaggeration, never fail to suggest to us individuals whom they resemble, or classes whom they typify. This can by no means be said of Hawthorne's. Some of them have scarcely any trait of humanity but the outward form, and even that not always so warmly clad in its habiliment of flesh and blood as to be taken into the reader's mind without a shiver.[32]

A quarter of a century later Thomas Bradfield found "Hawthorne's conceptions for the most part . . . deficient in human sympathy." Mentioning half a dozen English novels, including *Pickwick*, Bradfield maintained that

> in the works we have mentioned in contrast to those of Hawthorne, the

human interest is predominant and illustrated by rare delineation of character, in connection with stirring and varying incidents which go to make up life. . . . But with Hawthorne, human interest, the impulse and diversion of action, the conflicts of feeling, the ambitions, fascinations, meannesses and vices of the world are not the keys upon which his skilled fingers loved to play. . . . Hawthorne painted souls more than bodies, moods and impressions at the significant moments which affect the current of the after-life, rather than the ambitions and energies called forth by action and stimulated by contact with the world.[33]

A decade later, in the Hawthorne centenary year, two critics made similar comparative observations. George D. Latimer remarked that Poe and Hawthorne "had but slight interest in the delineation of open, cheerful, lovable characters such as Scott, Thackeray and Dickens chose to depict."[34] And M.E. Coleridge maintained: "We do not meet his characters in the street as we meet those of the other great novelists. How often have we not said: 'This family is by Dickens. . . .' and so on. Rarely do we come across the remote heroes, the yet more distant and ethereal heroines with whom Hawthorne brings us acquainted. Nature, so apt to take a hint from art, has turned a deaf ear to him; she will not be persuaded that there are any men and women like those of the enchanter."[35]

But not all the comparisons between Hawthorne and Dickens as character-creators were unfavourable to Hawthorne. It was not uncommon for Hawthorne's characterization to be seen as in some sense Shakespearean, as in this comment by G.P. Lathrop in 1876: "Men like Shakespeare and Hawthorne, however dissimilar their temperaments . . . grasp the two hemispheres of the human mind, the sane and the insane, and hold them perfectly reconciled in their gentle yet unsparing . . . insight. . . . We should place Dickens with them, for his variety of outlook, except that it is only the superficial distortions of mind which his genius chiefly concerns itself with; and we fancy in him at times a slightly fevered sensitiveness which leads to contamination from the phases he is describing."[36]

Howells, the Dean (or Pope) of American literature in the late nineteenth century, had no doubt of Hawthorne's superiority over Dickens as portrayer of women. "With Hawthorne there was a return, after a whole generation, to a conception of entire womanhood in fiction. His Zenobia and Hester Prynne are really women, and this cannot be unqualifiedly said of Scott's, or

Bulwer's, or Dickens's women. At the most it can be said that these novelists caught certain feminine traits and personified them, but femininity never posed for them in the *ensemble*."[37]

In one of the many Hawthorne centenary essays C.F. Adams also rated Hawthorne above Dickens: "I am inclined to think that, as a skilful portrait painter is entitled to artistic preference over a cartoonist — even the most ingenious, prolific, and generally accepted — as a delineator of character, taken at his absolute best, as in *The House of the Seven Gables* and *The Scarlet Letter*, truth to nature, real power, and delicacy of touch being the tests — I am inclined . . . to believe the world is likely to see another Dickens before it sees another Hawthorne."[38]

So, on balance, was F.P. Stearns, in a couple of scattered comments in his critical biography published in 1906. "Dickens was the great humanitarian writer of the nineteenth century, but he was also a caricaturist and a bohemian. He did not represent life as it is, but with a certain comical oddity. . . . As an author he is to Hawthorne what a peony is to a rose, or a garnet to a ruby."[39] "If power and versatility of characterization were to be the test of imaginative writing, Dickens would push closely on to Shakespeare, but we do not go to Shakespeare to read about Hamlet or Falstaff . . . but for the *tout ensemble*. . . . If it were not for the odd characters and variety of incident in Dickens's novels they would hardly be worth reading. Hawthorne's *dramatis personae* is not a long one . . . but his characters are finely drawn, and the fact that they have not become popular types is rather in their favour."[40]

As one would expect, many of the critical discussions of Hawthorne had a good deal to say about Hawthorne's conception of the romance as a kind of fiction distinct from the novel. Occasionally Dickens was introduced into discussions of this kind. One example is an 1888 essay by Maurice Thompson, who remarked that "the advocates of realism will not deal fairly with romance, but invariably pass by the Hawthornes and the Hugos to take a Jules Verne or a Rider Haggard as the typical romancer." Thompson continued:

> It would be quite fair, I think, to take Hawthorne and Dickens as standing about as wide apart as the breadth of legitimate romance, so far as novel-writing in the English language can exemplify it, and to use the work of these two great authors for the purpose of measuring the value of romance in

general. Hawthorne lacked the dramatic power of Dickens, but his art was so much greater in every other respect that comparisons can not be made. Still as both Hawthorne and Dickens kept well within the bounds of romance and never troubled themselves about photography, they stand as well set reference stones for the critical student.[41]

In partial contrast to this view is the claim of Andrew Lang, in the context of a discussion of Hawthorne as romancer, that the "widely different talents [of Hawthorne and Dickens] did really intersect each other, where the perverse, the grotesque and the terrible dwell."[42]

In what is certainly one of the most important general comparative discussions of the two writers, W.D. Howells insisted on the difference, rather than the similarities, between them. There was, Howells maintained,

the widest possible difference of ideal in Dickens and Hawthorne; the difference between the romanticistic and the romantic, which is almost as great as that between the romantic and the realistic. Romance, as in Hawthorne, seeks the effect of reality in visionary conditions; romanticism, as in Dickens, tries for a visionary effect in actual conditions. These different ideals eventuated with Hawthorne in characters being, doing and suffering as vitally as any we have known in the world; with Dickens in types, outwardly of our every-day acquaintance, but inwardly moved by a single propensity and existing to justify in some fantastic excess the attribution of their controlling quality. In their mystical world, withdrawn afar from us in the past, or apart from us in anomalous conditions, the characters of Hawthorne speak and act for themselves and from an authentic individuality compact of good and evil; in times, terms, and places analogous to those in which actual men have their being, the types of Dickens are always speaking for him, in fulfilment of a mechanical conception and a rigid limitation of their function in the drama. They are, in every sense, *parts*, and Hawthorne's creations are *persons* rounded, whole.[43]

As the foregoing anthology of extracts shows, many critics, both American and English, in the period of over sixty years from the early 1840s to the mid 1900s, made comparisons between Hawthorne and Dickens. But whether their comparisons were superficial and perfunctory, or more penetrating and elaborate; whether they considered the two novelists to be totally different or in some ways similar; whether they extolled one writer at the expense of the other, or whether they respected both equally; only a couple of these nineteenth-century critics hinted that one novelist might have influenced, or been influenced by, the other.

Critical Comparisons of Hawthorne and Dickens, 1950–1980

If Hawthorne did indeed significantly influence Dickens, and even if this influence passed virtually unnoticed in the novelists' own life-times and the following decades, one would not have expected it to have escaped the attention of the hosts of eager searchers for thesis topics in recent decades. But so far as I have been able to discover, there has been less comparative critical discussion of Hawthorne and Dickens since 1950 than before 1900. There has, of course, been a vast quantity of criticism of both novelists in recent years, especially associated with the centenaries of their deaths, in 1964 and 1970. But in the many recent books on Dickens I have found only two references to Hawthorne. One, by Grahame Smith, is only a passing mention. In discussing *Bleak House*, Smith, while not suggesting any critical influence of Hawthorne on Dickens, refers to the preface to *The House of the Seven Gables* as giving some indication of the nature of Dickens' novel: "But it is the romance, which presents its truths 'under circumstances . . . of the writer's own choosing or creation' which is relevant to the artistry of Dickens."[44]

The other, by Q.D. Leavis, is much more important. In her chapter on *Bleak House*, in *Dickens the Novelist*, Mrs Leavis suggests some indebtedness in *Bleak House* to Kingsley's *Alton Locke*, and comments: "It is impossible to read nineteenth century novels in bulk without coming to the conclusion . . . that the Victorian novelists read and used each other's work quite as freely as Elizabethan and Jacobean dramatists did theirs."[45] Mrs Leavis refers briefly to "cross-fertilization" between Dickens and Thackeray, George Eliot, Mrs Oliphant and Mrs Gaskell, Dickens and Charlotte Bronte, and quotes an 1852 letter of Dickens in which he commented on Harriet Beecher Stowe's appropriations, in *Uncle Tom's Cabin*, from himself, Mrs Gaskell's *Mary Barton*, and *The Children of the Mist*.

Later, in her chapter "How we must read *Great Expectations*", Mrs Leavis discusses the opening chapter in the churchyard, in which Pip, who knows of the existence on the marshes of the gibbet for hanging malefactors, "is to learn now that a prison hulk is part of his habitat."[46] Mrs Leavis comments:

Dickens like most great novelists was quick to pick up ideas and make them his own (not, in his case, at the conscious level probably) and we may note here substantial evidence for his expressed admiration for the opening scenes of Hawthorne's allegorical masterpiece *The Scarlet Letter* (1850) where Hawthorne had started by setting out the conditions of human society in the same terms but more forthrightly.... Whether Dickens adopted Hawthorne's ironic diagnosis of society or transferred the irony into the "great expectations" which such a society produces, he sets his scene in the same way, to investigate the human condition.[47]

In a footnote Mrs Leavis adds the comment: "*The Scarlet Letter* was so influential on English novelists and the Victorian reading public that it is really part of the English 19th century tradition, as witness its influence on, e.g. Dickens and George Eliot . . ." Continuing her discussion of *Great Expectations* and *The Scarlet Letter*, she comments: "The highly stylized settings and the schematic technique of *The Scarlet Letter* seem to have an affinity in the very deliberately selected simple settings of *Great Expectations*, as well as in its salvationist outcome and its exploration of the effects of guilt"; and concludes her brief discussion of similarities between the two novels with the remark that "Though the likeness of *Great Expectations* to Hawthorne's novel is pronounced in these respects, yet Dickens's masterpiece is unique — thus one creative genius can make use of another's work without being parasitic or even imitative."[48]

It is, of course, very welcome to find support for my belief in Hawthorne's influence on Dickens from such an authority as Q.D. Leavis; I agree that Dickens' indebtedness was "probably not at the conscious level" and that there was nothing "parasitic or even imitative" about it. But on two points I disagree with Mrs Leavis. In the first place, I think it is a mistake to see Hawthorne's influence on English novelists as confined to *The Scarlet Letter*; other romances, especially *The House of the Seven Gables*, were also influential. In the second place, I cannot accept as valid the implication in Mrs Leavis' comment ("as witness its influence on, e.g., Dickens and George Eliot. . . .") that Hawthorne's influence on Dickens has been as much "witnessed" as his influence on George Eliot. Q.D. Leavis mentions only one discussion of Hawthorne's influence on George Eliot — F.R. Leavis' essay, "*Adam Bede*"; but this essay, as I shall show in a later chapter, is only one item (though perhaps the most important) in a list going back to 1859. She cites no single discussion of Hawthorne's influence on Dickens; so far as I can discover, her assertion, in 1970, of the influence of *The Scarlet Letter* on Dickens, has only one published predecessor — an essay of my own[49] published in the previous year.

As well as the few references in books on Dickens, there have been a few articles which have, in one way or another, brought the two novelists together, without suggesting an influence of one on the other. Perhaps the most important of these is one to which I have previously referred, which appeared in the special Hawthorne issue (October 1964) of *Essex Institute Historical Collections* — Ghulam Ali Chaudhry's "Dickens and Hawthorne".

This writer begins by asserting: "A Dickens-Hawthorne study cannot be very ambitious, certainly not as ambitious as a Dickens-Irving or Dickens-Poe one" and maintains that "no such influential relationship [as that between Dickens and Poe] existed between Dickens and Hawthorne." He details the various references to Dickens in Hawthorne's work, and quotes Forster's report of Dickens' enthusiasm for Hawthorne's sketches and tales. Chaudhry comments:

> This enthusiastic appreciation of Hawthorne's early work by Dickens suggests some traits in which they both shared. In fact, in its radiant fancy, keen observation, and large sympathy *Twice Told Tales* is akin to *Sketches by Boz*. But in general tone and motive the two writers differ: Dickens is pronouncedly social and humanitarian, and Hawthorne markedly moral and intellectual. Thus, whereas Dickens informs his depiction of scene and character with a deeper sensibility, Hawthorne executes his overall design with a greater sense of form.[50]

Chaudhry considers of greater interest Dickens' opinion of *The Scarlet Letter*; the bulk of his essay is devoted to a defence of Hawthorne's masterpiece against Dickens' strictures. He maintains that there are other fine scenes besides the opening scene, notably the midnight scaffold scene; that Hester's and Dimmesdale's "suddenness of meeting and agreeing to go away together" is not really sudden or ill-prepared; that, "in his appraisal of the characterization, Dickens seems to overlook the deeper shades of Hester's nature" and that Dickens' "lack of recognition of [Hester] ... kept Dickens from reading Dimmesdale's character more correctly"; that "with the exception of Pearl, all main characters generally move along sound psychological lines, both in conception and execution."[51]

In discussing Pearl, Chaudhry admits that "one could point out instances where Pearl is indeed 'out of nature altogether' ", and suggests that "Hawthorne's failure with Pearl . . . helps to bring out the essential difference between his creative vision and Dickens'."[52] Chaudhry contends that

> whereas the link between the Dickens of the *Sketches* and the Dickens of the novels is chiefly of emotion and physical reality, that between the Hawthorne of the *Tales* and *Mosses* and the Hawthorne of the romances is primarily of idea and 'imagistic' reality. Almost all sorts of persons and places in the early Dickens flow easily into those in the later. . . . But in Hawthorne it is only a particular type of person or place that is fit for travel from the tale into the romance. . . . The fanciful realism of Dickens's *Sketches* brings even to his darker novels . . . a whole wealth of human comedy and the attendant voluble movement of life. Hawthorne, however, admits from the richly varied . . . world of his *Tales* and *Mosses* only intellectual reality into his romances, allowing it a dominance over the entire fabric, so that setting, scene, character, and atmosphere are marked by a dark heaviness, a severe and concentrated poetic style emerges — in *The Scarlet Letter* and *The House of the Seven Gables* in particular — and a precise overall unity of form — except perhaps in *The Marble Faun* — is achieved.[53]

I have summarized Ghulam Ali Chaudhry's essay chiefly to indicate that it does not at any point suggest the possibility of any influence of Hawthorne on the later Dickens. Indeed Chaudhry's argument, which posits a distinct similarity between the early work of the two writers, but a complete contrast between Dickens' novels and Hawthorne's romances, seems implicitly to deny any such possibility. I do not find this argument convincing. If one agrees with Chaudhry that the world of Hawthorne's *Tales* and *Mosses* is more varied than the world of the romances, one may question whether it is more "*richly* varied", as Chaudhry maintains. The elements of "playful fancy, sharp observation and generous sympathy" which Chaudhry sees in *Twice Told Tales* could be described, and have often been described, in less eulogistic terms — as insipid diluents rather than as enriching contrasts. Of the tales and sketches which, according to Chaudhry's description, present persons "the secret of [whose] creation lies . . . in their individual and physical reality", and places which "originate in real experience", Chaudhry refers to "The Village Uncle", "The Old Apple

Dealer", "Edward Fane's Rosebud", "Mr Higginbotham's Catastrophe", "Sights from a Steeple", and "Little Annie's Ramble". These sketches are pleasant, sympathetic, whimsical; some are perhaps even "exquisite". But it could hardly be seriously contended that they are as interesting, meaningful, or memorable as the other tales which are concerned with (in Chaudhry's view) "the particular type of person or place, that is fit for travel from the tale into the romance." Of such tales Chaudhry refers to "Endicott and the Red Cross", "The Great Carbuncle", "Dr Heidegger's Experiment", "The Birthmark", "Rappacini's Daughter" and "The Gray Champion". Chaudhry finds it possible to add only a few more sketches in the same fanciful — humorous — realistic vein as his first list, and none is more momentous — "The Toll-Gatherer's Day", "Snow Flakes" and "Footprints on the Sea Shore". But to the latter list of tales which pre-figure the romances in theme, character, setting, situation or atmosphere it is easy to add many more, some of which are clearly superior to Chaudhry's specimens — for example, "Young Goodman Brown", "The Maypole of Merry Mount", "The Hollow of the Three Hills", "Wakefield", "Roger Malvin's Burial", "The Artist of the Beautiful", "The Gentle Boy", "Ethan Brand", "The Minister's Black Veil", and "My Kinsman, Major Molineux". So one could argue that the most characteristic elements, and the most profound concerns of the tales are continued and developed in the longer romances, while the more conventional, sentimental and playfully fanciful elements fade away.

There is an even more fundamental objection to Chaudhry's argument, which assumes a close similarity between Hawthorne's four longer romances: "a dark heaviness, a severe and concentrated poetic style emerges, in *The Scarlet Letter* and *The House of the Seven Gables* in particular." To lump even Hawthorne's first two romances together in this way is to ignore the fact that after *The Scarlet Letter* Hawthorne set out, consciously and deliberately, to write something quite different. Hawthorne agreed with several of the contemporary reviewers who found *The Scarlet Letter* too unrelievedly gloomy and sombre; he wrote to his publisher, J.T. Fields: "I found it impossible to relieve the shadows of the story with so much light as I would gladly have thrown in" and "I will try to write a more genial book."[54] *The House of the Seven Gables* was, of course, Hawthorne's attempt "to write a more genial book", and "to throw in more light." The critics who had found *The Scarlet Letter* over-gloomy generally reacted favourably to *The House of the Seven Gables*. One of the best of them, E.P. Whipple, commented: "The error in *The Scarlet Letter* proceeded from the divorce of its humour from its pathos. . . . In *The House of the Seven Gables* the humour and the pathos are combined, and the whole book is stamped with the individuality of the author's genius in all its variety of power."[55] Twelve decades later, one of Hawthorne's most recent critics, J.C. Stubbs, subtitled his chapter on *The House of the Seven Gables*, "Hawthorne's Comedy", and defined the book's structure as depending on "a rhythm of straightforward presentation counterpointed with comic inversion."[56] (The same critic maintains that *The Blithedale Romance* holds "a careful fusion of the tragic Hawthorne, with the comic Hawthorne, in irony."[57])

Chaudhry suggests that Dickens probably reacted to *The Scarlet Letter* in the same way as Whipple and other contemporary critics. ("Probably Dickens looked for a larger measure of these ['touches of Hawthorne's earlier fanciful observation'] in *The Scarlet Letter*, and felt that Hawthorne's tales and sketches were more *fully* representative of him than this romance.")[58] Even if this was true, there is no evidence that Dickens' reaction to *The House of the Seven Gables* (if he read it) was the same; it seems more likely that his reaction would again have been similar to Whipple's, and that Hawthorne's second romance would have joined the tales in Dickens' mind as a body of themes, ideas, and images on which he could draw, and transform for his own purposes. That this did indeed happen I shall try to show. But I shall not be able to demonstrate Dickens' indebtedness either to the tales or to *The House of the Seven Gables* as conclusively as his indebtedness to *The Scarlet Letter*, for which he had so little good to say.

Only two other essays which associate Hawthorne and Dickens are listed in a recently published bibliography of Hawthorne criticism.[59] Both appeared in 1966 — M.L. Allen's "The Black Veil: Three Versions of a Symbol"[60] and Edward M. Passerini's "Hawthornesque Dickens".[61] Allen's essay is a comparative examination of Dickens' "The Black Veil" and Hawthorne's

"The Minister's Black Veil"; Allen sees both as versions of "the black veil dislodged by the heroine about a third of the way through *The Mysteries of Udolpho* [which] is central to the design"[62] of Mrs Radcliffe's novel. Allen does not suggest that either story influenced the other; the dates of publication would make anything of the kind impossible. ("The Minister's Black Veil" was included in *Twice Told Tales* (1837), but it had previously been published in the *Token* for 1836, which means that it must have been written before June 1835.[63] "The Black Veil" appeared in *Sketches by Boz* (1836); it had not been previously published. It was written in December 1835 specially for inclusion in the book.[64] So although Hawthorne's story was written several months before Dickens', it had not yet been published.)

Allen points out that "each tale is constructed around a single mystery in which the veil plays a part" and that "the reactions of susceptible observers to the veil again [as in *Udolpho*] provide the link between mystery and symbol." But Allen also suggests that "symbol, action and the perceiving sensibility are more closely fused in these tales, which added to the Radcliffean question 'what is the mystery of the veil?' a more specific one, 'why is the veil worn?' A greater depth of meaning is made possible than in *Udolpho* and as well as acting as a simple symbol of 'mystery' the veil contributes its various implications to the serious themes of the two stories."[65]

These serious themes are, however, quite different. Allen finds the stories interesting chiefly for

> the light they throw on the influence of the Gothic novel in America and Britain respectively. In both countries, novelists were finding in the Gothic mode the constituents of a symbolic convention, but the difference in *symbolic direction* shown by these two stories suggests one difference between the two traditions. "The Minister's Black Veil", like *The Scarlet Letter*. . . , uses symbol and mystery to explore the ambiguous relationship of the abstract (is evil metaphysical and universal?) and the psychological (or is it a manifestation of limitations and compulsions of the individual psyche?). 'The Black Veil', like . . . *Bleak House*, is less profoundly obsessed with these aspects of experience, but brings its symbolism directly to bear on a social situation.[66]

Allen's definition of the difference in "symbolic direction" between the fiction of Hawthorne and the fiction of Dickens is similar to Chaudhry's previously-quoted definition of the difference in general tone and motive of the two writers: "Dickens is pronouncedly social and humanitarian, and Hawthorne markedly moral and intellectual." This is unquestionably true; but that the differences in tone, motive and symbolic direction did not prevent Dickens from, perhaps unconsciously, making use of Hawthorne I shall try to show — particularly in *Bleak House*, and especially in the strand of *Bleak House* (that concerned with Lady Dedlock and her illegitimate child, Esther Summerson) in which Dickens is less concerned with contemporary, or near-contemporary social iniquities and inequities than with more universal themes of sin, guilt, betrayal, alienation, and expiation.

Edward M. Passerini, despite the challenging title of his essay, "Hawthornesque Dickens", and despite his challenging opening sentence: "Charles Dickens's best writing style resembles Hawthorne's",[67] does not assert a Hawthorne influence on Dickens, only a presumably accidental and occasional resemblance.

Passerini finds Dickens' best writing in "the sort of passage in which Dickens speaks of mighty themes in human terms, in which a very few three-dimensional figures enact the themes and in which the resolution is at once realistic and significant."[68] He takes as an example the opening chapter of *Our Mutual Friend*, in which he finds many Hawthornesque qualities:

(a) Concern with "a universal time". ("People are people and will behave the same way no matter what year it is.")[69]

(b) "Yet local time is very important" for "the setting of the mood."[70]

(c) Exact specification of place, establishing the importance of setting and of "symbols which will operate not only in the initial chapter but through the whole book."[71]

(d) A small number of characters, whose different attitudes illuminate the nature of the deed in which they are involved.[72]

(e) An ambiguous use of symbols; a pervasive sense of "strange ambiguity and perverse reality."[73]

(f) The theme of "estrangement as a result of crime"; and a concern with "development of personalities after the estrangement, rather than with the estrangement itself."[74]

Passerini concludes his discussion of the first chapter of *Our*

Mutual Friend with the comment: "The meanings of the symbols are various and the interactions of characters on each other are complex. The language is compact, the development sure. Hawthorne would have been proud."[75] It is rather surprising that Passerini does not take the farther step of suggesting that if Dickens at his best writes like Hawthorne, it may have been because he had read and learnt from Hawthorne.

Two important recent contributions (both published in 1978) to a study of the Hawthorne–Dickens relationship have already been mentioned (see note 9) — Jonathan Arac's article "The House and the Railroad: *Dombey and Son* and *The House of the Seven Gables*", and Edwin M. Eigner's book, *The Metaphysical Novel in England and America*. Both writers share the view of Nicolaus Mills (*American and English Fiction in the Nineteenth Century*, 1973) that the differences between these two bodies of fiction, English and American, have been greatly exaggerated by critics like Lionel Trilling, Richard Chase and Leslie Fiedler; both point to striking resemblances between Dickens and Hawthorne. But both, in so far as they are concerned with influences, see only the influence of Dickens on Hawthorne, not the equally important influence of Hawthorne on Dickens.

Hawthorne's Influence in *Bleak House*

It is, in my view, in *Bleak House* that evidence of Hawthorne's influence on Dickens is strongest. This is not surprising, since it was during the fifteen-month interval between the final number of *David Copperfield* (November 1850) and the first number of *Bleak House* (March 1852) that Dickens (in July 1851) read *The Scarlet Letter* (published in 1850); *The House of the Seven Gables* also appeared in this interval (in April 1851).

One may surmise, in the first place, that Dickens got from Hawthorne's two recently-published books general encouragement in the direction of sombre romance. The last curt single-sentence paragraph of Dickens' preface, written in August 1853, which is quite unconnected with the preceding comments on the Court of Chancery and Spontaneous Combustion ("In *Bleak House* I have purposely dwelt upon the romantic side of familiar things") seems like a shorthand version of what Hawthorne had said more fully in "The Custom-House" and the preface to *The House of the Seven Gables*. It reminds one, for example, of the famous passage in "The Custom-House" about the effect of moonlight and firelight on "familiar things".

> Moonlight, in a familiar room, falling so white upon the carpet, and showing all its figures so distinctly, — making every object so minutely visible, yet so unlike a morning or noontide visibility — is a medium the most suitable for a romance writer to get acquainted with his illusive guests. There is the little domestic scenery of the well-known apartment . . . all these details, so completely seen, are so spiritualized by the unusual light, that they seem to lose their actual substance, and become things of intellect. . . . Thus, therefore, the floor of our familiar room has become a neutral territory, somewhere between the real world and fairy-land, where the Actual and the Imaginary may meet, and each imbue itself with the nature of the other. Ghosts might enter here without affrighting us. . . .
>
>   The somewhat dim coal-fire has an essential influence in producing these effects which I would describe. It throws its unobtrusive tinge throughout the room. . . . This warmer light mingles itself with the cold spirituality of the moonbeams, and communicates, as it were, a heart and sensibilities of human tenderness to the forms which fancy summons up. It converts them from snow-images into men and women. . . .[76]

Whether or not Dickens, in the final sentence of his preface, also had in mind Hawthorne's opening sentence in his preface to *The House of the Seven Gables* ("When a writer calls his work a romance, it need hardly be observed that he wishes to claim a certain latitude, both as to its fashion and material, which he would not have felt himself entitled to assume, had he professed to be writing a novel"), it seems obvious that in *Bleak House* he did (to borrow other terms from Hawthorne's opening paragraph) "so manage his atmospherical medium as to bring out or mellow the lights and deepen and enrich the shadows of the picture" more consciously and carefully than he had ever done before. It seems likely that his mingling of "the Marvellous", especially in the "Ghost's Walk" at Chesney Wold, owes as much to Hawthorne's recent example as to the earlier Gothic romance which has frequently been considered a source. "The Legend of the Ghost's Walk", told by Mrs Rouncewell to her grandson, Wat, and Rosa (*Bleak House*, chapter 7) is exactly described in the second paragraph of Hawthorne's preface: "It is a Legend, prolonging itself, from an epoch now gray in the distance, down into our own broad daylight, and bringing along with it some of its legendary mist. . . ." The dying prophecy of the seventeenth-century Lady Dedlock, the Roundhead supporter accidentally crippled by her hated Royalist husband (" 'I will walk here, though I am in my grave. I will walk here, until the pride of this house is humbled. And when calamity, or when disgrace is coming to it, let the Dedlocks listen for my steps!' "), recalls the prophecy at the moment of execution of the seventeenth-century Mathew Maule, falsely accused of witchcraft by Colonel Pyncheon, in order to steal his land (" 'God will give him blood to drink!' "; *The House of the Seven Gables*, chapter 1.).

These resemblances to *The House of the Seven Gables* may be merely fortuitous, but those to *The Scarlet Letter* can hardly be. It is in chapter 41 of *Bleak House* ("In Mr Tulkinghorn's Room") that one is likely to become most aware of these resemblances. In this chapter Mr Tulkinghorn reveals to Lady Dedlock that he has pieced together her whole story and completed his case against her, but enjoins her to keep her secret, which he does not intend to expose for the moment. The dialogue between them ends with her question: " 'And I am to hide my guilt, as I have done so many years?' " and his reply " 'As you have done so many years' ", which may remind one that Hawthorne's sinner, Arthur Dimmesdale, hides his guilt for seven years. Lady Dedlock's earlier question: " 'I am to drag my present life on, holding its pains at your pleasure, day by day?' " is an accurate description of Dimmesdale's long ordeal, his life preserved by Chillingworth only that Chillingworth may protract the unholy pleasure of his revenge. (Hester says to Chillingworth, in chapter 14 of *The Scarlet Letter*: " 'Your clutch is on his life, and you cause him to die daily a living death.' ") Her following question: " 'I am to remain on this gaudy platform, on which my miserable deception has been so long acted, and it is to fall beneath me when you give the signal?' " seems to establish definitely the connection between these two novels. Lady Dedlock's image of the "gaudy platform" is appropriate enough to describe the place of exposed social eminence which she occupies as the wife of Sir Leicester who "is only a baronet, but there is no mightier baronet than he" (*Bleak House*, chapter 2). But it can hardly fail to remind anyone who has read *The Scarlet Letter* both of the scaffold, the "pedestal of infamy", on which Hester and her child are publicly exposed for three hours at the beginning of the novel, on which, seven years later, Dimmesdale stands with Hester and Pearl in the darkness, and is revealed to Chillingworth by the lurid light of the meteor, and on which, at the end of the novel, Dimmesdale at last public-ly confesses his guilt and dies; and of the pulpit, from which Dimmesdale preaches with "sad, persuasive eloquence", seem-ing to his congregation "a miracle of holiness", while he is to himself "utterly a pollution and a lie" (*The Scarlet Letter*, chapter 11).

Any doubts that memories of *The Scarlet Letter* were strongly present in Dickens' mind when he wrote *Bleak House* should be dispelled by a passage a few chapters later: "Mr Vholes . . . took his long thin shadow away. I thought of it on the outside of the coach, passing over all the sunny landscape between us and London, chilling the seed in the ground as it glided along" (*Bleak House*, chapter 45). Surely Esther's fancy about the black-garbed legal vampire, Vholes (which Q.D. Leavis describes as "that blood-curdling image"),[77] is too strikingly similar to Hester's fancy about the blighting blackness and coldness of her necromancer-husband Chillingworth, to be merely coincidental?

> Hester gazed after him a little while, looking with a half-fantastic curiosity to see whether the tender grass of early spring would not be blighted beneath him, and show the wavering track of his footsteps, sere and brown, across its cheerful verdure. . . . Did the sun, which shone so brightly everywhere else, really fall upon him? Or was there, as it rather seemed, a circle of ominous shadow moving along with his deformity, whichever way he turned himself? Would he not suddenly sink into the earth, leaving a barren and blasted spot . . .? (*The Scarlet Letter*, chapter 15).

The passages I have cited provide the most conspicuous evidence of Dickens' indebtedness to Hawthorne, but this in-debtedness, I believe, extends far beyond particular isolated passages. I believe that Dickens, whether consciously or not, in the part of *Bleak House* centred on Lady Dedlock, borrowed quite extensively from *The Scarlet Letter*; that several situations and scenes in *Bleak House* are strongly reminiscent of situations and scenes in *The Scarlet Letter*; and, particularly, that one of Dickens' major characters, Tulkinghorn, is modelled on one of Hawthorne's, Chillingworth. I shall now examine the similarities, and the differences, in situation and action.

The basic similarities are that in both novels one of the major characters is a woman who has borne an illegitimate child (I doubt that it is mere coincidence that in one the mother's name is Hester, in the other the daughter's name is Esther); that in both cases the child's paternity is known only to the mother; and that in both cases another main character devotes himself to the task of discovering what has been concealed — in *The Scarlet Letter*, the identity of the father, in *Bleak House* the whole secret — and to the further task of in some way punishing the gulty. There is, of course, the important difference that while Hester's "shame" is known to all, and publicly displayed at the beginning of the novel, Lady Dedlock's remains unsuspected until she betrays interest in the handwriting of her former lover, seen by chance in a copy of a legal document. In *Bleak House* there is the further mystery that the child's identity is unknown to herself, and her existence unsuspected by her mother, who has been led to believe that the child died at birth.

A further difference is that whereas Dimmesdale, the father of Pearl, is one of the major characters (some, including Henry James, would say *the* major character) of *The Scarlet Letter*, Captain Hawdon, the father of Esther, has never seen his child, does not know of its existence, and appears in *Bleak House* only as the corpse of a drug-addicted drop-out. I suggest, however, that what Dickens does, in effect, though probably not in conscious intention, is to combine in the person of Lady Dedlock the roles of both Hester and Dimmesdale. It is Lady Dedlock who, like Hester, has committed the sin of passionate love before the action of the novel begins; but it is also she who, like Dimmesdale, hides her guilt and lives a life of hypocrisy and self-torment. As the beautiful wife of the elderly Sir Leicester Dedlock she has become a leading figure in fashionable society, but her social eminence brings her no satisfaction, for she is haunted by a double guilt. There is, in Edgar Johnson's words, "the false guilt imposed by a conventional standard of ethics", but there is also, as Johnson remarks, "the real guilt of her submission to its standards, her hidden cowardice, her failure to be faithful to her lover and child."[78] I quote this comment of an eminent Dickens scholar because, while its accuracy as a summary of Lady Dedlock's emotional and spiritual condition as actually realized in *Bleak House* may be debatable, it has (with the necessary change of pronoun) a clear relevance to Dimmesdale's condition.

I do not contend that Lady Dedlock has much resemblance to Hester Prynne, beyond the fact that both are proud and passionate women of strong and independent spirit. But there are at least three more specific points of similarity in their own actions and reactions, and others' reactions to them. In the first place, both enter reluctantly into some kind of pact with the investigator-persecutor figure. Hester agrees to keep her husband's presence and identity a secret, even from her lover; Lady Dedlock agrees not to run away, but to go on living as usual until Tulkinghorn has decided what to do with the knowledge he has gained. Tulkinghorn's admonitions (*Bleak House*, chapter 41): " 'I must request you, in the meantime, to keep your secret as you have kept it so long, and not to wonder that I keep it too' "; and " 'In the meantime I must beg you to keep your own counsel, and I will keep mine' " recall Chillingworth's adjuration of Hester (*The Scarlet Letter*, chapter 4): " 'Thou hast kept the secret of thy paramour. Keep likewise mine!' " In the second place, both women make some attempt to atone for the wrong they have done their lover — Hester, by revoking her contract with Chillingworth, informing Dimmesdale that his trusted physician is really his vengeful enemy, and persuading him to flee with her; Lady Dedlock by her visit, with Jo as guide, to the loathsome, rat-infested graveyard where Hawdon's body lies under a few inches of dirt. Thirdly, both extort an unwilling admiration from their antagonists. " 'Woman, I could well nigh pity thee!' said Roger Chillingworth, unable to restrain a thrill of admiration too; for there was a quality almost majestic in the despair which she expressed. 'Thou hadst great elements. . . . I pity thee, for the good that has been wasted in thy nature' " (*The Scarlet Letter*, chapter 14). Tulkinghorn "thinks with the interest of attentive curiosity, as he watches the struggle in her breast, 'The power and force of this woman are astonishing' " (*Bleak House*, chapter 41).

Neither do I contend that there is much similarity between Lady Dedlock and Arthur Dimmesdale, beyond the fact that both conceal their guilt and suffer as a result. Obviously the mask of aristocratic boredom and cold, supercilious hauteur which Lady Dedlock adopts to hide her sense of guilt and her self-contempt is very different from "the anguish in [Dimmesdale's] inmost soul, and the undissembled expression of it in his aspect", and the "vague confession" of his guilt in his sermons, in which, "subtle but remorseful hypocrite that he was", "he has spoken the very truth, and transformed it into the veriest falsehood" (*The Scarlet Letter*, chapter 11).

What I do contend is that Dickens devised a character who is something like Hester Prynne, put her in a situation that is something like Arthur Dimmesdale's, and subjected her to something like the ordeal that Dimmesdale suffers from the ministrations of his physician-tormenter. That all this is not a purely coincidental use of a conventional dramatic or melodramatic situation is, I believe, made plain in the confrontation scene between Chillingworth and Lady Dedlock, previously referred to.

The most important parallel between the two novels, however, is the striking similarity between Tulkinghorn and Chillingworth which I shall now try to demonstrate.

In the first place there is an evident similarity between the two names. Both have three syllables, of which the central syllable is identical. Unlike many of the names in *Bleak House* (Dedlock, Vholes, Smallweed, Guppy, Turveydrop, Boythorn, Skimpole, etc.), Tulkinghorn's name does not seem especially appropriate to him; it is certainly not as appropriate as Chillingworth's assumed name, with its suggestions of blighting coldness and former worthiness, is to him.[79] This suggests that Dickens may have unconsciously adopted the sound of Chillingworth's name rather than devised one to suggest the quality of his own character.

In the second place there is a similarity in appearance. Tulkinghorn's old-fashioned, rusty, threadbare attire owes nothing directly to Chillingworth, whose dress is never precisely specified. But another feature of Tulkinghorn's garb, its blackness, is at once noted ("One feature of his black clothes, and of his black stockings, be they silk or worsted, is that they never shine" (*Bleak House*, chapter 2)) and is re-emphasized at every appearance, e.g. "His black figure may be seen walking before breakfast like a larger species of rook" (chapter 12); "Mr Tulkinghorn, such a foil in his old-fashioned rusty black to Lady Dedlock's brightness" (chapter 33). Tulkinghorn's dress, it seems to me, is Dickens' attempt to find a realistic counterpart for the quality of darkness or blackness, that is so frequently emphasized in Chillingworth. For example, when Hester sees Chillingworth after three years she is startled to perceive that "his dark complexion seemed to have grown duskier" (*The Scarlet Letter*, chapter 7). Later he is described by the narrator as a "dark miner", and a "low, dark and misshapen figure" (chapter 10); by the ship's captain as the "black-a-visaged, hump-shouldered old doctor" (chapter 22) and by Dimmesdale as "yonder dark and terrible old man" (chapter 23).

Tulkinghorn's "blackness" is not a mere matter of outer garb. He comes to be a black shadow over the life of Lady Dedlock. "Interposed between her and the fading light of day in the now quiet street, his shadow falls upon her, and he darkens all before her. Even so does he darken her life" (*Bleak House*, chapter 48). This image is strongly reminiscent of such passages in *The Scarlet Letter* as the account, in chapter 10, of Chillingworth's "search into the minister's dim interior", when, despite his care, "the shadow of his presence, in a forbidden proximity, would be thrown across his victim."

Thirdly, both men have defective vision. Tulkinghorn, in his turret-room at Chesny Wold "happens not to be in business mind. After a glance at the documents awaiting his notice — with his head bent low over the table, the old man's sight for print or writing being defective at night — he opens the French window and steps out upon the leads" (*Bleak House*, chapter 41). Hester, standing on "the scaffold of the pillory" recalls her native village, in England. "There she beheld another countenance of a man well stricken in years, a pale, thin, scholar-like visage, with eyes dim and bleared by the lamplight that had served them to pore over many ponderous books" (*The Scarlet Letter*, chapter 2). Both men, nevertheless, have extraordinarily acute powers of observation and perception. Hester's recollections of Chillingworth continue: "Yet those same bleared optics had a strange penetrating power, when it was their owner's purpose to read the human soul." After Chillingworth's discovery of Dimmesdale's guilt, "not merely the external presence, but the very inmost soul of the latter seemed to be brought out before his eyes, so that he could see and comprehend its every moment" (*The Scarlet Letter*, chapter 11). Of Tulkinghorn we are told, "While Mr Tulkinghorn may not know what is passing in the Dedlock mind at present, it is very possible that he may" (*Bleak*

House, chapter 2), and later (chapter 29): "It may be that my Lady had better have five thousand pairs of fashionable eyes upon her, in distrustful vigilance, than the two eyes of this rusty lawyer. . ."

Fourthly, the two characters are alike in their outward demeanour. Chillingworth first speaks to a stranger in the Boston market-place in a "formal and courteous manner" (*The Scarlet Letter*, chapter 3). He enters Hester's room in the prison "with the characteristic quietude of the profession to which he announced himself as belonging"; he looks into her eyes "with calm and intent scrutiny" and replies "with the same cold composure" (chapter 4). He speaks to Dimmesdale "with that quietness which, whether imposed or natural, marked all his deportment" (chapter 9). After he has discovered Dimmesdale's guilt he still appears "calm, gentle, passionless" (chapter 10). What Hester "best remembered in him" was "the aspect of an intellectual and studious man, calm and quiet" (chapter 45).

Similarly Dickens again and again stresses Tulkinghorn's calm inscrutability. He is "mute, close, irresponsive to any glancing light" (*Bleak House*, chapter 2). "His imperturbable face has been as inexpressive as his rusty clothes. . ." (chapter 11). He is "a hard-grained man, close, dry and silent" and "more impenetrable than ever" (chapter 22); "outwardly quite undisturbed" (chapter 29). He shows "the same formal politeness, the same composed deference . . . the whole man the same dark, cold object, at the same distance, which nothing has ever diminished" (chapter 41).

Fifthly, in both men this air of quiet composure is a mask behind which they conceal strong emotions. When Chillingworth first appears in Boston, and sees his wife on the scaffold, with the infant in her arms, "His face darkened with some powerful emotion, which nevertheless he so instantaneously controlled by some effort of his will, that, save for a single moment, his expression might have passed for calmness" (*The Scarlet Letter*, chapter 3). In his interview with Hester in prison, "The eyes of the wrinkled scholar glowed so intensely upon her, that Hester Prynne clasped her hands over her heart, dreading that he should read her secret there at once" (chapter 4). It is, of course, only after this interview that Chillingworth adopts his new name and his mask, and that the demeanour of quiet, calm studious composure which has been "natural" becomes "imposed". Even after he has discovered Dimmesdale's guilt, and has become "a chief actor in the poor minister's interior world", Dimmesdale, though intuitively distrusting and abhorring him, sees nothing in Chillingworth's demeanour to justify his "distrust and abhorrence" (chapter 11). But Hester in her second private interview with Chillingworth (chapter 14) easily sees through the mask.

> But the former aspect of an intellectual and studious man . . . had altogether vanished, and been succeeded by an eager, searching, almost fierce, yet carefully guarded look. It seemed to be his wish and purpose to mask this expression with a smile, but the latter played him false, and flickered over his visage so derisively, that the spectator could see his blackness all the better for it. Even and anon, too, there came a glare of red light out of his eyes; as if the old man's soul were on fire, and kept on smouldering duskily within his breast, until, by some casual puff of passion, it was blown into a monetary flame. This he repressed as speedily as possible, and strove to look as if nothing of the kind had happened.

Similarly Dickens again and again makes it known that Tulkinghorn's habitual demeanour gives no indication of his emotions and motives. "He has shown nothing but his shell. As easily might the tone of a delicate musical instrument be inferred from its case, as the tone of Mr Tulkinghorn from *his* case" (*Bleak House*, chapter 11). " 'He wears his usual expressionless mask — if it be a mask' " (chapter 12). "In face watchful behind a blind. . ."; he "looks (from behind that blind which is always down) . . ." (chapter 27). The mask slips momentarily on only a couple of occasions in his dealings with Lady Dedlock. "One glance between the old man and the lady; and for an instant the blind that is always down flies up. Suspicion, eager and sharp, looks out. Another instant, down again" (chapter 33). "The blood has not flushed into his face so suddenly and redly for many a long year as when he recognizes Lady Dedlock" (chapter 41). But, occasionally also, with people like George (chapter 27) and Hortense (chapter 41), from whom he thinks he has nothing to fear, he drops the mask.

Sixthly, both characters are repeatedly associated with images of mortality and burial, related to images of secrecy and concealment. In his prison visit to Hester Chillingworth exhorts her: "Let, therefore, thy husband be to the world as one already dead" (*The Scarlet Letter*, chapter 4). He answers Dimmesdale's inquiry about his "bundle of unsightly plants": " 'I found them growing on a grave, which bore no tombstone, nor other memorial of the dead man, save these ugly weeds . . . They grew out of his heart, and typify, it may be, some hideous secret that was buried with him . . .' " Chillingworth, we have already been told, "now dug into the poor clergyman's heart, like a miner, searching for gold, or rather like a sexton delving into a grave, possibly in quest of a jewel that had been buried on the dead man's bosom, but likely to find nothing save mortality and corruption. Alas for his own soul, if these were what he sought!" (chapter 10). This extended simile is obviously applicable to Tulkinghorn's investigation into the past of the dead Nemo, in search of evidence of Lady Dedlock's guilt.

At Tulkinghorn's first introduction we are told "there are noble Mausoleums . . . which perhaps hold fewer secrets, than walk abroad among men, shut up in the heart of Mr Tulkinghorn"; and "he receives these salutations with gravity, and buries them along with the rest of his knowledge" (*Bleak House*, chapter 2). "He is always the same speechless repository of noble confidences" (chapter 12). He sits "in his lowering magazine of dust, the universal article into which his papers and himself, and all his clients, and all things of earth . . . are resolving"; he returns from his wine-cellar "encircled by an earthy atmosphere", and as he sips his port, thinks of his one bachelor friend, "a man of the same *mould*" (my italics) who "one summer evening . . . walked leisurely home to the Temple, and hanged himself" (chapter 22). As he sleeps in the turret-room at Chesney Wold, after his confrontation with Lady Dedlock, "he looks as if the digger and the spade were both commissioned, and would soon be digging" (chapter 41).

There are other touches in the portrayal of Tulkinghorn which may have been suggested by *The Scarlet Letter*. For example this passage has the distinct flavour of Hawthorne: "His manner of coming and going between the two places is one of his impenetrabilities. He walks into Chesney Wold as if it were next to his chambers, and returns to his chambers as if he had never been out of Lincoln's Inn Fields. . . . He melted out of his turret-room this morning, just as now, in the late twilight, he melts into his own square" (*Bleak House*, chapter 42). This is reminiscent of Hawthorne's flirtings with the supernatural in such passages as the account of Hester Prynne's return to her cottage after years of absence. "In all those years it had never once been opened; but either she unlocked it, or the decaying wood and iron yielded to her hand, or she glided shadow-like through these impediments . . ." (*The Scarlet Letter*, chapter 24). When Dickens comments, as Tulkinghorn walks up and down on the leads at Chesney Wold: "The time was once, when men as knowing as Mr Tulkinghorn would walk on turret-tops in the starlight, and look up into the sky to read their fortunes there . . . If he be seeking his own star, as he methodically turns and turns upon the leads, it should be but a pale one to be so rustily represented below. If he be tracing out his destiny, that may be written in other characters nearer to his hand" (*Bleak House*, chapter 41), he may have been half-remembering a paragraph from *The Scarlet Letter* (chapter 12).

> Nothing was more common, in those days, than to interpret all meteoric appearances, and other natural phenomena, that occurred with less regularity than the rise and set of sun and moon, as so many revelations from a supernatural source . . . We doubt whether any marked events, for good or evil, ever befell New England, from its settlement down to Revolutionary times, of which the inhabitants had not been previously warned by some spectacle of this nature. . . . It was, indeed, a majestic idea that the destiny of nations should be revealed, in these awful hieroglyphics, on the cope of heaven . . . But what shall we say, when an individual discovers a revelation, addressed to himself alone, on the same vast sheet of record!

I think the case for regarding Chillingworth as the prototype of Tulkinghorn has been established. Both these similarly-named characters are elderly men, "black" in appearance, dim-eyed but acutely perceptive, whose cold, formal and inscrutable demeanours are masks maintained to hide their passions, who carry with them an aura of death and decay, and who are fancifully credited with semi-supernatural powers. To this, of course, must be added the even more important fact that their parts in the actions of their respective novels are closely similar: both Chillingworth and Tulkinghorn combine the roles of pertinacious investigator of secret guilt and self-ordained agent of retribution. Chillingworth attaches himself, as constant companion and trusted medical adviser, to Dimmesdale; he is convinced that Dimmesdale's bodily disease is "but a symptom of some ailment in the spiritual part" (*The Scarlet Letter*, chapter 10); and when, by an unusual chance, his suspicion that Dimmesdale was his wife's paramour is confirmed, he applies all the resources of his knowledge of humanity, his intellectual subtlety, and his medical skill to the sole purpose of revenge, and of keeping his victim alive to prolong his revenge. Tulkinghorn, the trusted legal adviser of the Dedlock family, becomes suspicious of some guilty secret in Lady Dedlock's past; he ferrets out the identity of the dead Nemo, whose handwriting has startled Lady Dedlock out of her customary glacial calm; and when, through a combination of persistent investigation and chance, he has discovered the truth of Lady Dedlock's illicit affair with Captain Hawdon, he plays cat-and-mouse with Lady Dedlock, first compelling her to go on acting her miserable deception on her "gaudy platform", and then, when she dares to defy him by dismissing her maid Rosa from her potentially contaminating presence, announces his intention of revealing her past to her husband.

This summary indicates that, as well as the strong resemblances between Chillingworth and Tulkinghorn, there are important differences between their respective roles. Chillingworth, the physician-necromancer, is the wronged husband of Hester; Tulkinghorn, the Chancery lawyer, is not personally involved with Lady Dedlock, and is wronged by her only insofar as she is the most glittering representative of the class that treats him as "the butler of the legal cellar" (*Bleak House*, chapter 2).

It is certainly not my intention to suggest that Dickens' use of Chillingworth was a matter of slavish imitation. I suggest, however, that, even though Dickens summarily and cryptically dismissed Chillingworth as "very poor", Hawthorne's dark and mis-shapen, preternaturally acute and implacably sadistic old avenger made a powerful impact on Dickens' imagination, and that, whether consciously or not, he recognized Chillingworth as a figure that he could use and adapt for his own very different purpose in *Bleak House*.

It is not necessary to my case to consider whether Dickens, in adapting Chillingworth, created a character who is equally convincing and psychologically plausible. But it is, I think, worth mentioning that the critical histories of the two characters have been remarkably similar. Chillingworth, in the words of William Bysshe Stein, used generally to be "treated as a piece of machinery",[80] or regarded as an almost purely allegorical figure representing evil, or guilt, or "man's bitter and diseased past."[81] But it has been shown by critics like Stein and Darrel Abel that "Hawthorne logically motivates all the physician's actions",[82] that Chillingworth is "not badness incarnate, but goodness perverted"[83] (as his name suggests), and that the course of his development, or degeneration, is quite explicable and fully analyzed.

Similarly, it often used to be alleged that Tulkinghorn's gratuitous detective activity and apparently unprovoked persecution of Lady Dedlock constituted one of the most serious weaknesses of *Bleak House*, and phrases like "motiveless malignancy" were commonly used about him. But critics like Joseph I. Fradin and Eugene F. Quirk have shown that "the main outlines of his psychological motivation are quite clear",[84] and that the reasons for his pursuit of Lady Dedlock are not merely his desire for power, and his passion for learning secrets; these are themselves the symptoms of his "dislike and suspicion of women" and his "fierce resentment of the overbearing pride of the fashionable world which sees him only as a valuable appendage to the estates and positions of its members."[85] These deeper motives are revealed, dramatically and usually without explicit comment, in many scenes.

The difference between the two characters is not that one is adequately motivated and the other is not. The difference between them reflects a basic difference between the art of Hawthorne and the art of Dickens. Whereas Chillingworth develops and alters in the course of the action, Tulkinghorn, like the great majority of Dickens' characters, is seen as a character formed, fixed and consistent.

Chillingworth is, in Hawthorne's own words, "a striking evidence of man's faculty of transforming himself into a devil, if he will only for a reasonable space of time undertake a devil's office" (*The Scarlet Letter*, chapter 14). The reason for his undertaking a devil's office is clear — the traumatic experience, when he at last reaches Boston and is greeted by the sight of his wife on the scaffold with the baby in her arms. For Chillingworth, "a man thoughtful for others, craving little for himself, — kind, true, just, and of constant, if not warm affections" (chapter 11), Hester had epitomized sympathy, tenderness and love; having lived alone and apart he had clutched at the dream of ideal love which would give him life, and make him part of the general life of humanity. The dream violently shattered, Chillingworth, for whom (in Abel's words) "goodness had been rather a matter of deliberate choice and policy, so long as he had no motive to do ill, than of strong inclination,"[86] dedicates himself to vengeance against the shatterer of his dream. But because he recognizes his own part in Hester's guilt — " 'Mine was the first wrong, when I betrayed thy budding youth into a false and unnatural relation with my decay' " (chapter 4) — he seeks no revenge against her; but out of injured self-love, jealousy of his supplanter, and the terrible sense that Hester's betrayal has doomed him to eternal isolation, he is determined to seek out and spiritually destroy her paramour. So although Chillingworth, though not naturally fiend-like, becomes a fiend, we can understand why he does, and to a degree, sympathize with him.

In contrast, Tulkinghorn has become a "devil" before we first encounter him, and we are never shown directly what caused his diabolization. But it does become clear enough that in his case it was not a particular personal disillusionment which embittered and distorted him. Rather, as Fradin contends, we are made to recognize that "his disease is in a general way the disease of the community, 'inbred in the body itself' "; "that the repression and distortion of the personality we find in Tulkinghorn is the necessary condition of his success in the world"; and that "Tulkinghorn's will to power has its roots in the denial of the sexual life."[87]

An important reason why readers have tended to feel that Tulkinghorn is less adequately motivated than Chillingworth is the difference in the manner of presentation of the two characters. Not only does Chillingworth himself recognize and define the change that has occured in him (in chapter 14), but Hawthorne in several extended passages provides a perceptive analysis of Chillingworth's motives, and of the development of his monomaniacal obsession. "He had begun an investigation, as he imagined, with the severe and equal integrity of a judge, desirous only of truth, even as if the question involved no more than the air-drawn lines and figures of a geometrical problem, instead of human passions and wrongs inflicted on himself. But, as he proceeded, a terrible fascination, a kind of fierce, though calm, necessity seized the old man within its gripe, and never let him free again until he had done all its bidding" (chapter 10). "Calm, gentle, passionless, as he appeared, there was yet, we fear, a quiet depth of malice, hitherto latent, but active now, in this unfortunate old man, which led him to imagine a more intimate revenge than any mortal had ever wreaked upon an enemy" (chapter 11).

In contrast to Hawthorne's minute and searching scrunties of Chillingworth, of which the quoted sentences are only samples (and which, no doubt, were among those which caused Dickens to describe "the psychological part" of *The Scarlet Letter* as "very much overdone"), Dickens hardly ever goes inside Tulkinghorn's mind, to show us how he regards the world, and what are the springs of his behaviour. What Dickens does is to show Tulkinghorn's behaviour, and occasionally to speculate (or rather to pretend to speculate) about his motives. The most important passage occurs in chapter 29.

> It may be that he pursues her doggedly and steadily, with no touch of compunction, remorse or pity. It may be that her beauty, and all the state and brilliancy surrounding her, only gives him the greater zest for what he is set upon, and makes him the more inflexible in it. Whether he be cold or cruel, whether immovable in what he has made his duty, whether absorbed in love of power, whether determined to have nothing hidden from him in ground where he has burrowed among secrets all his life, whether he in his heart despises the splendour of which he is a distant beam, whether he is always treasuring up slights and offences in the affability of his gorgeous clients — whether he be any of this or all of this, it may be that my Lady had better have five thousand pairs of fashionable eyes upon her, in distrustful vigilance, than the two eyes of this rusty lawyer . . .

This passage, which has some at least superficial resemblance to Hawthorne's use of what F.O. Mathiessen described as "the device of multiple choice",[88] provoked Robert Garis to comment:

> This splendid array of possible motives figures merely as the *material* which the theatrical mystification-artist is manipulating for his desired effect . . . But this whole procedure — the trifling with the "mystery" of human motivation only in order to work up our thrilled acceptance of a theatrical tableau — this amounts by ordinary standards of serious art to an exploitation of our moral stupidity. If we co-operate with it, it is because we are not

at the moment, and Dickens almost never is, interested in moral intelligence as George Eliot would understand it.[89]

This comment is unjust; though couched in the form of a series of alternatives, the real effect of the passage in question is to provide a summary of Tulkinghorn's complicated *actual* motives. No two of the apparently alternative motives are mutually exclusive, not even what Tulkinghorn "*has made* his duty" (my italics) and his "love of power"; what Tulkinghorn "has made his duty" has been called into question earlier, in chapter 12, in another transparent set of alternatives — "Whether his whole soul is devoted to the great or whether he yields them nothing beyond the services he sells, is his personal secret." Eugene Quirk is right in claiming that "the passage supplies not only the more obvious reasons for Tulkinghorn's conduct ... but, in what is almost surely an ascending order both psychologically and rhetorically, it makes clear that Tulkinghorn does despise 'the splendour of which he is a distant beam' ".[90]

I do not, therefore, now maintain (as I have done elsewhere)[91] that Tulkinghorn is a less psychologically convincing character than Chillingworth, and that Tulkinghorn's inferiority in this regard is further negative evidence of Dickens' indebtedness. No more than Hawthorne does Dickens commit the unpardonable sin of swerving aside from the truth of the human heart (to borrow Hawthorne's phrases in the preface to *The House of the Seven Gables*); but the means which he adopts to present the truth are not Hawthorne's, but typically Dickensian.

I have suggested certain resemblances, both in character and situation, between Hawthorne's Hester Prynne and Dickens' Honoria Dedlock; I have also questioned whether it is mere coincidence that in one novel the "guilty" mother's name is Hester, and in the other the illegitimate daughter's name is Esther. It might seem rather absurd to suggest that two such apparently different characters as Lady Dedlock and her daughter both owe much to Hawthorne's Hester, but it must be remembered that Hester herself is — or appears to be — almost two different characters, as the titles of chapters 5 and 13, "Hester at her Needle" and "Another View of Hester", suggest. Moreover, as one of the most recent vindicators of Esther, Alex Zwerdling, has pointed out: "The two women [Lady Dedlock and Esther] seem totally different yet are in a similar position. Each is alienated from her true self and unable to acknowledge her deepest feelings. Each is incomplete: Lady Dedlock searches for a child; Esther for a mother. Lady Dedlock has given up her lover and married an affectionate and protecting man a generation older than herself, whom she respects but does not love — the very doom that Esther narrowly escapes."[92]

Neither novelist is likely to have named his character without intending some reference to the Old Testament Esther, the beautiful Jewish maid, the ward of her older cousin, Mordecai, who was chosen as the wife of the Persian King, Ahasuerus, and who, at the risk of her own life, interceded with Ahasuerus on behalf of her oppressed people, condemned to destruction through the machinations of Haman, the nobleman who feared and was bitterly jealous of Mordecai, whose name had been entered in the chronicles of the King's house for his service in discovering and revealing a plot against the King's life.

Neither novelist, of course, tried to make the life of his character, in seventeenth century New England, or in nineteenth century England, an exact parallel to that of the biblical Esther. But in each case, as critics have pointed out, the fictional character does, in some ways, recall the biblical figure (who was herself probably a fictional character). Of Hester Prynne, H.H. Waggoner has commented: " 'Hester' is a modern form of 'Esther'; and the Old Testament Esther is gifted with beauty, strength, and dignity. Courageous and loyal, she defends a weak and oppressed people. The obvious parallel between the two women contributes one more implication that Hester is to be seen as finally 'in the right'. And it offers another bit of evidence to those who like to stress the feminist implications of the novel, for we may see the 'weaker sex' defended by Hester as but a variant of the weak people defended by Esther."[93] Of Esther Summerson, William Axton has remarked: " 'Esther' is no less appropriate [that her surname, Summerson], for this name links the heroine of *Bleak House* to the Old Testament orphan girl who was adopted and raised by a kindly and wise older man, Mordecai, the counterpart of Mr Jarndyce. Furthermore, Esther and Mr Jarndyce, like Esther and Mordecai before them, join forces to protect their persecuted brethren — the neglected children of the novel — from false ministers who threaten to destroy them — in this case all the irresponsible and falsely charitable characters and institutions."[94]

The common factor in Esther, Hester and Esther Summerson is, of course, defence of "a weak and oppressed people", or protection of "persecuted brethren." What Esther Summerson derives from Hester Prynne is not championship of the feminist cause, but self-denying service to others. In chapter 13 of *The Scarlet Letter*, "Another View of Hester", Hawthorne gives an account of what Hester's life is like, seven years after the birth of Pearl:

> She never battled with the public, but submitted uncomplainingly to its worst usage. . . . While Hester never put forward even the humblest title to share in the world's privileges, — farther than to breathe the common air, and earn daily bread for little Pearl and herself by the faithful labor of her hands, — she was quick to acknowledge her sisterhood with the race of man, whenever benefits were to be conferred. None so ready as she to give of her little substance to every demand of poverty; even though the bitter-hearted pauper threw back a gibe in requital of the food brought regularly to his door. . . . None so self-devoted as Hester, when pestilence stalked through the town. In all seasons of calamity, indeed, whether general or of individuals, the outcast of society at once found her place. She came, not as a guest, but as a rightful inmate, into the household that was darkened by trouble. . . . In such emergencies, Hester's nature showed itself warm and rich; a well-spring of human tenderness, unfailing to every real demand, and inexhaustible by the largest. . . . She was self-ordained a Sister of Mercy; or, we may rather say, — the world's heavy hand had so ordained her. . . .Such helpfulness was found in her, — so much power to do, and power to sympathize, — that many people refused to interpret the scarlet A by its original signification. They said it meant Able, so strong was Hester Prynne, with a woman's strength.

This passage virtually provides a summary of Esther Summerson's life also, in the years between her arrival in London, to become John Jarndyce's housekeeper, and her marriage to Alan Woodcourt. She too is uncomplaining, warm, tender, merciful, charitable, helpful, sympathetic, and "able", in all her dealings with Jarndyce, Ada Clare, Richard Carstone, Miss Flite, the Jellybys (especially Peepy and Caddy), the Neckett children, Prince Turveydrop, the brick-makers' wives, Jenny and Liz. She is "ready to give of her little substance to every demand of poverty" — even Harold Skimpole's; when "pestilence stalked through the town" she contracts it from nursing Charly Neckett, who caught it from the crossing-sweeper Jo. Esther too is "self-ordained a Sister of Mercy; or, we may rather say, the world's heavy hand had so ordained her."

This is not the place to undertake any detailed investigation of the complex psychological motivations either of Hester Prynne, which have been endlessly debated, or of Esther Summerson, which have also been much discussed. I wish only to suggest that there are strong similarities. In both cases there is a strong sense of guilt which leads to a long period of self-abnegating service to others. It is true that in chapter 17 of *The Scarlet Letter* Hester says to Dimmesdale: " 'What we did had a consecration of its own." But it is equally true that in the previous chapter, only a few minutes before, she had said to Pearl: " 'Once in my life I met the Black Man. . . . This scarlet letter is his mark!' " And in earlier chapters: "Here she said to herself, had been the scene of her guilt, and here should be the scene of her earthly punishment; and so perchance, the torture of her daily shame would at length purge her soul . . ." "Much of the time . . . she employed in making coarse garments for the poor. It was probable that there was an idea of penance in this mode of occupation . . ." (chapter 5). "She knew that her deed had been evil . . ." (chapter 6). Even though her reason "for continuing a resident of New England . . . was half a truth and half a self-delusion" (chapter 5), her life as "a Sister of Mercy" is undertaken at least partly as a form of penitence and expiation for an admitted sin (whether against herself, Dimmesdale, Chillingworth, God or the community).

Esther's case, of course, is different. She has herself committed no sin, but one of her earliest recollection is of the birthday on which her harshly Calvinistic aunt and godmother, Miss Barbary, tells her that she has inherited an ineradicable moral taint from the sin of her parents, that she has been "orphaned and degraded from the first "of these evil anniversaries", that she is "different from other children . . . not born, like them, in common sinfulness and wrath" but "set apart" (*Bleak House*, chapter 3). (Just so, it is worth interpolating, is Hester's Pearl "a born outcast of the infantile world. An imp of evil, emblem and product of sin, she had no right among christened infants" [*The Scarlet Letter*, chapter 6]. And Miss Barbary's charming opening conversational gambit: " 'It would have been far better, little Esther, that you had no birthday; that you had never been born!' " recalls Hester's unspoken thought about Pearl: "The child's own nature had something wrong in it, which continually betokened that she had been born amiss, — the effluence of her mother's lawless passion, — and often impelled Hester to ask, in bitterness of heart, whether it were for good or ill that the poor little creature had been born at all" [*The Scarlet Letter*, chapter 13].) Miss Barbary, the equivalent of the "world's heavy hand" which ordains Hester a "Sister of Mercy", adjures Esther that "submission, self-denial, diligent work, are the preparation for a life begun with such a shadow on it." Esther's reaction, she recalls, was to resolve to "try as hard as ever I could, to repair the fault I had been born with (of which I confessedly felt guilty and yet innocent), and would strive as I grew up to be industrious, contented and kind-hearted, and to do some good to some one, and win some love to myself if I could." As William Axton remarks, "From the beginning of *Bleak House*, then, and throughout the novel, Esther's character is defined by an inner struggle between a sense of an inherited moral taint and personal worthlessness prompted by her illegitimate birth, which urges her towards self-abnegating service to others, and a contrary awareness of her innocent and personal responsibility for her moral state, which expresses itself in the desire to experience normal self-realization and fulfilled identity in love and marriage."[95] This inner struggle, I suggest, is similar to the conflict in Hester Prynne between a sense of guilt prompted by her sin of adultery, which urges her toward self-abnegating service to others, and a hidden but passionate commitment to love, which causes and enables her, in the forest scene, to inspire the wretched Dimmesdale with her hope (vain and foredoomed as it is) that it is possible to salvage happiness from the wreckage of their lives ("to do some good to some one, and win some love for [her]self").

Despite these similarities between Hester and Esther, it is obvious that Esther has none of Hester's grandeur. Esther has in her nature no "rich, voluptuous, Oriental characteristic", and one can hardly imagine her assuming, as Hester did, "a freedom of speculation" which might have made her "a prophetess", and brought her "death from the stern tribunals of the period, for attempting to undermine the foundation of the Puritan establishment" (*The Scarlet Letter*, chapter 13). Few would now dismiss Esther as she generally used to be dismissed, as "the most detestable of all Dickens' heroines",[96] or as a merely sentimental indulgence on Dickens' part, or as an often-discarded ventriloquist's doll; most would probably agree with William Axton that "Esther's personal inconsistencies comprise an objective study of a character divided against herself by contending forces clearly discernible in her personal history", whose ambiguities of character "find direct expression in [her] narrative style."[97] Nevertheless, in the total context of *Bleak House*, what one remembers most about Esther is not her inner conflicts, but her sympathetic helpfulness. This, I suspect, owes less to Hester Prynne's "Sister of Mercy" role than to the essential uncomplicated nature of the heroine of Hawthorne's second romance, Phoebe Pyncheon.

I have suggested previously that, while Dickens seems not to have mentioned *The House of the Seven Gables*, it is very likely that he would have read it. The likeness between Esther and Phoebe seems to me too strong to be coincidental. Consider first these two comments, taken almost at random from the Hawthorne and Dickens critics. "In many ways Phoebe is the central figure in the *Seven Gables*. Not only does she have the largest number of lines to speak, but her sunny cheerfulness shines pervasively on each of the other characters. . . . No one and nothing that matters remains untouched by her genial influence."[98] "Esther is more central" to *Bleak House*'s structure" "than any other heroine . . . that Dickens produced." "Cheerfully sane and domestic, and much loved by those nearest to her", she "spread[s] sanity and healing in other people's misfortunes."[99]

Esther's surname, Summerson (who gave it to her, by the way — surely not Miss Barbary?) is one of the strongest pieces of evidence of her partial derivation from Phoebe; it could almost be taken as an admission by Dickens of his indebtedness. Her name, as Axton remarks, "is of course meant to pun on 'summer sun', emblematic of the cheerful brightness the girl brings to Bleak House in consequence of her desire to be 'industrious, contented and kind-hearted.' "[100] Phoebe's name is the feminine form of Phoebus, the god who for many centuries has been associated with the sun. Even before she enters the gloomy old mansion, it is clear what her role is to be: "The sordid and ugly luxuriance of gigantic weeds . . . and the heavy projection that overshadowed her . . . none of these things belonged to her sphere. But — even as a ray of sunshine, fall into what dismal place it may, creates for itself, a propriety in being there — so did it seem altogether fit that the girl should be standing at the threshold" (*The House of the Seven Gables*, chapter 4). The image recurs in the following chapter, when we are told that she is "as pleasant, about the house, as a gleam of sunshine falling on the floor"; it is her office "to move in the midst of practical affairs, and to gild them all . . . with an atmosphere of loveliness and joy" (chapter 5). When Phoebe leaves to make a brief visit to her country village "an easterly storm . . . set in and indefatigably applied itself to the task of making the black roof and walls of the old house look more cheerless than ever before . . . Phoebe was not there; nor did the sunshine fall upon the floor" (chapter 15). When she returns the sky is "genial once more with sunshine" (chapter 19). "In fine", as Rudolph Von Abele remarks, "she is continuously linked with that life-giving thing, the sun."[101]

In chapter 5 ("May and November") Hawthorne carefully establishes the symbolic basis for Phoebe's future actions. We are told that she "has a kind of natural magic", "the gift of practical arrangement", which enables her to throw "a kindly and hospitable smile" over her "waste, cheerless and dusky chamber", to "exorcise the gloom"; "the genial activity pervading her character" "impelled her forth . . . to seek her fortune, but with a self-respecting purpose to confer as much benefit as she could anywise receive"; she is (as she answers Hepzibah "smiling, and yet with a kind of gentle dignity") " 'a cheerful little body' "; she is "bright, cheerful and efficient", with "the cheeriness of an active temperament, finding joy in its activity, and therefore rendering it beautiful"; she wins Hepzibah's praise as "a nice little housewife", and her "truth and sagacity" make her "as nice a little saleswoman"; she is "admirably in keeping with herself, and never jar[s] against surrounding circumstances"; there is "a spiritual quality in Phoebe's activity"; like an angel, she does not toil "but let[s] her good works grow out" of her.

Virtually every comment made about Phoebe is equally applicable to Esther Summerson, and many of them are actually made, in paraphrase. When Esther expresses the fear that she is not clever enough to be Bleak House's housekeeper, Jarndyce reassures her: " 'You are clever enough to be the good little

woman of our lives here, my dear, . . . the little old woman of the
Child's . . . Rhyme:

> "Little old woman, and whither so high?" —
> "To sweep the cobwebs out of the sky."
> You will sweep them so neatly out of *our* sky, in the course of your
> housekeeping, Esther, that one of these days, we shall have to abandon the
> Growlery, and nail up the door' "   (*Bleak House*, chapter 8).

The effect that Jarndyce accurately prophesies Esther will have
in Bleak House, is the effect that Phoebe has in the House of the
Seven Gables: "The grime and sordidness of the House of the
Seven Gables seemed to have vanished, since her appearance
there; the gnawing tooth of the dry-rot was stayed, among the old
timbers of its skeleton-frame; the dust had ceased to settle down
so densely from the antique ceilings, upon the floors and fur-
niture of the rooms below; — or, at any rate, there was a little
housewife, as light-footed as the breeze, that sweeps a garden-
walk, gliding hither and thither, to brush it all away". And
Phoebe's moral-spiritual effect is equally potent. "The shadows
of gloomy events . . . the heavy, breathless scent which Death
had left . . . were less powerful than the purifying influence . . .
of one, youthful, fresh, and thoroughly wholesome heart"
(chapter 9).

Esther, in her narrative, adds that Jarndyce's quoting the
Child's Rhyme "was the beginning of my being called Old
Woman, and Little Old Woman, and Cobweb, and Mrs Shipton,
and Mother Hubbard, and Dame Durden, and . . . many other
names of that sort" (*Bleak House*, chapter 8). William Axton
points out that " 'Little Old Woman' or 'Mother Cobweb' . . .
has associations which reinforce those of Esther's last name,
Summerson or 'summer sun'. Like Mother Cobweb, Esther
brings good spirits and order to Bleak House, once darkened and
abandoned by the law's delay."[102] It is to be noted, however, that
not all of Esther's nicknames are derived from nursery rhyme
and folklore; one, more august, comes from Greek mythology.
Richard Carstone often calls Esther "Minerva"; Esther, Axton
remarks, "is a Minerva-like figure in her commonsense wisdom
and her devotion to the domestic virtues. An unwed orphan like
her mythic counterpart, Esther assumes the role of protectress of
hearth and family . . . as mistress of Bleak House, as foster-
parent to the Neckett and Jellyby children, and as an epitome of

. . . dutiful responsibility toward the unfortunate like Jo, the crossing-sweeper . . ."[103]

Phoebe, too, "assumes the role of protectress of hearth and family". Holgrave says to her " 'Whatever health, comfort and natural life, exists in this house, is embodied in your person. These blessings came along with you and will vanish when you leave the threshold.' " Phoebe modestly agrees that her " 'small abilities were precisely what they [Hepzibah and Clifford] needed; and I have a real interest in their welfare — an odd kind of motherly sentiment — which I wish you would not laugh at!' " And in the same conversation Phoebe explicitly but unselfconsciously states the basic tenet of the religion of love which she instinctively practises: " 'How is it possible to see people in distress, without desiring, more than anything else, to help and comfort them?' " (chapter 14). For Esther, no less than for Phoebe, the Christian injunction to "love thy neighbour" is a basic principle of life.

Despite the lack of external evidence that Dickens read *The House of the Seven Gables*, published in April 1851, before the first instalment of *Bleak House* appeared, in March 1852, I find it difficult to regard as purely coincidental the similarities between the heroines of the two novels, in their actual and symbolic roles, as suggested by their names. Esther is certainly the more complex and self-conscious character, because of her sense of inherited guilt; Phoebe, though a member of a family afflicted by the wrong-doing of an earlier generation, has little of the Pyncheon in her, knows little of the family history, and seems to have forgotten most of what she has been told.

It is worth mentioning that, as with Chillingworth and Tulkinghorn, the two characters have been subjected to similar criticism, and denounced as sentimental and unreal idealizations; and both have been effectively defended against such charges (in Esther's case by critics like Axton, Dyson and Zwerdling; in Phoebe's case by critics like Alfred J. Levy[104]). Phoebe's effect on the action of Hawthorne's romance has generally been underrated, but at least she has not been stigmatized as hypocritical and mock-modest as Esther often has. Hawthorne's narrative method does not require her to draw attention to her own virtues or record the praises of other people, as Dickens' method does with Esther. But despite the differences in presentation, the two characters seem to me quite startlingly similar.

One contemporary English critic, an anonymous writer in *Blackwood's Magazine*, detected a similarity between another of the five main characters of *The House of the Seven Gables* and one of those who figures prominently in Esther's part of *Bleak House*. He made this comment:

Clifford's perfect selfishness is only an intense development of his love for the beautiful, says his biographer. Hephzibah's [sic] shy and awkward tenderness disgusts and irritates rather than delights him, because it is his natural instinct to seek beauty, and there is nothing lovely in the withered ancient lady, in spite of the deep love at her heart. If we are not mistaken, Mr Hawthorne calls this "poetic", this heartlessness of his hero, and certainly endeavours to elevate it into something higher than the common hard selfishness which we are accustomed to. . . . Whatever it may be in America, we should be greatly disappointed to find the poetic temperament resolved into this vulgar sensationalism in our own more sober world. A nice eye for external beauty, and a heart closed to all perception of the beauty of other hearts, may make a voluptuary, but will never, with any amount of talent added thereto, make a poet. The character is fit enough for Harold Skimpole, and comes in admirablly to make up that capital sham, but we entirely reject and disbelieve it in any personage of more serious pretensions.[105]

Almost thirty-five years later, another British critic, Andrew Lang, in the course of a discussion of similarities between Hawthorne and Dickens, also noticed a likeness between Clifford Pyncheon and Harold Skimpole.

Perhaps it is really the beautiful, gentle, oppressed Clifford who haunts our memory most, a kind of tragic and thwarted Harold Skimpole. "How pleasant! — how delightful!", he murmured, but not as if addressing anyone. "Will it last? How balmy the atmosphere, through that open window! An open window! How beautiful that play of sunshine! Those flowers, how very fragrant! That young girl's face, how cheerful, how blooming; a flower with the dew on it, and sunbeams in the dewdrops!" This comparison with Skimpole may sound like an unkind criticism of Clifford's character and place in the story — it is only a chance note of a chance resemblance. Indeed it may be that Hawthorne himself was aware of the resemblance. "An individual of his [Clifford's] temper can always be pricked more acutely through his sense of the beautiful and harmonious, than through his heart." And he suggests that, if Clifford had not been so long in prison, his aesthetic zeal "might have eaten out or filed away his affections". This is what befell Harold Skimpole — though "in prisons often" — at Coavinses![106]

Lang's suggestion that Hawthorne may have been "aware of the resemblance" is, of course, absurd, since Harold Skimpole made his first appearance in print in April 1852, a year after *The House of the Seven Gables* was published. But the converse may well have been true — Dickens may have been aware of the resemblance. There is certainly a distinct similarity between Clifford's quoted speech (chapter 7), on his first morning in the old house, after some thirty years of imprisonment for a murder which he did not commit (which, indeed, was no murder), and Skimpole's conversation with "Coavinses" (*Bleak House*, chapter 6) after Esther and Richard have paid, on his behalf, the "twenty-four pound, sixteen, and seven-pence ha' penny" to save him from arrest for debt.

> "But when you came down here", proceeded Mr Skimpole, "it was a fine day. The sun was shining, the wind was blowing, the lights and shadows were passing across the fields, the birds were singing" and "Then you didn't think, at all events," proceeded Mr Skimpole, "to this effect. 'Harold Skimpole loves to see the sun shine; loves to hear the wind blow; loves to watch the changing lights and shadows; loves to hear the birds, those choristers in Nature's great cathedral. And does it seem to me that I am to deprive Harold Skimpole of his share in such possessions, which are his only birthright!' You thought nothing to that effect?"

There are, of course, great differences between these two sybaritic aesthetes. Clifford Pyncheon has been reduced to a state of torpid near-idiocy by thirty years in prison; Skimpole makes a career of idleness, as a gentleman amateur in various arts, parasitically battening on benefactors like Jarndyce to keep him out, or get him out, of prison. In the course of *The House of the Seven Gables* Clifford is transformed (whether convincingly or not is another matter) from an emotional and spiritual cripple to a vigorous and aware adult; in the course of *Bleak House*, Skimpole is not transformed, but through his heartless conniving with Bucket to have the desperately ill Jo "moved on", through his abetting of, and feeding on, Richard Carstone's hopes of achieving riches from Jarndyce and Jarndyce, he is revealed to be, not an entertaining and charmingly irresponsible critic of society, but a viciously selfish and callous monster. And there is a great difference between Hawthorne's sympathetic and compassionate treatment of Clifford, and Dickens' contemptuous dislike of Skimpole, which comes clearly through Esther's narrative.

Skimpole, moreover, as Louis Crompton remarks, "was, of course, widely recognized as a thinly disguised portrait of [Leigh] Hunt by contemporary critics, most of whom objected to the sketch as wildly unjust."[107] Crompton contends that despite

Dickens' claim, in a letter in 1853, that Skimpole "is the most exact portrait that was ever painted in words", Dickens "worked largely by exaggeration and exclusion. He takes Hunt's lightest vein [especially in his 1844 Christmas book, *A Jar of Honey from Mount Hybla*], removes the qualifications from his statements, and succeeds in converting a writer of tepid charm into a diabolically scintillating caricature."[108]

Even though Hunt was, undoubtedly, the chief model for Skimpole, and despite the differences I have mentioned between Skimpole and Clifford Pyncheon, it seems possible that Dickens received some hints from Hawthorne's character. There is, particularly, their "childishness". Donald Junkins, in an essay on *The House of the Seven Gables*, has assembled some of the "myriad references to Clifford's childish qualities."[109] When Hepzibah shows Phoebe the miniature (chapter 5), Phoebe remarks: " 'It has something of a child's expression. . . . He ought never to suffer anything.' " Phoebe tells the Judge (chapter 8); " 'There is no frightful guest in the house, but only a poor, gentle, childlike man. . . .' " For Hepzibah (chapter 10) "The more Clifford seemed to taste the happiness of a child, the sadder was the difference to be recognized." Clifford takes "childish delight in the music" of the barrel-organ. "He had no burthen of care upon him; there were none of those questions and contingencies with the future to be settled, which wear away all other lives. . . . In this respect, he was a child; a child for the whole term of his existence, be it long or short. . . . He sometimes told Phoebe and Hepzibah his dreams, in which he invariably played the part of a child, or a very young man" (chapter 11). To Holgrave's enquiry (chapter 12) whether Clifford seems happy, Phoebe answers " 'As happy as a child . . . but — like a child, too — very easily disturbed.' "

When Esther, Ada and Richard first arrive at Bleak House (chapter 6), Jarndyce tells them: " 'There's no one here but the finest creature upon earth — a child' " and then explains " 'I don't mean literally a child . . . but a child in years. He is grown up . . . but in simplicity, and freshness, and enthusiasm, and a fine guileless inaptitude for all wordly affairs he is a perfect child.' " Skimpole, who "had more the appearance . . . of a damaged young man, than a well-preserved elderly one" loses no time in candidly elaborating on his "childishness": " 'Then, for

Heaven's sake, having Harold Skimpole, a confiding child, peti-
tioning you, the world, an agglomeration of practical people of
business habits, to let him live and admire the human family, do
it somehow or other, like good souls, and suffer him to ride his
rocking horse!' " He couldn't practise medicine, because "he had
always been a mere child in point of weights and measures"; he
failed in every opening to which his good friends helped him,
because, like a child, "he had no idea of time [and] . . . no idea of
money."

There is the obvious difference that Clifford has regressed to a
childlike state as the result of decades of imprisonment, while
Skimpole's frequently asserted childishness is a manifestation of
total moral irresponsibility — whether excuse, mask, or symptom
it is impossible to tell, since Skimpole appears only in Esther's
narrative (and she admits, in chapter 15, "I never really
understood him well enough to know" whether he was "politic"
and "divined" "that his off-hand professions of childishness and
carelessness were a great relief to my guardian", "since to find
one perfectly undesigning and candid man, among many op-
posites could not fail to give him pleasure"). But it is worth mentioning that Q.D. Leavis has remarked that "except in his claims
to be childlike Skimpole is a recognisable later Victorian type, an
aesthete, who systematically substitutes aesthetic reactions for
human ones."[110] The least than can be said is that Hawthorne
preceded Dickens in creating such a character, and aroused the
bluff and misguided ire of the *Blackwoods* critic — misguided
because Hawthorne does not anywhere suggest, any more than
Dickens does, that "a nice eye for external beauty, and a heart
closed to all perception of the beauty of other hearts" will ever
"make a poet". But it is tempting to go further, and suggest that
Dickens saw in Clifford's childishness (a state from which
Clifford emerges with the death of his cousin Jaffrey, and
through the revitalizing influence of Phoebe) a pose for Skimpole
to adopt as justification for his using the world, in George Eliot's
famous phrase, as "an udder to feed our supreme selves."

It may even be that Dickens derived Skimpole's often repeated
and fancifully embroidered assertion that the world owes him a
living because he is a person of taste and exquisite sensibilities
(As Q.D. Leavis comments: "Other people don't exist for
Skimpole in their own right, and yet he demands their services

since he can't, being a social parasite, exist without them. Skimpole's claim to preferential treatment is that as an artist he *has* sensibility, and he needs to feed it ... but at the cost of excluding human considerations")[111] partly from Hawthorne's extended comment on Clifford:

> Not to speak it harshly or scornfully, it seemed Clifford's nature to be a Sybarite. It was perceptible, even there, in the dark, old parlour, in the inevitable polarity with which his eyes were attracted towards the quivering play of sunbeams through the shadowy foliage. It was seen in his appreciative notice of the vase of flowers, the scent of which he inhaled with a zest, almost peculiar to a physical organization so refined that spiritual ingredients are moulded in with it. It was betrayed in the unconscious smile with which he regarded Phoebe, whose fresh and maidenly figure was both sunshine and flowers, their essence in a prettier and more agreeable mode of manifestation. [Compare Skimpole's speeches about Ada Clare " 'She is like the morning ... with that golden hair, those blue eyes, and that fresh bloom on her cheeks she is like the summer morning. ... If I had [my way] there should be no brambles of sordid realities in such a path as that. It should be strewn with roses; it should lie through bowers, where there was no spring, autumn, nor winter, but perpetual summer' " *Bleak House*, chapter 6.] Not less evident was this love and necessity for the Beautiful, in the instinctive caution with which, even so soon, his eyes turned away from his hostess, and wandered to any quarter, rather than come back. It was Hepzibah's misfortune; not Clifford's fault. How could he — so yellow as she was, so wrinkled, so sad of mien ... how could he love to gaze at her! But, did he owe her no affection for so much as she had silently given? He owed her nothing. A nature like Clifford's can contract no debts of that kind. It is — we say it without censure, nor in diminution of the claim which it indefeasibly possesses on beings of another mould — it is always selfish in its essence; and we must give it leave to be so, and heap up our heroic and disinterested love upon it, so much the more, without a recompense (*The House of the Seven Gables*, chapter 7).

Isn't this parodied in Skimpole's speech (*Bleak House*, chapter 6): " 'It's only you, the generous creatures, whom I envy. ... I envy you your power of doing what you do. ... I don't feel any vulgar gratitude to you. I almost feel as if *you* ought to be grateful to *me*, for giving you the opportunity of enjoying the luxury of generosity. ... For anything I can tell, I may have come into the world expressly for the purpose of increasing your stock of happiness. I may have been born to be a benefactor to you, by sometimes giving you an opportunity of assisting me in my little perplexities' "?

There is one other episode in *The House of the Seven Gables* which was seen by contemporary critics as Dickensian, but which might, with at least equal justification, have been seen as influencing Dickens. One anonymous critic (presumably British) remarked in 1855: "Only the pen that flung that strange, terrible gloom over the closing scenes of *Bleak House* could rival the incidental touches immediately antecedent to the death of Judge Pyncheon."[112] Five years later, another anonymous critic (presumably American) commented: "The eighteenth chapter of this novel, in which the author describes all the schemes of an ambitious man cut short by his sudden death is full of a grim irony such as we find nowhere so well sustained except in some of the best passages of Dickens."[113] G.E. Woodberry, in 1902, also saw a resemblance to Dickens, but not at his best: "In the long chapter which serves as [Jaffrey Pyncheon's] requiem, and in which there is the suggestion of Dickens not in the best phase of his art, the jubilation is somewhat diabolic; it affects one as if Hawthorne's thoughts were executing a dance upon a grave."[114]

Chapter 18 of *The House of the Seven Gables*, entitled "Governor Pyncheon" was generally regarded as one of the show-pieces of the novel. Jaffrey Pyncheon, who has allowed his cousin to rot in gaol for thirty years for Jaffrey's crime, sits dead in his seventeenth century ancestor's chair, dead of the same disease which killed the ruthless and rapacious Colonel; he sits through the long day, while the narrator rehearses all the important engagements he is missing (especially the dinner at which he is to be nominated for the Governorship of Massachusetts). He sits throughout the night, in darkness and in moonlight, while the narrator "makes a little sport" with the "ridiculous legend that, at midnight, all the dead Pyncheons . . . assemble in this parlour." He sits as "the dreary night . . . gives place to a fresh, transparent, cloudless morn", and a house-fly creeps "over the bridge of his nose, towards the would-be chief-magistrate's wide-open eyes."

It is not my purpose to consider whether this long chapter is reminiscent of "some of the best passages of Dickens", or "of Dickens not in the best phase of his art", but rather to suggest that to it Dickens was in some degree indebted for the conception (*Bleak House*, chapter 47) of his villain, Tulkinghorn, lying dead, shot through the heart, with "foreshortened Allegory" pointing helplessly at the body, "at the empty chair, and at a stain upon the ground before it that might almost be covered by a hand." Dickens' treatment is much more economical -- only a few paragraphs; indeed much of Hawthorne's chapter is summarized in a single sentence: "Moonlight, darkness, dawn, sunrise, day. There he is still, eagerly pointing, and no one minds him." But the similarities in the basic conceptions (both Judge Pyncheon and Tulkinghorn are on the point of destroying their victims when death frustrates them) seem too great to be coincidental.

Hawthorne's Influence in *Hard Times*

As I have said, it is in *Bleak House*, especially in the Lady Dedlock strand, that the Hawthorne influence on Dickens is strongest. But it seems to me that the influence of Hawthorne is also considerable in Dickens' next novel, *Hard Times* — in character, situation, theme and symbolism. But it also seems to me that in this case the Hawthorne influence was not really beneficial; here I consider that Dickens picked up some of Hawthorne's ideas without really making them his own.

In some obvious ways *Hard Times*, which was originally published in twenty weekly instalments in *Household Words*, is more like a Hawthorne romance than any of Dickens' previous novels. There is, first of all, the similarity of length. *Hard Times* is little more than one-fourth the length of the twenty-part novels like *Dombey and Son*, *David Copperfield*, *Bleak House* and *Little Dorrit*. Even so, it is considerably longer than *The Scarlet Letter*, and about the same length as *The House of the Seven Gables*. (The Norton Critical Edition of *Hard Times* runs to 226 pages; *The Scarlet Letter*, in identical format and type face, runs to only 181 pages, and excluding "The Custom-House" to only 149; *The House of the Seven Gables* is about 25 per cent longer than *The Scarlet Letter*, including "The Custom House", and would be about 224 pages in the same format.)

I am not going to suggest that Dickens decided to follow Hawthorne's example and write a novel of the same approximate dimensions. The circumstances of the writing and publication of *Hard Times* are well-known; Dickens had intended to take a year off novel-writing after completing *Bleak House* in September 1853, but, as he wrote in a letter to Angela Burdett-Coutts in

January 1854, when he had written one page of *Hard Times* (still one of fourteen possible titles): "There is such a fixed idea on the part of my printers and co-partners in Household Words, that a story by me, continued from week to week, would make some unheard of effect with it, that I am going to write one. It will be as long as five numbers of *Bleak House*, and will be five months in progress. . . ."[115]

Why Dickens decided in advance that *Hard Times* was to be the length of only five numbers of *Bleak House* (rather than six, or eight, or ten) is not clear; but, having made the decision, he stuck to it — except that he decided that the weekly numbers after No. 16 would be "enlarged to ten of my sides each-about"[116] (instead of "about seven pages and a half of my writing").[117] The result was that the last four weekly instalments, which became Book 3 ("Garnering") in the one-volume edition, are approximately equivalent to the final so-called "double number" of the long novels, which in fact was not twice the length of the preceding eighteen, but equal to one and a half numbers (forty-eight pages instead of thirty-two). He stuck to the decision, but soon found himself severely constricted by the projected total length of the novel, and exasperated by the brevity of the individual weekly units. In February 1854, he wrote to Forster: "The difficulty of the space is CRUSHING. Nobody can have an idea of it who has not had an experience of patient fiction-writing with some elbow-room always, and open places in perspective."[118] And in April, to H.W. Wills: "I am in a dreary state, planning and planning the story of Hard Times (out of materials for I don't know how long a story), and consequently writing little."[119]

Though I did not suggest that Dickens, in writing an uncharacteristically short novel, was consciously following Hawthorne's example, I do suggest that the self-imposed restrictions almost inevitably produced a work which, in structure and methods, has distinct similarities to *The Scarlet Letter*, and *The House of the Seven Gables*.

Whether the restriction in length, and the consequent adoption of a more carefully controlled and articulated structure, had beneficial or deleterious effects is one of the basic critical questions about the novel. The question has, of course, received every conceivable answer. At one extreme is F.R. Leavis's elevation of *Hard Times* to the top of the Dickens canon, as "of all Dickens's works . . . the one that has all the strength of his genius, together with a strength no other one of them can show — that of a completely serious work of art";[120] as "a moral fable", in which "the representative significance of everything . . . — character, episode and so on — is immediately apparent as we read", but in which "the Dickensian vitality is [present], in its varied characteristic modes, which have the more force because they are free of redundance";[121] and as a work which "by texture, imaginative mode, symbolic method, and the resulting concentration, . . . affects us as belonging with formally poetic works."[122] At the other extreme is A.J.A. Waldock's rejoinder (quoted because it was the earliest, made even before Leavis's essay became part of *The Great Tradition*) that "*Hard Times* undoubtedly is a moral fable, and no one need raise any question about the perseverance with which Dickens sticks to the task he has set himself";[123] but that is just what is wrong with the book. "The basic fact . . . is simply that Dickens is trying to do two contradictory things at once. He cannot forget that he is ostensibly writing a novel so he goes through the pretence of moving 'characters' about as if they were real. But what his heart is really set on is the writing of a pamphlet, and come what may, he is determined to write it. How could such a misdirected enterprise end in anything but the most crashing of failures?"[124] In the middle are verdicts like Angus Wilson's — that *Hard Times* is exceptional among Dickens' novels in its careful structuring, but that it is "equally shaped and impoverished by discipline"; that "Bounderby, Mrs Sparsit and above all James Harthouse offer more flesh to the skeleton than has usually been recognized; but the novel remains a skeleton"; that it is not one of Dickens' feasts but "merely a menu card."[125]

I quote these divergent appraisals, not to adjudicate between them, but to point to what they agree about — "moral fable", "insistent intention", "coherent whole", "representative significance", "persevering sticking to task", "shaped and impoverished by discipline", "skeleton". The point I wish to make is that most comments on *Hard Times*, whether eulogistic, objurgatory or impartial, strongly remind me of Hawthorne's rather disparaging comments on his own work, in contrast to that of Dickens and other serial novelists, which I have quoted previously: "In all my stories, I think, *there is one idea running through them like an iron rod* and to which all other ideas are referred and subordinate; and the circumstance gives the narrative a character of monotony; which possibly may strengthen the impression which it makes, . . . but [may] become intolerably wearisome." (Italics mine.) Critics, it seems to me, praise or blame *Hard Times* because it approaches Hawthorne's description of his own work.

It is of some interest that Dickens in his letters uses the term "idea" in much the same way as Hawthorne does. In the letter to Angela Burdett-Coutts, previously quoted, Dickens continued: "*The main idea* of it, is one on which you and I . . . have often spoken; and I know it will interest you *as a purpose*." In a later letter (to Mrs Richard Watson) in November 1854, some months after the novel was finished, he remarked that he had "intended to do nothing in that way for a year, when *the idea* laid hold of me by the throat in a very violent manner."[126] (Italics mine.) Though undeveloped, these comments suggest Dickens' awareness that the motivating and controlling force behind *Hard Times* was different from the impulse behind his other novels — that in Hawthorne's terms, "there is one idea running through [it] like an iron rod"; and his complaints to Mrs Watson about "the compression and close condensation necessary" shows his recognition that "all other ideas" had to be "referred and subordinate" to this idea.

Dickens did not anywhere define "the main idea" which would interest Angela Burdett-Coutts "as a purpose", but some of the possible titles which he listed in a letter to Forster probably give a clearer indication of it than does the title eventually chosen — for example, *Mr Gradgrind's Facts, The Grindstone, Two and Two are Four, Something Tangible, Simple Arithmetic, A Matter of Calculation, A Mere Question of Arithmetic*.[127] All of these titles suggest that the book is to be a polemical work, an exposure of, and attack on, materialism and hard-headed, inhumane practicality. David Lodge has effectively abstracted the argument behind the novel: "The argument has two stages: (1) that the dominant philosophy of Utilitarianism, particularly as it expresses itself in education, results in a damaging impoverishment of the moral and emotional life of the individual; and (2) that this leads in turn to social and economic injustice, since individuals thus conditioned are incapable of dealing with the human problems created by industrialism."[128]

But there were a few other possible titles which Dickens listed on the first page of his working memoranda (*Mems.* as he called them) for *Hard Times*, but did not include in the list sent to Forster. One, the curt monosyllable, *Fact*, is similar to those cited. Two others, however, suggest a greater complexity of theme — *Heads and Tales* and *Hard heads and soft hearts*.[129] The first punningly suggest the antithesis between "fact" and "fancy" which is explicitly stated in the opening sentence of chapter 5, significantly titled "The Key-note". "Coketown . . . was a triumph of fact; it had no greater taint of fancy than Mrs Gradgrind herself." The second more explicitly indicates that there is an obverse to the main thesis, a counter-argument which maintains that England has not yet been totally undermined, corrupted and dehumanized by the "hard heads" of Utilitarianism, materialism, self-interest, acquisitiveness; there are still "soft hearts" who believe, and act on their beliefs (as the bleary and sleasy Mr Sleary states them in the second-last chapter): " 'One, that, there ith a love in the world, not all Thelf-interetht after all, but thomething very different; t'other, that it hath a way of ith own of calculating or not calculating, which . . . ith . . . hard to give a name to.' "

In one of the best discussions of *Hard Times*, David Sonstroem has commented on "the somewhat conflicting impulses that moved Dickens as he wrote it."[130] These two rejected titles seem, however, to indicate Dickens' awareness, even before he had written the first page, that the "idea" of the novel was to include two sets of antitheses (heads and tales; heads and hearts). Sonstroem elaborates the point: "The first sentence of *Hard Times* discloses the villain of the piece: Facts — narrow, dry statistics and definitions imperiously presented as a sufficient, and the only sufficient, explanation of the world and all living things. Not so obvious is the beleaguered alternative that Dickens champions. The predominant word for it is Fancy, but what he means by it is decidedly sweeping and variable, and therefore unclear." After listing various linked and synonymous terms which Dickens uses, Sonstroem points out: "Two areas of meaning emerge from this cluster. The one is imaginative play: mental play unhindered by the strictures of reality. The other is fellow feeling: compassion, sentiment."[131]

This is quite true. It is not difficult to construct from the text two lists of contending forces and qualities, ranged under each of the rejected titles. Under "Heads v Hearts", there is Hardness v Tenderness; Sterility v Fertility; Destruction v Creation; Materialism v Spirituality; Calculation v Affection; Self-Interest v Sympathy; Egotism (Number One) v Fellow-feeling; Isolation v Communion. Under "Heads v Tales" there is Fact v Fancy (given concrete embodiment in Coketown v Sleary's Circus); Reason v Imagination; Statistics v Romance; Definition v Dream; "Ologies" v "Childish Lore".

It is not my purpose to consider whether Dickens succeeds in bringing the two opponents of "heads" and "facts" (i.e. "hearts" and "fancy" — or, in Sonstroem's formulation, "fellow feeling" and "imaginative play") into effective alliance, or whether, as Sonstroem claims, they are "not always in league, and in fact sometimes work at cross-purposes."[132] My first purpose is to suggest that both of these conflicts had previously been treated, and more profoundly treated, by Hawthorne in tales like "The Maypole of Merry Mount", and in *The Scarlet Letter* and *The House of the Seven Gables*. And secondly, I want to suggest that Dickens was in some degree indebted to Hawthorne both for the "idea" of *Hard Times*, and for some of the details of its treatment.

I quote first from a passage in chapter 2 of *Hard Times* which F.R. Leavis found especially impressive, for the force "with which the moral and spiritual differences are rendered ... in terms of sensation, so that the symbolic intention emerges out of metaphor and the vivid evocation of the concrete."[133]

"The square finger, moving here and there, lighted suddenly on Bitzer, perhaps because he chanced to sit in the same ray of sunlight which ... irradiated Sissy. ... But, whereas the girl was so dark-eyed and dark-haired, that she seemed to receive *a deeper and more lustrous colour* from the sun when it shone upon her, the boy was so light-eyed and light-haired that the self-same rays appeared to draw out of him what little colour he ever possessed." (My italics.)

I have not found anything in Hawthorne analogous to the effect of the sun in accentuating Bitzer's sterile albinism, but I suggest that the description of Sissy owes a good deal to Hester Prynne, who "had dark and abundant hair, so glossy that it threw off the sunshine with a gleam" (*The Scarlet Letter*, chapter 2), and who, in the chapter entitled "A Flood of Sunshine" (18) "took off the formal cap that confined her hair; and down it fell upon her shoulders, dark and rich, with at once *a shadow and a light* in its abundance . . ." (My italics.)

The image is no doubt, as Leavis says, intended to suggest that "Sissy stands for vitality as well as goodness", for "life that is lived truly and richly from the deep instinctive and emotional springs." But does Sissy really live up to the image; does she achieve "a potently symbolic role"? Does she not dwindle into an insipid shadow of Esther Summerson, who herself, I have suggested, is Dickens' version of Phoebe Pyncheon? Part of the trouble with Sissy is that she is, literally, "not there" for most of the novel. We see and hear very little of her, after she joins the Gradgrind household. In book 1, chapter 9, Louisa tells her " 'You are more useful to my mother, and more pleasant with her than I can ever be . . . You are pleasanter to yourself, than *I* am to *my*self.' " In book 1, chapter 14, Mr Gradgrind, terminating her education, tells her: " 'You are an affectionate, earnest, good young woman. . . . You are useful to Mrs Gradgrind, and (in a generally pervading way) you are serviceable to this family also. . . .' " But we never actually see her being "pleasant and useful" to Mrs Gradgrind and "serviceable to the family". Apart from glimpsing her, in book 2, chapter 1, with Jane's arm round her neck, we are given no evidence that "some change may have been slowly working about me in this house, by mere love and gratitude", as Gradgrind thinks he has noticed (book 3, chapter 1).

In making their comments on Sissy's beneficial effect, Louisa and her father are virtually repeating a conversation between Phoebe Pyncheon and Holgrave (*The House of the Seven Gables*, chapter 14), after the first dawning of love between them. Phoebe says:

> "It is pleasant to live where one is much desired, and very useful; and I think I may have the satisfaction of feeling myself so, here."
> "You surely may, and more than you imagine", said the artist.
> "Whatever health, comfort, and natural life, exists in the house, is embodied in your person. These blessings came along with you, and will vanish when you leave the threshold. Miss Hepzibah, by secluding herself from society, has lost all true relation with it, and is in fact dead. . . . Your cousin

> Clifford is another dead and long-buried person. . . . I should not wonder if
> he were to crumble away, some morning, after you are gone. . . . Miss
> Hepzibah, at any rate, will lose what little flexibility she has. . ."

The great difference is that we have *seen* Phoebe in her friendly, helpful and sympathetic intercourse with her elderly relatives;
we have seen that she gives them life and hope by her very being.
Hawthorne has provided several passages of imaginative analysis
of Phoebe's nature and its effect on Hepzibah and Clifford,
notably in chapter 9.

> The shadows of gloomy events . . . were less powerful than the purifying in-
> fluence, scattered throughout the atmosphere of the household by the
> presence of one, youthful, fresh and thoroughly wholesome heart. [Compare
> Gradgrind's "In a generally pervading way, you are serviceable to the family
> also."] There was no morbidness in Phoebe. . . . But, now, her spirit
> resembled, in its potency, a minute quantity of attar of roses in one of
> Hepzibah's huge, iron-bound trunks, diffusing its fragrance through the
> various articles of linen . . . treasured there. As every article in the great
> trunk was the sweeter for the rose-scent, so did all the thoughts and emotions
> of Hepzibah and Clifford, sombre as they might seem, acquire a subtle at-
> tribute of happiness from Phoebe's intermixture with them. Her activity of
> body, intellect, and heart, impelled her continually to perform the ordinary
> little toils that offered themselves around her, and to think the thought,
> proper for the moment, and to sympathize . . . with Hepzibah's dark
> anxiety, or the vague moan of her brother.

But such expository passages serve essentially as corroboration of
the human realities, sensitively presented in a series of scenes in
the chapters entitled "May and November", "Clifford and
Phoebe" and "the Pyncheon-Garden". Hawthorne convinces us
of Phoebe's reality as a warm, palpable, human presence; this
Dickens never does with Sissy. And because Dickens does not
really believe in Sissy, he is quite prepared, when the plot
requires someone to send Harthouse packing, to bring on
someone with Sissy's name to perform the function, in the scene
which no one but F.R. Leavis has found "wholly convincing".[134]
John W. Gibson comments: "The young girl that prevails
against James Harthouse is not the emotionally-oriented, intuitive child of the circus. The master of rhetorical passion
opposing the weary dandy is more reminiscent of an Edith
Dombey, crushing Carker to death, than any female of
simplicity."[135] Even more trenchantly, but no less justly, David
H. Hirsch: "Now the simple girl who previously was unable to

string three syllables together . . . speaks fluently in the flowery rhetoric of a cultured and refined eighteenth-century heroine. The words 'reparation' and 'mitigate', 'compensation' and 'obligation' flow from her lips with a readiness that Clarissa herself would have envied. . . . Sissy now speaks the language of the sentimental romance of seduction, and her action is complemented by all the cliches of that genre."[136]

What I am suggesting, then, is that Dickens tries to give Sissy Jupe in Stone Lodge the same symbolic role as Phoebe Pyncheon in the house of the seven gables, as the representative and embodiment of spontaneous tenderness and affection, intuitive sympathy and fellow-feeling; but where Hawthorne created a believable being, Dickens produced a dim, sentimentalized wraith, who is equally unconvincing on the realistic and symbolic levels, and whose only vitality derives from the image with which she is first introduced, itself probably borrowed from Hawthorne.

Another small piece of evidence of Hawthorne's influence in *Hard Times* is the very name of the languid would-be seducer whom Sissy so easily defeats — James Harthouse. Hawthorne, of course, frequently imaged the human heart as a house or mansion, and occasionally reversed the process. There is, for example, Chillingworth's assertion to Hester (*The Scarlet Letter*, chapter 4): " 'My heart was a habitation large enough for many guests, but lonely and chill, and without a household fire.' " And, in reverse, there is the description of the Pyncheon mansion (*The House of the Seven Gables*, chapter 1): "So much of mankind's varied experience had passed there, — so much had been suffered, and something, too, enjoyed; — that the very timbers were oozy, as with the moisture of a heart. It was itself like a great human heart, with a life of its own, and full of rich and sombre associations."

One can't help suspecting that Dickens was remembering passages like these in naming Harthouse. But if the name has a distinctly Hawthornean flavour, it hardly seems an appropriate name for one who is "heartless". In the interview with Sissy, we are told: "He was touched in the cavity where his heart should have been — in that nest of addled eggs, where the birds of heaven would have lived if they had not been whistled away — by the fervour of this reproach." But whether appropriate or not,

Harthouse's name suggests to me a considerable indebtedness to Hawthorne for the whole "head versus heart" theme of *Hard Times*.

It would be foolish to contend that Hawthorne was the first writer of fiction to employ these antithetical terms for the conflict between thought and emotion, reason and passion. Marvin Laser points out that "Hawthorne might have found ample precedent for his favourite terms in earlier novelists like Richardson, Sterne, Godwin, Jane Austen, and even in his avowed early idol, Sir Walter Scott."[137] So too, presumably, might Dickens. But I suspect more than coincidence in the emergence into explicit prominence of the theme in Dickens, so soon after the publication of *The Scarlet Letter* and *The House of the Seven Gables*.

The theme becomes most baldly explicit in *Hard Times*, in the opening chapter of Book the Third, titled "Another Thing Needful". Louisa has escaped from her detested husband and the seductions of Harthouse, and fainted at her father's feet. Gradgrind's faith in facts and statistics is destroyed by the sight of "the triumph of his system, lying, an insensible heap, at his feet." When he visits her next day, he announces: "Some persons hold that there is a wisdom of the Head, and that there is a wisdom of the Heart. I have not supposed so; but, as I have said, I mistrust myself now. I have supposed the head to be all-sufficient. It may not be all-sufficient. . . ." In the succeeding scene Sissy Jupe, the representative of the wisdom of the heart, refuses to be repelled by Louisa's angry resentment; and, eventually, Louisa

> fell upon her knees, and clinging to this stroller's child looked up at her almost with veneration.
> "Forgive me, pity me, help me! Have compassion on my great need, and let me lay this head of mine upon a loving heart!"
> "O lay it here!" cried Sissy, "Lay it here, my dear."

David Hirsch's comment is harsh, but not unjust. "This should be a moving scene, for it suggests the power of Christian self-sacrifice, humility, and love to overcome the ruin wrought by a sterile materialism. As the scene materializes, however, it is actually ludicrous. The language is excessive, trite, and empty. The same is true of the gestures. No doubt Dickens intends the laying of Louisa's 'head' on Sissy's 'loving heart' to bristle with symbolic significance. But any significance is lost in the tiredness of the sentimental rhetoric."[138]

In Hawthorne the "head versus heart" theme is treated with great subtlety and profundity. As shown by the journal entry which was the seed of the portrayal of Ethan Brand and Chillingworth, for him "the Unpardonable Sin might consist in a want of love and reverence for the human soul . . . the separation of the intellect from the heart."[139] But though he believed that the purely rational, intellectual, scientifically-minded man was in danger of committing the sin of prideful isolation from humanity, which would damn and destroy him, Hawthorne had no sentimental faith in the heart (which he frequently referred to as a foul cavern) as the pure source of all good. As Matthiessen remarked, he "believed disequilibrium between the two to be the chief source of tragedy."[140] And, conversely, one solution to the problem of human happiness and fulfilment is the achievement of a balance between head and heart. (It is this which saves Phoebe Pyncheon, with "her activity of body, *intellect and heart*", from being a sentimentalized figment.)

It seems to me that the strength of *Hard Times* is almost entirely outside "the main idea" — particularly in the characterization of Bounderby, Harthouse and Mrs Sparsit. In developing "the main idea" (*Hard Heads and Soft Hearts*) Dickens cheapened and vulgarized Hawthorne's psychology of the head and the heart. He reduced to a threadbare, vapid and simplistic allegory of heartlessness versus mindlessness what in Hawthorne was a means of investigating the complexities of human beings and their inter-relations. I believe that Dickens was indebted to Hawthorne; but in *Hard Times* (far more than in *Bleak House, Little Dorrit, Great Expectations* or *Our Mutual Friend*) what he produced was a banal caricature.

Hawthorne's Influence in Dickens' Last Novels

I do not think that Hawthorne's influence is as readily identifiable in Dickens' four last-written novels as in *Hard Times* and, especially, in *Bleak House*. In each there are characters, themes, images, symbols which strike one as Hawthornesque, but it is not usually possible to adduce specific passages from Hawthorne to substantiate this impression.

In *Little Dorrit*, now generally regarded as Dickens' masterpiece, everyone recognizes, with J.C. Reid, that "the prison image is ubiquitous"[141]. There are the literal prisons of the Marseilles gaol of the opening chapter, and the Marshalsea; but more importantly the prison becomes a metaphor for Victorian society, in which men and women are trammelled and frustrated by social conventions, class divisions, legal institutions, bureaucratic obstruction. Most importantly, as Reid remarks, "the prisons in *Little Dorrit* are not only physical and social ones; they are psychological as well. Men are prisoners of their own fears, guilts, inhibitions."[142]

It is chiefly the psychological prisoners, those who are isolated and alienated from humanity, who remind one of Hawthorne's characters — especially three of them. In ascending order of importance, first there is Ellen Wade, the self-tormenting, illegitimate orphan who, convinced that she is unwanted and unloved, chooses to be hateful, and enlists as disciple the passionately rebellious, similarly-situated Tattycoram (whose very nickname indicates the patronizing, belittling attitude to her of the well-meaning Meagles), who, incidentally, has the "rich black hair" (chapter 2) of Sissy Jupe (and Hester Prynne). There is not, I think, any Hawthorne character quite like Miss Wade; but does not the image used to describe her, in her first scene with Tattycoram, irresistibly remind us of *The Scarlet Letter*: "The observer stood with her hand upon her own bosom, looking at the girl, as one afflicted with a diseased part might curiously watch the dissection and exposition of an analogous case" (chapter 2)? Does not the image bring together all three of those involved in Hawthorne's drama of guilt and expiation? Hester "had always this dreadful agony in feeling a human eye upon the token; the spot never grew callous; it seemed, on the contrary, to grow more sensitive with daily torture"; but "she felt or fancied . . . that the scarlet letter had endowed her with a new sense. She shuddered to believe . . . that it gave her a sympathetic knowledge of the hidden sin in other hearts" (*The Scarlet Letter*, chapter 5). "To Hester's eye, the Reverend Mr Dimmesdale exhibited no symptom of positive and vivacious suffering, except that, as little Pearl had remarked, he kept his hand over his heart" (chapter 16). After Chillingworth has had his "revelation", "by its aid, in all the subsequent relations betwixt him and Mr Dimmesdale . . . the very inmost soul of the latter seemed to be brought out before his eyes" in (chapter 11).

There is Mrs Clennam, who for many years has been imprisoned in her chair by paralysis, a psychosomatic condition with its source in her grim self-righteousness and her gloomy retributive religion, and her sense of guilt for the wrong she has done to Arthur, his mother, and Amy Dorrit, by suppressing the codicil to Gilbert Clennam's will. Again there is no Hawthorne character quite like her; but again there are touches in the portrayal which remind of Hawthorne. For example, the comment made about her, in chapter 5 ("Her severe face had no thread of relaxation in it, by which any explorer could have been guided to the gloomy labyrinth of her thoughts") recalls such passages from *The Scarlet Letter* as "Thus Hester Prynne . . . wandered without a clew in the dark labyrinth of mind" (chapter 13) and "She had wandered . . . in a moral wilderness; as vast, intricate and shadowy, as the untamed forest, amid the gloom of which they were now holding a colloquy" (chapter 18).

There is William Dorrit, imprisoned for debt for twenty-three years, while unknown to him he is the heir to a large fortune. Released from prison, he remains a prisoner; and, eventually, in one of the greatest and most terrible scenes Dickens ever created, his mind crumbles under the strain of his pretence of ignorance of the prison, and he reverts to his old role of father of the Marshalsea. John Holloway remarks that "what was true for . . . Dorrit . . . is true for all the major characters. All are prisoners through the force of an idea characteristic of the mid-nineteenth century, with its deep sense of causal law and long temporal continuity: *the present is imprisoned in the past*."[143] This, it is worth mentioning, is exactly the theme that Holgrave expounds to Phoebe in the Pyncheon garden:

> Without directly answering her, he turned from the Future . . . and began to speak of the influences of the Past. One subject, indeed, is but the reverberation of the other.
> "Shall we never, never get rid of this Past!. . . . It lies upon the Present like a giant's dead body! In fact, the case is just as if a young giant were compelled to waste all his strength in carrying about the corpse of the old giant, his grandfather, who died a long while ago, and only needs to be decently buried" (*The House of the Seven Gables*, chapter 12).

More specifically, William Dorrit's situation and experience reminds of that of Clifford Pyncheon, imprisoned for thirty years, wrongly condemned for the death of his uncle. The developments of the two prisoners after release are almost diametrically opposite. Clifford, a shattered, childish semi-imbecile after his release, develops into an aware and intelligent adulthood (asserted, however, rather than demonstrated). Dorrit, on his release is (somewhat improbably) able to assume the facade of the wealthy gentleman, but, under the strain of the pretence relapses into a state of semi-imbecile amnesia. Dorrit is undoubtedly one of the greatest of all Dickens' characters; comments like John Lucas' are fully justified. ("It is remarkable but true, that although Dorrit is presented to us in all his faults of selfishness, weakness, vanity, self-deception, yet he never entirely forfeits our sympathy. Compassion is a word that is over-used and consequently degraded in critical discussion, but no other will do justice to Dickens's treatment of Dorrit").[144] It would be absurd to suggest that the character is in any way derivative or imitative; but it is, I hope, not absurd to suggest that, in his wonderfully sure and delicate examination of Dorrit's disintegration, Dickens may have received some hints from such passages about Clifford Pyncheon as this: "Then his face darkened, as if the shadow of a cavern or a dungeon had come over it; there was no more light in its expression than might have come through the iron grates of a prison-window — still lessening, too, as if he were sinking farther into the depths" (*The House of the Seven Gables*, chapter 7).

I would say, however, that there is a clearer, more definite connection between Clifford Pyncheon and the prisoner of Dickens' next novel, Doctor Manette. John Lucas expresses a common enough view in maintaining that "if *Little Dorrit* is Dickens's greatest novel, [*A Tale of Two Cities*] is his worst";[145] and Philip Hobsbawm another, in suggesting that "what one can pick out . . . is the original concept of a man emerging into the world after many years of solitary confinement. Somewhere within the tuppence-coloured landscape of *A Tale of Two Cities* is a short story of remarkable psychological insight called 'Buried Alive' . . . The imaginative core of the book centres upon the plight of Doctor Manette."[146]

Hawthorne's creation of Clifford Pyncheon, eight years before

A Tale of Two Cities, means that "the concept of a man emerging into the world after many years of solitary confinement" was not "original" in the sense of "created, invented for the first time". There seem to be enough similarities between the two characters to raise doubts as to whether the concept was wholly "original" in the sense of "not derived or copied from something or someone else." I adduce a couple of passages from each novel.

From *The House of the Seven Gables*: "Phoebe heard that strange, vague murmur, which might be likened to an indistinct shadow of human utterance" (chapter 6).

> Phoebe saw an elderly personage . . . wearing his gray, or almost white hair, of an unusual length. . . . After a very brief inspection of his face, it was easy to conceive that his footstep must necessarily be such an one as that which — slowly, and with as indefinite an aim as a child's first journey across a floor — had just brought him hitherward. Yet there were no tokens that his physical strength might not have sufficed for a free and determined gait. It was the spirit of the man that could not walk. The expression of his countenance — while, notwithstanding, it had the light of reason in it — seemed to waver, and glimmer, and nearly to die away, and feebly to recover itself again. It was like a flame which we see twinkling among half-extinguished embers . . .
>
> 'Phoebe?' repeated the guest with a strange, sluggish, ill-defined utterance. . . .
>
> Continually . . . he faded away out of his place, or, in other words, his mind and consciousness took their departure, leaving his wasted, gray, and melancholy figure — a substantial emptiness, a material ghost — to occupy his seat at table. Again, after a blank moment, there would be a flickering taper-gleam in his eyeballs.
>
> This old, faded garment, with all its pristine brilliancy extinct, seemed . . . to translate the wearer's untold misfortune. . . . It was the better to be discerned, by this exterior type, how worn and old were the soul's more immediate garments, that form and countenance, the beauty of which had almost transcended the skill of the most exquisite of artists. . . . There he seemed to sit, with a dim veil of decay and ruin betwixt him and the world . . . (chapter 7).

From *A Tale of Two Cities*: "The faintness of the voice was pitiable and dreadful. It was not the faintness of physical weakness. . . . Its deplorable peculiarity was, that it was the faintness of solitude and disuse. It was like the last feeble echo of a sound made long and long ago. So entirely had it lost the life and resonance of the human voice, that it affected the senses like a once beautiful colour, faded away into a poor weak stain."

"The task of recalling him from the vacancy into which he

always sank when he had spoken, was like recalling some very weak person from a swoon. . . ."

". . . Some long obliterated marks of an actively intent intelligence in the middle of the forehead, gradually forced themselves through the black mist that had fallen on him. They were over-clouded again, they were fainter, they were gone; but they had been there." (Book the First. chapter 6).

". . . the abstraction that overclouded him fitfully, without any apparent reason" (Book the Second. chapter 4).

No doubt, as Hobsbawm claims, Dickens' portrayal of Manette showed the "incalculable harm . . . done by loneliness and neglect";[147] but so had Hawthorne's portrayal of Clifford Pyncheon. It seems to me that the passages I have cited provide substantial evidence of Dickens' indebtedness to Hawthorne in what is generally considered the only valuable part of his poorest work.

As previously mentioned,[148] *Great Expectations* seems to be the only one of Dickens' novels in which a Hawthorne influence has previously been detected (though Q.D. Leavis, finding in the opening chapter of *Great Expectations* "substantial evidence for [Dickens'] expressed admiration for the opening scenes of Hawthorne's allegorical masterpiece, *The Scarlet Letter*" implies that the influence of *The Scarlet Letter* on Dickens, as well as on George Eliot, has been generally recognized). Mrs Leavis argues that in his opening chapter, in which Pip gives his earliest memory of himself crying in the churchyard, at his parents' grave, and in which he is to learn that a prison hulk, as well as the gibbet, is part of his habitat, Dickens was picking up an idea from Hawthorne's opening chapter in which Hawthorne had "in the same terms, but more forthrightly" set out the conditions of human life. "However Utopian a new colony may be in intention, he states, 'the founders . . . have invariably recognized it among their earliest practical necessities to allot a portion of the virgin soil as a cemetery, and another portion as the site of a prison' — that is, death, and sin or crime (offences against the laws of God and man) are the basic facts of any society and, Hawthorne adds, therefore not only is a burial ground needed but the settlement's soil invariably bears 'the black flower of civilized society, a prison.' "[149]

I must admit that to me the connection seems too tenuous to

provide "substantial evidence" of Hawthorne's influence. Nor, I must confess, do I find Mrs Leavis' further discussion, in a footnote, of "the pronounced likeness of *Great Expectations* to Hawthorne's novel" overwhelmingly convincing.

> Hawthorne opens his novel outside the prison, uses the Scaffold for public expiation, has his little settlement surrounded by woods where lurk the Devil and his instruments, all as a background for the sinful consciousness of Hester Prynne and Arthur Dimmesdale, with the incidental revelation by Hawthorne, with devastating irony, that the society that condemns the sinners is far more really evil. The two characters have to work out their own salvation by suffering, contrition, confession, self-abnegation and atonement, and, in the case of Hester the survivor, by a life of useful work and humble acceptance of her lot. Miss Havisham's being seen by Pip in a vision as first and last hanging from a beam reminds one of Hester forced to stand on the Scaffold at the beginning and end of her sufferings.[150]

Pip's repeated hallucination seems to me a piece of gratuitous gothicism, which has little or no connection or analogy with the series of three scaffold scenes which are of such paramount importance in the structure and meaning of *The Scarlet Letter*.

Nevertheless, Miss Havisham, like Mrs Clennam in her voluntary self-imprisonment in embittered solitude, and her obsessive hatred of life, is a distinctly Hawthornesque character — a strange, semi-demented combination of Hepzibah Pyncheon and Roger Chillingworth. She has committed what, for Hawthorne, are three of the worst sins — wilful self-separation from humanity, self-dedication to one ruling passion, and "a want of love and reverence for the Human Soul". Like Hawthorne's Ethan Brand, who, in the process of "converting man and woman to be his puppets" became a "fiend", Miss Havisham shapes Estella to be "the cold instrument of her revenge on human passion and on life itself",[151] and maliciously encourages Pip in the mistaken belief that she is his benefactor.

There is one passage, in chapter 49, when Miss Havisham has confessed to Pip her sins against him and Estella, and has begged his forgiveness, which seems to me more substantial evidence of Dickens' indebtedness to Hawthorne than anything suggested by Q.D. Leavis. Lucas may be right in remarking that in this passage "we recognize Dickens' own voice beginning to edge into Pip's thoughts";[152] if so it may be because Dickens (unwittingly, no doubt) was borrowing the terms of his moral-psychological analysis from Hawthorne.

I knew not how to answer or how to comfort her. That she had done a grievous thing in taking an impressionable child to mould into the form that her wild resentment, spurned affection, and wounded pride found vengeance in, I knew full well. But, that, in shutting out the light of day, she had shut out infinitely more; that, in seclusion, she had secluded herself from a thousand natural and healing influences; that her mind, brooding solitary, had grown diseased, as all minds do and must and will that reverse the appointed order of their Maker, I knew equally well. And could I look upon her without compassion, seeing her punishment in the ruin she was, in the profound unfitness for this earth in which she was placed, in the vanity of sorrow which had become a master mania . . .?

One could point to a host of passage in Hawthorne's tales and romances which Dickens, or Pip, seems to be unconsciously paraphrasing and adapting. I content myself with four, chosen almost at random.

Meanwhile, Roderick seemed aware how generally he had become the subject of curiosity and conjecture, and, with a morbid repugnance to such notice, or to any notice whatsoever, estranged himself from all companionship. Not merely the eye of man was a horror to him; not merely the light of a friend's countenance; but even the blessed sunshine, likewise, which in its universal beneficence typifies the radiance of the Creator's face, expressing his love for all the creatures of his hand. . . .
All persons chronically diseased are egotists, whether the disease be of the mind of body; whether it be sin, sorrow, or merely the more tolerable calamity of some endless pain, or mischief among the cords of mortal life ("Egotism; or, the Bosom Serpent").
That daughter . . . was . . . Esther [Estella, a coincidence?] the very girl whom, with such cold and remorseless purpose, Ethan Brand had made the subject of a psychological experiment, and wasted, absorbed, and perhaps annihilated her soul, in the process. . . .
But where was the heart? That, indeed had withered, — had contracted, — had hardened — had perished! It had ceased to partake of the universal throb. He had lost his hold of the magnetic chain of humanity. . . . He was now a cold observer, looking on mankind as the subject of his experiment, and, at length, converting man and woman to be his puppets. . . . ("Ethan Brand").
Some attribute had departed from her, the permanence of which had been essential to keep her a woman. Such is frequently the fate . . . of the feminine character and person, when the woman has encountered, and lived through, an experience of peculiar severity. . . . If she survive, the tenderness will either be crushed out of her, or . . . crushed so deeply into her heart tht it can never show itself more. . . .
Standing alone in the world . . . she cast away the fragments of the broken chain (*The Scarlet Letter*, chapter 13).
Hepzibah . . . had grown to be a kind of lunatic, by imprisoning herself so long in one place, with no other company than a single series of ideas, and

but one affection, and one bitter sense of wrong (*The House of the Seven Gables*, chapter 12).

Not only is Pip's judgment of Miss Havisham couched in terms reminiscent of Hawthorne's comments on several of his isolated characters, but Miss Havisham's death by fire, immediately after she has acknowledged the heinousness of her crimes against life, is reminiscent of Ethan Brand's suicide in the lime-kiln, immediately after he has recognized that he has committed the Unpardonable Sin.

I have referred previously to Edward M. Passerini's essay, "Hawthornesque Dickens", which finds many similarities to Hawthorne in Dickens' "best writing", as exemplified in the opening chapters of *Our Mutual Friend*, without suggesting that the resemblances are more than coincidental.[153] I do not think that a strong case can be made for Hawthornean influence on *Our Mutual Friend*, but there are a few points which I'd like to make, without wishing to make too much of any of them.

In the first place, *Our Mutual Friend* is, essentially, a four-person novel; its structure is based on the developing and contrasted relationships between two pairs of lovers — John Harmon and Bella Wilfer; Eugene Wrayburn and Lizzie Hexam. This last-completed of Dickens' novels was the first in which he used such a structure, though he complicated it by introducing a large number of characters, not only those related to one or other of the main strands (the Boffins, the Wilfers, Silas Wegg, and Mr Venus; Gaffer and Charly Hexam, Bradley Headstone, Rogue Riderhood, and "Jenny Wren") but a third, fiercely satirized "choric" group — the Veneerings, the Podsnaps, the Lammles, Twemlow and Lady Tippins.

Variations of the same basic form were to be used by novelists as different as George Eliot (who had, indeed, already used a very similar form in *Adam Bede*), particularly in *Daniel Deronda*; James, especially in *The Golden Bowl*; Hardy, in such novels as *The Return of the Native* and *The Woodlanders*; and Lawrence, especially in *Women in Love*. It may be no more than coincidence that Hawthorne had twice used such a form, in *The Blithedale Romance* and *The Marble Faun*.

In the second place, there is a distinct thematic similarity between at least one strand of *Our Mutual Friend* (the Harmon-Wilfer-Boffin strand) and *The House of the Seven Gables*. I have

previously quoted part of Holgrave's fulmination against the
dead body of the past crushing the present. The first example
that Holgrave gives of life's enslavement to death is: "A Dead
Man, if he happens to have made a will, disposes of wealth no
longer his own . . ." (*The House of the Seven Gables*, chapter 12).
John Harmon's father in his grasping, suspicious reluctance to
release his clutch on the money he has amassed from "dirt", has
made not one, but a whole series of contradictory wills — all
designed to punish or repressively control his descendants and
beneficiaries. The Harmon story is certainly related (not
necessarily by deliberate intent) to the avowed "moral" of *The
House of the Seven Gables*, as explicitly stated in Hawthorne's
preface — "the folly of tumbling down an avalanche of ill-gotten
gold, or real estate, on the heads of an unfortunate posterity,
thereby to maim and crush them. . . ." The intended, actual, or
potential effects of Harmon's wills include reducing Bella Wilfer
to a chattel, punishing his son by making his inheritance condi-
tional on his marriage to a girl whom he expected to become a
viciously selfish virago, corrupting Boffin into a miserly image of
Harmon himself, and attracting to the noxious pile of filthy lucre
a swarm of predatory flies and vultures.

   It is worth noting too that both novelists have been accused of
"going soft", of denying the full implications of their own
"morals" (Hawthorne's as quoted above, Dickens' "Money,
money, money, and what money can make of life"). The other
part of Hawthorne's moral, as stated in the preface is that "the
wrong-doing of one generation lives into the successive ones,
and, divesting itself of every temporary advantage, becomes a
pure and uncontrollable mischief". The conclusion of *The House
of the Seven Gables*, in which Hepzibah and Clifford, Phoebe and
Holgrave (now self-revealed as the descendant of Matthew
Maule, who was virtually murdered for his land by the original
Pyncheon) ride off in a "handsome dark-green barouche" to the
dead Jaffrey's country estate, there to enjoy the hundreds of
thousands of dollars they have inherited from him, through the
timely death of his son, seems to contradict the moral. Moreover,
so F.O. Matthiessen claims, "In the poetic justice of bestowing
opulence on all those who had previously been deprived of it by
the Judge, Hawthorne overlooked the fact that he was sowing all
over again the same seeds of evil."[154]

K.J. Fielding's criticism of *Our Mutual Friend* is similar. "The foul dust-heap, composed of vast quantities of refuse, does represent wealth. But . . . its more unsavoury aspects are glossed over. . . . Then . . . we are not allowed to forget that the golden-hearted Boffin also helped to build them up, that he inherits them, and that they are passed on to Bella Wilfer and the miser's son with the evident approval of the author." The deduction drawn by Fielding is "that there is no objection to inheriting wealth without working for it, and that it is only wrong for a man like Harmon to build it up by providing an honest service for the community."[155]

Both criticisms are, to some extent at least, mistaken. In quoting Hawthorne's avowed moral, I omitted the important qualifying clause. What he actually says is that ill-gotten gold or real estate would maim and crush its inheritors "until the accumulated moss shall be scattered abroad in its original atoms." Francis Joseph Battaglia contends that "the inference is quite definite that when the pilfered wealth has gotten back to its original owners, the evil of its acquisition will cease to vex those who have been inheriting it. In terms of Hawthorne's plot, when the House of the Seven Gables, dishonestly wrested from the Maules, shall have been returned to them [as it is through Phoebe's marriage to Holgrave], the curse acquired with its illicit possession will cease to plague the Pyncheons."[156] Holgrave certainly does not propose to Phoebe for mercenary motives; it is not until a week after Jaffrey's death that it is learnt that his son is also dead. So it is difficult to see why Matthiessen should maintain that Hawthorne was, unwittingly, "sowing again the same seeds of evil"; the Maule fortune will not have been founded on any "wrong-doing", but rather on reparation for wrong-doing.

Rather similarly, Dickens does not censure old Harmon either because his fortune was founded on wrong-doing, or because it was built up "by providing an honest service," the collection of refuse. As Kenneth Muir points out, old Harmon is criticized "because he uses the wealth he has amassed in immoral ways. He is a miser; he has no sense of stewardship or of responsibility to society; he treats his children badly; and he tries to control the actions of his son from the grave. Boffin, on the other hand, is generous with the money he has inherited; and he uses it to give happiness to others."[157] It is not money in itself that Dickens is attacking, but the uses to which it may be put, and the dehumanizing cupidity with which it may be sought. *Our Mutual Friend* is about "what money *can* make of life", not what it inevitably must make of life. Much of the novel — the whole elaborate deception of Bella by Boffin's masquerade as a miser, and her renunciation of mercenariness in utter revulsion at his moral degeneration — is designed to demonstrate that money is not an all-powerful corruptor.

Yet when all this has been said, it remains true that the endings of both novels are vitiated by a sentimental, fairy-tale unreality. Harmon's introduction of Bella to the refurbished Boffin mansion, "tastefully ornamented with the most beautiful flowers", with its "charming aviary" "gold and silver fish, and mosses, and water-lilies, and a fountain, and all manner of wonders" (chapter 62), is all too like the departure of Phoebe and her husband for "the elegant country-seat of the late Judge Pyncheon", where the two decrepit hens are already indulging in an orgy of egg-laying, and a gingerbread cottage is to be fitted up for Uncle Venner (chapter 21). The trouble is not so much that the two happy young couples have acquired wealth, through no effort or particular merit of their own, but that it is hard for the reader to imagine what they will do with it. Matthiessen's criticism of the end of *The House of the Seven Gables* applies equally to that of *Our Mutual Friend*: "Hawthorne's comparatively flimsy interpretation of the young lovers derives from the fact that he has not visualized their future with any precision. . . . The fact that he hardly cast a glance at what would prevail at the Holgraves' country seat, prevented him from suggesting their participation in any definite state of existence."[158] But, presumably, what will prevail at the Holgrave country seat is very much what Orwell sees as the ideal striven after by Dickens' heroes, including John Harmon: "A hundred thousand pounds, a quaint old house with plenty of ivy on it, a sweet womanly wife, a horde of children, and no work. Everything is safe, soft, peaceful, and, above all, domestic."[159]

The House of the Seven Gables and *Our Mutual Friend* are very different novels, but they are at least alike in this: in Hawthorne's novel, and in one of the two main strands of Dickens', a young man and a young woman, initially divided by powerful pressures from the past (a family feud with overtones of class conflict — aristocrat v plebeian; the appalling will of a malicious old tyrant) through selfless and disinterested love gain the strength to overcome the evil forces working on and through them, achieve happiness and prosperity, and disappear from view into a state of paradisal domestic euphoria.

If there are any characters in *Our Mutual Friend* who at all resemble characters of Hawthorne, they appear in the other, far better, and almost totally separate, part of the novel — the two rivals for the love of Lizzie Hexam, Eugene Wrayburn and Bradley Headstone. Despite Henry James, who, in his anonymous review, dismissed both as "simply figures",[160] Wrayburn and Headstone are generally recognized as among Dickens' most percipiently understood characters. The main reason is that both the "well-bred, careless, elegant, sceptical and idle gentleman", Wrayburn, and the "high-tempered, hard-working, ambitious young schoolmaster", Headstone (to borrow James' thoroughly inadequate tags) are intimately related to Dickens' own life. Philip Hobsbawm suggests that "Eugene . . . is something Dickens would have liked to be, the gentleman born, so certain of his place in society as to be able to treat it with disdain" but "beneath his nonchalance . . . haunted by lack of ready money and fear of disaffection from his class"; but that Headstone, motivated by a "devouring paranoia", is closer to Dickens, for it is he "who has most to conceal; who is least socially safe; who is imbued with passions his author dare not own; who lives in order to subjugate another to his will; who therefore comes across like a blast from the inferno of his author's secret life."[161]

If the conflict between Wrayburn and Headstone has its origins in conflict within Dickens himself, as Hobsbawn and others suggest, it may be sheer delusion to see it prefigured in the main male characters of Hawthorne's *The Blithedale Romance*, Coverdale and Hollingsworth. If so, I confess to delusion.

There are great differences between Coverdale and Wrayburn, but they are similar in being aristocratic, supercilious, cool, detached, sceptical; in his repudiation of aggressive competitiveness, his lack of purpose, Coverdale seems to end where Wrayburn begins. On the last page of his narrative, several years after the Blithedale experience, Coverdale confides that the want of [a purpose], I occasionally suspect, has rendered my own life an emptiness. I by no means wish to die. Yet were there any cause, in this whole chaos of human struggle, worth a sane man's dying for, and which my death would benefit, then — provided, however, the effort did not involve an unreasonable amount of trouble, I might be bold to offer up my life. If Kossuth, for example, would pitch the battlefield of Hungarian rights within an easy ride of my abode, and choose a mild, sunny morning, after breakfast, for the conflict, Miles Coverdale would gladly be his man, for one brave rush upon the levelled bayonets. Further than that, I should be loath to pledge myself.

In substance and tone this seems to me very like the conservation between Wrayburn and Mortimer Lightwood (who is little more than Wrayburn's shadow) in the cab, on the way to view the body thought to be John Harmon's.

" 'Then idiots talk, said Eugene . . . 'of Energy. If there is a word in the dictionary under any letter from A to Z that I abominate, it is energy. It is such a conventional superstition, such parrot gabble!'

'Precisely my view . . . Eugene. But show me a good opportunity, show me something really worth being energetic about, and *I'll* show you energy.'

'And so will I' said Eugene."

Similarly, there are great differences between Hollingsworth and Headstone, but they are similar in being of plebeian origin (Hollingsworth is an ex-blacksmith), strenuous, passionate, hot-tempered, obsessed. Their obsessions are different; Hollingsworth is obsessed with his plans for the reformation of criminals, Headstone is obsessed by his passion for Lizzie and jealous hatred for Eugene. But in the pursuit of his philanthropic obsession Hollingsworth is no less ruthlessly determined than Headstone to subjugate others to his will; he is quite prepared to exploit, sacrifice and discard Priscilla, Zenobia and Coverdale. Coverdale does not taunt and bait Hollingsworth, as Wrayburn does Headstone; and Hollingsworth does not try to murder him. But when Coverdale finally refuses to devote himself to Hollingsworth's cause, "Hollingsworth looked at me fiercely, and with glowing eyes. He could not have shown any other kind of expression than that, had he meant to strike me with a sword" (chapter 15). Westervelt's malicious description of Hollingsworth, to Coverdale (chapter 11) is a pretty accurate description of Headstone: "a man of iron, in more senses than one; a rough, cross-grained individual, rather boorish in his manners . . . and by no means of the highest intellectual cultivation." For Headstone, no less than for Hollingsworth, Zenobia's passionate denunciation that "It is all self . . . nothing but self, self, self!" (chapter 25) is true. And there is surely something Hawthornean in the account of Headstone walking the streets "with a bent head hammering at one fixed idea", and in Dickens' comment: "Love at first sight is a trite expression; enough that, in certain smouldering natures like this man's, that passion leaps into a blaze and make such head as fire does in a rage of wind . . ." (chapter 28). Compare, for example, the description of Chillingworth (*The Scarlet Letter*, chapter 14). "Ever and anon, too, there came a glare of red light out of his eyes; as if the old man's soul were on fire, and kept on smouldering duskily within his breast, until, by some casual puff of passion, it was blown into a momentary flame."

It seems to me, then, that certain features of structure and theme, and a few of the characters, of *Our Mutual Friend*, suggest that there is at least a residual influence of Hawthorne in Dickens' last completed novel.

Conclusion

Everyone agrees that, after his first marvellously prolific decade as a novelist, Dickens' art matured and developed in various ways. It became much more disciplined in form and structure. There was far less of the old comic and melodramatic improvisation; though still (generally) long and highly elaborate, the later novels were much more thought out in advance, their plots more carefully shaped and designed to articulate dominant themes and ideas — the inter-relatedness of human lives; the constraints on life of rigid systems of thought, arbitrary conventions, self-perpetuating institutions; the distortions in the individual psyche caused by such constraints. He began to use large symbols, or emblems, not artificially imposed, but developing out of the naturalistic facts, to amplify and reinforce vision and meaning by non-narrative means. While he remained an often angry and bitter critic and satirist of particular aspects of contemporary society, his vision became more comprehensive; he tended more to see his contemporary world as a manifestation of a universal and timeless human drama. While still believing, or at least proclaiming his belief, in the redemptive power of self-abnegating love, he became much more pre-occupied with themes of loneliness, guilt, alienation, obsession, and expiation; so while many of his characters are two-dimensional representations and embodiments of abstract ideas and social attitudes, many others have a far greater inwardness and psychological depth than those of his previous novels.

Critics have used various terms to describe Dickens' later work. The Leavises favour the term "dramatic poem". J.C. Reid suggests that Dickens moved "towards that form called the meta-novel, which, by its use of symbol and imagery, its complexity of significance, and its several levels, approaches the nature of poetry."[162] If one were to use only terms that were current in Dickens' own time, however, one would have to say that he moved towards allegory and psychological romance.

Dickens, a great original genius, may well have developed in much the same way if he had been the only writer in the world (or if Shakespeare had been the only other). But I believe that the appearance, in 1850 and 1851, of Hawthorne's *The Scarlet Letter* and *The House of the Seven Gables*, with their accompanying introductions and prefaces, which insist that these books are not novels, but romances — that they do not aim at a minute fidelity to the ordinary, but present human truths under poetically heightened circumstances — had a significant effect, at least in encouraging Dickens in almost every one of the directions in which he was beginning to move.

I have tried to show that in *Bleak House*, the first novel Dickens wrote after the publication of *The Scarlet Letter* (the first longer work of a writer whose shorter fiction he warmly admired), there is conclusive evidence for this belief. I have more tentatively suggested that in each of the succeeding novels there is, at least, some evidence of Hawthorne's influence.

Part II

Hawthorne and George Eliot

There is no great novelty in proposing that all of George Eliot's work, from *Scenes of Clerical Life* to *Daniel Deronda*, was, in varying degrees, influenced by Hawthorne. Many critics, from 1859 on, have detected resemblances between one or other of George Eliot's novels, and one or other of Hawthorne's romances; a few have suggested that these resemblances are evidence of actual indebtedness on George Eliot's part. I shall provide a good deal of new evidence of Hawthorne's influence, but this chapter will be largely a work of consolidation and systematization of discoveries already made.

Introduction

In the Hawthorne-George Eliot relationship, unlike the Hawthorne-Dickens relationship, there can hardly be any question of reciprocal influence. Marian Evans, born in November 1819, was more than fifteen years younger than Hawthorne. Hawthorne had been writing fiction for thirty years, had published *Fanshawe* (and suppressed it), *Twice Told Tales*, *Mosses from an Old Manse*, *The Scarlet Letter*, *The Snow-Image and other Twice-Told Tales*, *The House of the Seven Gables* and *The Blithedale Romance*, before Marian Evans, in September 1856, began to write "The Sad Fortunes of the Reverend Amos Barton".

In the next few years Marian Evans completed "Amos Barton", and its companion-pieces, "Mr Gilfil's Love-Story" and "Janet's Repentance", which were published first in *Blackwood's Edinburgh Magazine* during 1857, and then as *Scenes of Clerical Life*, under the pseudonym George Eliot in 1858; and her first full-length novel, *Adam Bede*, published in three volumes in 1859. Her second novel, *The Mill on the Floss*, appeared almost simultaneously with Hawthorne's last completed romance, *The Marble Faun*, in 1860. So of Hawthorne's work only *The Marble Faun* could have been in any way influenced by George Eliot, and only, of course, by *Scenes of Clerical Life* and *Adam Bede*. There seems to be no evidence, either internal or external, that it was, though it is probable that Hawthorne read at least *Adam Bede*.

Hawthorne was United States consul in Liverpool from July 1853 to the end of 1857. But he left England for Italy in January 1858, and did not return to England until the middle of 1859, after *Scenes of Clerical Life* and *Adam Bede* had been published, and the advent of a new major novelist had been immediately recognized. In the following year both novelists left England, George Eliot in March for Italy, Hawthorne in June for America. During the ten months or so of 1859 and 1860 when both were in England they did not meet. Back in America, according to Moncure D. Conway, Hawthorne expressed disappointment at not having met George Eliot. In an essay published in 1904, Conway quoted Hawthorne as having said: "I mentioned my wish to meet her to several ladies in London in whose houses I was a guest, but none of them was on visiting terms with her." Conway added: "He ascribed this to her irregular marriage to — or relations with — G.H. Lewes."[1]

In his biography of Hawthorne, published in 1890, Conway had previously recorded, however, that Hawthorne had met at least one lady, one of George Eliot's oldest friends, who could almost certainly have arranged for the two novelists to meet. Referring to Hawthorne's visit, in February 1860, to Coventry "where he met the Brays and Hennells" Conway added, in a footnote, "My friend, Mrs Charles Bray writes: 'My husband and I were invited to meet him at dinner; and as he took me in to dinner he sat next to me, and I think talked exclusively about Miss Evans, asking questions of all kinds about her, which I was very glad to answer to one so appreciative and so interesting as himself.' "[2] Hawthorne's own account of the conversation with Mrs Bray (which took place on February 15, 1860) gives a slightly different impression.

> She talked to me about the author of 'Adam Bede' whom she has known intimately all her life. Her intimations were somewhat mysterious; but I inferred from them that the lady in question had really been the mistress of Mr Lewes, though it seems that they are now married. Miss Evans (the name of

the 'Adam Bede' lady) was the daughter of a steward and gained her exact knowledge of rural life by the connection into which this origin brought her with the farmers. She was entirely self-educated, and has made herself an admirable scholar, in classical as well as in modern languages. Those who knew her had always recognized her wonderful endowments, and only watched to see in what way they would develop themselves. She is a person of the simplest manners and character, amiable and unpretending, and Mrs Bray seemed to speak of her with great affection and respect, notwithstanding all that may have been amiss or awry in the conduct of her life. By the by she is no longer young.[3]

This seems to be Hawthorne's only recorded reference to George Eliot. Although it includes no explicit comment on her work, Hawthorne's interest, and the wish to meet her (which was probably somewhat qualified by his apparent concern about "all that may have been amiss or awry in the conduct of her life", even though he somehow gained the impression that she was now married to Lewes) make it virtually certain that he must have read *Adam Bede* at least. It would be interesting to know whether he had read the anonymous review of *Adam Bede*, in the *Edinburgh Review*, in July 1859, which noted several resemblances between "Mr Eliot" and "Hawthorne, the American author" (to which I shall refer again).

Evidence of George Eliot's Knowledge of Hawthorne's Work

There is ample evidence, in George Eliot's letters and journals, of her interest in, and admiration of, the work of Hawthorne. There is no record of her immediate reactions to either *The Scarlet Letter* or *The House of the Seven Gables*, but the earliest letter, written on 19 August 1852, which refers to Hawthorne, clearly implies that she had already read at least one (and probably both) of them. From Broadstairs she wrote to Mrs Peter Taylor: "One see no novels less than a year old at the sea-side, so I am unacquainted with the 'Blithedale Romance', except through the reviews, which have whetted my curiosity more than usual. Hawthorne is a grand favourite of mine, and I shall be sorry if he does not go on surpassing himself."[4] Three weeks later, back in London, a letter to Mrs Bray (September 11, 1852) equally clearly implies that she had now read Hawthorne's third novel, though it gives no indication of what she thought of it: "You may as well expect news from an old spider or bat as from me. I can only tell you what I think of the 'Blithedale Romance', of 'Uncle Tom's Cabin', and the American Fishery Dispute — all which, I am very sure, you don't want to know."[5]

The following month's issue of the *Westminster Review*, of which Marian Evans had become assistant editor (in effect, the managing editor) in 1851, included in the "Contemporary Literature of America" section, a six-page review of *The Blithedale Romance*.[6]

In an essay published in 1955, James D. Rust begins by claiming that there is "good reason to believe" that this review "was written by George Eliot." Rust produces three pieces of evidence for attributing the review to George Eliot:

(a) Although it had been agreed, when Marian Evans became assistant editor of the *Westminster Review*, that she should write the articles on foreign literature, "before 1852 had ended almost the only writing she did for the magazine was the reviewing of American books";

(b) The review "shows clear marks of her style";

(c) The second letter quoted above shows that George Eliot had read Hawthorne's novel by September 11; like the letter, the review also mentions *Uncle Tom's Cabin*.

To Rust, the evidence was apparently strong enough for him, in his second sentence, to assert that "this review is interesting, first because it reveals what a great novelist thought of the work of a fellow artist, and second, because of the light it throws upon the development of George Eliot's thought about the art of fiction."[7]

In a subsequent essay, "The Art of Fiction in George Eliot's Reviews",[8] Rust again assumes, as established beyond question, George Eliot's authorship of the review of *The Blithedale Romance*, and uses it as a principal document in his exposition of George Eliot's theory of fiction.

Some of Hawthorne's biographers and critics, notably Edward Wagenknecht,[9] have accepted Rust's attribution of the review to George Eliot; but several George Eliot scholars, including Gordon Haight, Richard Stang and Thomas Pinney, have questioned or rejected the attribution.

Haight, in a footnote to the September 1852 letter to Mrs Bray, remarked,

> It might be G E who reviewed Hawthorne's *The Blithedale Romance* in the 'Contemporary Literature of America' section, *Westminster Review*, 58 (October 1852), 592–598, in which she calls it "unmistakably the finest production of genius in either hemisphere, for this quarter at least." But she finds that Hawthorne's moral faculty is "morbid as well as weak; and his characters partake of the same infirmity." Objecting to his failure to exhibit the working of the socialistic settlement, she says: "He confines himself to the delineation of its picturesque phases as 'a thing of beauty' and either has no particular convictions, respecting its deeper relations, or hesitates to express them" (p. 597). The rhetorical style makes G E's authorship doubtful.[10]

If Haight thought George Eliot's authorship doubtful, one wonders why he so definitely speaks of the author as "she", clearly meaning George Eliot.

Two years later, in an article entitled "George Eliot's Theory of Fiction",[11] which reviews Rust's two essays and Alice R. Kaminsky's "George Eliot, George Henry Lewes, and the Novel",[12] Haight seems to lean even further towards accepting the attribution of the article to George Eliot, which had, in the meantime, been made by Rust. He remarks that "In the absence of positive evidence — acknowledgment in a letter, bibliography, or biography, records of payment, or a marked file of the periodical — the greatest caution should be used in attributing these *Westminster* articles to particular authors."[13] He points out that Rust's first article ("George Eliot on *The Blithedale Romance*") "is not quite accurate in its statement about George Eliot's connection with the *Westminster*: she could not have become editor in May 1851, for Chapman did not buy it until October, nor was her reviewing ever limited to American books." He continues: "Though he gives no reasons, Mr Rust does not hesitate to accept the review of Hawthorne's *The Blithedale Romance* in October 1852 as George Eliot's. In spite of some journalistic crudities which seem to me below the level of her writing, it is very tempting to ascribe it to her." After a transitional sentence in which Haight acknowledges that "Mr Rust gives a clear summary of it and an able analysis of its significance", Haight apparently finds the temptation irresistible, despite the lack of evidence and the "journalistic crudities": "Appearing five years before the *Scenes of Clerical Life*, it indicates, as he says, that when she came to the writing of fiction, she had 'thought long and deeply about the problems of the novelist, and had arrived at definite opinions concerning the form, style, and purpose of the novel.' It foreshadows her concern with the moral element in fiction and with realism."[14]

Richard Stang, much more decisively, rejects the attribution, quoting Haight's comments (in the *Letters*), and adding: "Moreover, the content is not reconcilable with [George Eliot's] critical position at this time. For example, we find in this review, 'Reality should only be so far introduced as to give effect to the bright ideal which Hope pictures in the future.' "[15]

Thomas Pinney, in his edition of George Eliot's essays, includes the review among "Articles Wrongly or Doubtfully Attributed to George Eliot", and suggests that it is "perhaps by R.W. Griswold." Pinney claims that "the internal, as well as the slight external, evidence is rather against than for George Eliot's authorship. As Richard Stang . . . has pointed out, the content of the review contradicts everything known of George Eliot's critical position at that date. The attribution is also questioned on different grounds, by Gordon S. Haight. . . . It seems worth while to enter at least a strong *caveat* against this attribution. . . ."[16]

The question can hardly be said to have been settled; but I find it very difficult to believe that George Eliot, so committed to realism in the novel, would have written the sentence quoted by Stang (or many similar ones), or would have described her "grand favourite" as morbid, as well as weak in moral faculty, a cynical exploiter of "the beauty of deformity", and "not even a Jeremiah" but "a Mephistopheles".

The next certain evidence of George Eliot's interest in Hawthorne's work comes nearly five years later, after "Amos Barton" had been published in *Blackwood's Magazine*. In late March 1857, George Eliot and George Henry Lewes, weather-bound in Penzance, read aloud several novels to one another — including *The Scarlet Letter*.[17] From George Eliot's description of Hawthorne, in 1852, as "a grand favourite of mine", it seems virtually certain that this was not the first time she had read Hawthorne's masterpiece; but it is, of course, of special significance that she re-read the book only five months or so before she began work on her own first novel, *Adam Bede*, and just before she started on the third of the Scenes, "Janet's Repentance."

Three years later, again, in May 1860, shortly after the publication of *The Mill on the Floss*, George Eliot wrote to her publisher, William Blackwood, from Florence: "There has been a crescendo of enjoyment in our travels, for Florence from its relation to the history of modern art has aroused a keener interest in us even than Rome, and has stimulated me to entertain rather an ambitious project. . . " This was the first hint of George Eliot's Italian novel, *Romola*; it is, therefore, of particular interest that, later in the same letter, George Eliot remarked: "Literature travels slowly even to this Italian Athens. Hawthorne's book is not to be found here yet in the Tauchnitz edition!"[18] George Eliot was obviously referring to *The Marble Faun*, which had also just been published. As Ellin Jane Ringler comments, in an unpublished doctoral thesis which is the fullest comparative study of the two novelists: "It is certain that George Eliot wished to read Hawthorne's Italian novel when she first began contemplating her own book about Italy; and it is highly probable that she did read it in the two years between its publication and that of *Romola*. That she was ultimately familiar with *The Marble Faun* is clear, for, in 1873 she commented approvingly on a reference to Hilda, the heroine of *The Marble Faun*, made in a letter to her by an American schoolgirl."[19] *Romola* itself, as we shall see, provides ample evidence of George Eliot's knowledge of *The Marble Faun*.

Ellin Jane Ringler (the purpose of whose thesis is "to illuminate certain aspects of the novels of Nathaniel Hawthorne and George Eliot by exploring their methods of handling similar themes"[20] rather than to demonstrate Hawthorne's "appreciable influence" on George Eliot) summarizes her account of George Eliot's specific references to Hawthorne thus:

> It can be said with certainty that Eliot was familiar with three of Hawthorne's four major novels: *The Scarlet Letter*, *The Blithedale Romance*, and *The Marble Faun*. The first and the last of these were read or re-read by Eliot just before she started writing novels that were, at least in their broader aspects, similar to Hawthorne's. . . . Whether Eliot read Hawthorne's tales or *The House of the Seven Gables* cannot be ascertained, though the fact that she called the American 'a grand favourite' suggests that, by 1852, and before reading *The Blithedale Romance*, she had read enough of Hawthorne's writing to make a fairly sweeping judgment.[21]

Critical Comparisons of Hawthorne and George Eliot, 1859–1910

As with Hawthorne and Dickens, comparisons between Hawthorne and George Eliot began to appear in the reviews very promptly. Coincidentally, the earliest comparative comment was, like Duyckinck's about Hawthorne and Dickens in 1842, one of the few which explicitly suggested that George Eliot had been influenced by Hawthorne. This occurred in a long anonymous review of *Adam Bede*, in the *Edinburgh Review* for July 1859, now ascribed to Caroline E.S. Norton.

> Apart from all delineations of character, apart from all progress in the story, stand passages of wit which charm us by their poetry, or make us smile by their humour. In this last quality Mr Eliot resembles Hawthorne, the American author, more than any other writer with whom we are acquainted. The sentence describing Mr Craig the gardener, "the man of sober passions" who is also one of Hetty's suitors (though not a very eager one), and who, after an extra glass of grog, had been heard to say of her, that "the lass was well enough" and "that a man might do worse" *but on convivial occasions men are apt to express themselves strongly* . . . has all the scent of the Hawthorne bough.

In the following paragraph Caroline Norton used another "punning conceit at the expense of the American author's surname"[22] in suggesting Hawthorne's influence on *Scenes of Clerical Life*:

> And so have many others, more especially in his earlier work, the 'Scenes of Clerical Life.' In a certain minute, yet not tedious, habit of description he also resembles Hawthorne; the clerical meeting at Milby Vicarage, — the description of Knebly Church, — the delightful narrowness of Mrs Patten's soul, — the account of Miss Pratt, — of large fair mild-eyed Milly and the lithe dark thin-lipped countess, — the wonderful account of the pauper audience Milly's husband endeavours to enlighten, — all seem written under the same vigorous yet blossomy shade, and to be flowers of the Hawthorne species.[23]

Caroline Norton's examples, it is worth noting, are taken from all three of the *Scenes*.

It is not known whether either Hawthorne or George Eliot read the *Edinburgh Review* article. But in the following year, George Eliot, at least, read another anonymous article, concerned mainly with *The Mill on the Floss* and *The Marble Faun*.

In September 1860 she wrote to John Blackwood: "I wonder if you know who is the writer of the article in the N. British, in which I am reviewed along with Hawthorne . . . it is so unmixed in its praise that if I had any friends, I should be uneasy lest a friend should have written it."[24]

It is still not known whether it was a friend of George Eliot who wrote the article headed "Imaginative Literature. The Author of *Adam Bede* and Nathaniel Hawthorne",[25] to which Allan Casson re-directed attention (though mistakenly describing it as "doubtless the first comparison of Hawthorne and George Eliot")[26]. This anonymous writer, in contrast to Caroline Norton, did not suggest any Hawthorne influence on George Eliot; indeed only a small fraction of the article compares the two writers, and the comparison is very much in favour of George Eliot, whom the critic considered to be an imaginative writer of a higher order than Hawthorne.

The basic thesis of the article is that "the imagination in diffeent men works under different laws. The more powerful intellects keep it in subjection, but it takes the feebler captive. In the one case it vitalizes and exalts; in the other it discolours and exaggerates. The author of *Adam Bede* represents the first class; Nathaniel Hawthorne, the second."[27] When, after several pages of eulogy of George Eliot (never actually referred to by her pseudonym) the writer turns his attention to Hawthorne, he acknowledges Hawthorne's "grave sympathy, the homely insight, the classic Puritanism, the rich and meditative intellect", and recognizes that "his imagination is vivid and affluent, and capable of sustaining an impassioned and lofty flight"; but clearly considers Hawthorne's imagination inferior because "it takes the colour of what it feeds on."

The actual comparison between the two novelists is confined to a single long paragraph, in which two aspects, style and characterization, are examined, in general and impressionistic terms.

> Mr Hawthorne is an admirable writer; but his style (where both are so pre-eminently good) is curiously unlike that of the lady of whose works we have spoken. *Hers* has a crystal-like purity; his is dyed with rich and vivid colours. The rhetoric of *Adam Bede*, untouched by the heart or the imagination, might become bald; with these, — exactly as we have it, in short, — it is the perfection of natural eloquence. But even without original thought or deep

feeling, Mr Hawthorne's style — rich, fragrant, and mixed with flowers of many hues, like Attic honey — would be always delightful. Even in this matter of language the contrast we have insisted upon asserts itself, while, as respects the relative power of these writers to delineate *character*, the evidence is still more decisive. In the one book it grows like a flower; in the other it is constructed like a machine. Mr Hawthorne, starting with some moral or intellectual conception, adapts his characters to it, fits them into the framework he has prepared, and expands or compresses them until they fill the mould. Thus there is in his representation a want of the ease, *abandon*, and lawlessness of life, — they are too symmetrical to be natural, too exact to be true. A character may accidentally or incidentally illustrate a law; but the writer who models the character upon the law, produces a moral or intellectual monster. If there are no actual 'monsters' in *Transformation*, there is at least very little flesh and blood in it, — very little except the affluent fancy, the fine analysis, and the perfect taste of an admirable *critic*; no life but only a great deal of very delightful talk about life.[28]

After devoting two pages to quoting five descriptive passages from Hawthorne's romance, the reviewer has time only to note that "one trait of Mr Hawthorne's habit of thought re-appears." As in *The House with [sic] the Seven Gables* and *The Scarlet Letter* "the commonplace events of the present are shrouded in the ghost-like shadows of the past. The influences of the dead haunt and afflict the footsteps of living men. . . . The crime of yesterday is curiously interwrought with the retribution of to-day. It follows the present with menacing tenacity, and clings to it with an immitigable grasp."[29] It is a little surprising that the critic did not recognize that this "trait of Mr Hawthorne's habit of thought" was also a trait of the habit of thought of the lady of whose works he had been speaking.

It was this trait of thought which, ten years later, a French critic, L. Etienne, noted as common to George Eliot and Hawthorne. In the course of a discussion of *The Spanish Gypsy*, Etienne commented (my translation):

The author of *Adam Bede* and *Scenes of Clerical Life* once again finds here her favourite source of inspiration. Without being Calvinist or puritan, George Eliot takes pleasure in the portrayal of the soul of the sinner in the presence of the evil he has done, irremediable evil according to the hopeless dogma of the church in which he grew up, even though he may no longer be its disciple. Silva is delivered up to the sufferings of the damned, the torments of hell possess him throughout his life. No salvation, no outlet, no hope for the criminal! Thus it is that the philosopher freed from the narrow beliefs of his ancestors still keeps the same gloomy ideas about evil done, the same tendency towards the cult of fatality. Almost all the author's novels have as their centre a theme of repentance without outlet. It is the basis of the sad story of poor Janet in "Janet's Repentance"; it is the main theme of the book which made the author's great reputation; Hetty, guilty of infanticide and forced to confess her crime, holds the reader's interest much more than the worthy and irreproachable Adam Bede. A secret crime is the crux of *Silas Marner*, and *Romola* would not be a novel at all without the story of the remorse of the hero because of a theft which he has managed to conceal. George Eliot again and again recounts the drama of sin, not that of appeasement — of the moral law violated, not of divine justice satisfied. Calvinism has so firmly implanted in the consciousness the idea of inexpiable crime that it remains even in those who have ceased to be Calvinists. The American novelist, Nathaniel Hawthorne, a free and purely philosophical spirit, was nurtured on this dogma; his novels furnish irrefutable proof of this. I do not know whether George Eliot, more subtle in moral analysis, has not pushed farther the art of making use of that fearful repentance which, like Prometheus' vulture, rends a heart perpetually reborn for its torment."[30]

Ellin Ringler remarks that "one comes across no other contrast between Hawthorne and Eliot [than the *Edinburgh Review* and *North British Review* articles] again in the nineteenth century, unless the indirect comparison made by Henry James in his review '*Daniel Deronda*: a Conversation' might be counted."[31] I don't think that the James reference counts for much. It is made by Pulcheria, the flippant, "sadly aesthetic", and determinedly irreverent anti-George Eliot spokesman in James' dialogue. Near the end of the dialogue, quite unconvinced by Theodora's rather gushing admiration, and Constantius' more judicious and qualified approval, she says: "All that is very fine, but you cannot persuade me that *Deronda* is not a very awkward and ill-made story. It has nothing that one can call a subject. A silly young girl and a heavy, overwise young man who don't fall in love with her. That is the *donnee* of eight monthly volumes. I call it very flat. Is that what the exquisite art of Thackeray and Miss Austen and Hawthorne has come to? I would as soon read a German novel outright."[32]

There were, in fact, several other nineteenth-century and early twentieth-century comments, as well as Etienne's, which associated Hawthorne and George Eliot in some way. For example, Robert Collyer, in an 1869 essay on Hawthorne, remarked that Hawthorne "had written some books of a quality and flavour as separate, unique and rare as the 'Heart of Mid Lothian' or 'Adam Bede' and had done more than any other man, except Emerson, to establish our claim to a literature of our own."[33] J. Nicholl, in a book on American literature, in 1882, described *The Scarlet Letter* as "the most profound, the boldest, the most riveting analytical romance of our tongue, in our century — followed, I think, at an interval by *Wuthering Heights* and by *Silas Marner*";[34] and remarked that the end of *The Blithedale Romance* is "a fit close to the wreck of idealisms and the holocaust of aspirations, that leaves us with a deeper sense of the mockery of life, of more utter hopelessness than any other English work of fiction, excepting perhaps *Middlemarch*."[35]

Near the end of the century, William Dean Howells acknowledged the great and similar effects of the two novelists on himself:

> The life and character I have found portrayed [in novels] had appealed always to the consciousness of right and wrong implanted in me; and from no one has this appeal been stronger than from George Eliot. Her influence continued through many years, and I can question it now only in the undue burden she seems to throw upon the individual, and her failure to account largely enough for motive from the social environment. There her work seems to me unphilosophical.
>
> It shares whatever error there is in its perspective with that of Hawthorne, whose *Marble Faun* was a new book at the same time that *Adam Bede* was new, and whose books now come into my life. . . . He was always dealing with the problem of evil, too, and I found a more potent charm in his more artistic handling of it than I found in George Eliot. Of course, I then preferred the region of pure romance where he liked to place his action.[36]

In the same year (1895), J.A. Noble, while not suggesting a Hawthorne influence on George Eliot, also commented on the similarity of their ideas and concerns. Noble quoted an entry from Hawthorne's *American Notebooks*: "Selfishness is one of the qualities apt to inspire love." He claimed that

> Though Hawthorne did not elaborate his own text [In saying this, Noble seems to have overlooked, for example, Clifford Pyncheon] it has been elaborated by other writers of fiction. Charles Dickens . . . in [his] portrait of Harold Skimpole [has] done justice to the selfishness which cunningly plays the part of the grown-up baby . . . and in Tito Melema, George Eliot has given us a subtle and veracious study of the other and more complex type. . . . Tito is an admirable embodiment of Hawthorne's thought. An inferior author would have told us that Tito was fascinating and loveable, but the value of George Eliot's portraiture lies in the subtle manner in which she enables us to feel his power, and analyse the elements out of which it was evolved. She has shown us how his peculiar attractiveness was the inevitable result of his peculiar form of selfishness.[37]

But the most important nineteenth-century comparison of Hawthorne and George Eliot which I have come across occurred a decade earlier, in an essay on Hawthorne by H.S. Salt. In discussing *The Marble Faun*, Salt remarked that

> books written in a foreign country, under the impulse of travel and passing observation rather than life-long intimacy, can seldom attain to the same excellence as those which are inspired by the natural objects which the writer has known from childhood. There never lived a keener observer than George Eliot; yet how slight and artificial is her Italian study, *Romola*, elaborate as it is, compared with her simple, but immortal, delineations of homely English life. So, too, it was with Hawthorne. He set himself with great earnestness and considerable success to study Italian art; yet, with all his pains in founding a romance on this subject, he failed to wield the same power as in his stories of Puritan life.[38]

This is probably the earliest comment bringing together the Italian novels of Hawthorne and George Eliot. Even more interesting is the next paragraph, in which Salt was probably the first to point out specific similarities between *The Scarlet Letter* and *Adam Bede*.

> It can hardly be doubted that *The Scarlet Letter* is the best of all Hawthorne's productions. . . . The resemblances of its general structure to that of Lockhart's *Adam Blair* had been more than once commented on; it is also worth remark that *The Scarlet Letter* offers one or two very striking points of comparison with George Eliot's *Adam Bede*. The relations existing between the two guilty characters are almost identical in the two books; a forbidden love; a fatal secret, a disgrace borne at first by the woman alone, but finally shared by her lover — these form a strange coincidence in the plans of the novels, which is maintained even in the names of the characters, Hester Prynne and Hester Sorrel, Arthur Dimmesdale and Arthur Donnithorne. But with the names and situations of the characters the similarity ends; for Hawthorne's beautiful and pathetic story is happily free from the sensational incidents which so sadly mar the latter part of *Adam Bede*. In *The Scarlet Letter* the moral is not obtruded on the reader, yet the tone is altogether more lofty and spiritual, and aided by a power of poetical imagination of which George Eliot was wholly destitute. Nor can it be said that Hawthorne, on his side, was deficient in that keen insight and subtle analysis of character for which George Eliot is justly renowned. Indeed, this is one of the most striking features of *The Scarlet Letter*. . . .[39]

Salt was wrong in thinking that the similarity did not extend beyond "the names and situations of the characters". Knowing as we do that George Eliot had re-read *The Scarlet Letter* shortly before beginning to write *Adam Bede*, we can be almost certain that he was also wrong in thinking the resemblances coincidental.

Before the end of the century, at least one other critic, William Cranston Lawton, saw similarities between *The Scarlet Letter* and *Adam Bede*. Lawton wrote, in 1898:

> It is true that in *The Scarlet Letter*, as in *Adam Bede*, the chief action of the drama is set in motion by a grievous sin. But sin, evil, — and here we touch the heart of Hawthorne's, of George Eliot's, of Emerson's creed — is no malignant, demoniacal power contradicting and thwarting the will of Heaven, and accomplishing at last its own purposes. It is but estrangement, distortion, misuse, of impulses not in themselves accurst; and therefore through repentance, atonement and penance it may work out to blessedness, even of the sinner. Hester and Arthur fell through passionate mutual love; and that love, though so sin-stained, is never actually destroyed, but, purified and spiritualized, supports Arthur in death, and Hester in the heavier trial of life. This is not, indeed, a truth that would have been tolerated by the grim Puritans of Endicott's day; but it is undoubtedly what Hawthorne, like George Eliot ... indeed nearly all the true artists and liberal-minded thinkers of our century, believe and teach.[40]

G.E. Woodberry, a few years later, also saw Hawthorne and George Eliot as sharing the same ethical views, but defined them very differently from Lawton. Remarking that Hawthorne's Hester "recognized the impossibility that any mission . . . should be confided to a woman stained with sin", Woodberry commented: "That was never the Christian gospel nor the Puritan faith. Indeed, Hawthorne here and elsewhere anticipates those ethical views which are the burden of George Eliot's moral genius, and contain scientific pessimism. This stoicism, which was in Hawthorne, is a primary element in his moral nature, in him as well as in his work; it is visited with few touches of tenderness and pity; the pity one feels is not in him, it is in the pitiful thing which he presents objectively, sternly, unrelentingly."[41]

A couple of other critics contrasted Hawthorne's "detachment" with George Eliot's (and therefore her readers') greater involvement with her characters. Hamilton Wright Mabie asserted (in 1904): "We seem always to be looking at Hawthorne's figures from a distance; we never touch hands with them; they never speak directly to us; we do not expect to come upon them in any of those chance meetings which sometimes bring us face to face with Becky Sharp, Maggie Tulliver or Silas Lapham."[42] And Samuel McChord Crothers (in 1910): "In his treatment of sin there is always a sense of moral detachment. We are not made to see, as George Eliot makes us see, the struggles with temptation, — the soul, like a wild thing, seeing the tempting bait and drawing nearer to the trap. Hawthorne begins after the deed is done. He shows us the wild thing taken in a trap which sees the trapper coming through the wood."[43]

A couple of others, again, asserted the greater stature of Hester Prynne, at least, over George Eliot's characters. D.F. Hannigan, in 1901, maintained: "The woman, Hester Prynne, is a heroine as great as Magdalen. Her moral martyrdom raises the story to the highest level of tragedy. Even George Eliot has never presented to us the heroic possibilities of a woman's nature so vividly or thoroughly as Hawthorne has in *The Scarlet Letter*"[44] And F.P. Stearns in his 1906 biography of Hawthorne: "Hester does not collapse into a pitiful nonentity like Scott's Effie Deans, nor is she maddened to crime like George Eliot's Hetty Sorrel."[45] (Stearns added a footnote suggesting that the name of George Eliot's character was "apparently compounded from Hester Prynne and Schiller's Agnes Sorrel.")

Finally, in 1905, two writers — one obscure and one famous — asserted the pre-eminence of Hawthorne and George Eliot among nineteenth-century novelists. Anton E. Schonbach claimed: "Next to George Eliot, or rather with her, Hawthorne is the first English prose writer of the nineteenth century."[46] And William Dean Howells: "None of these writers (Dickens, Thackeray, Trollope, Reade) can match with the author of *Adam Bede*, *The Mill on the Floss*, *Romola* and *Middlemarch* in the things which give a novelist the highest claim to a reader's interest. Hawthorne, arriving at effects of equal seriousness from a quarter so opposite to hers, among her contemporaries can alone rival her in the respect, not to say, the reverence, of criticism."[47]

For about half a century, then, from George Eliot's first appearance as a novelist until some thirty years after her death in 1880, it seemed natural for critics to associate her with Hawthorne. It is a little surprising, however, that scarcely anyone, after Caroline Norton in 1859, explicitly suggested the possibility of any indebtedness to Hawthorne; even H.S. Salt considered the similarities between *The Scarlet Letter* and *Adam Bede* to be coincidental.

Critical Comparisons of Hawthorne and George Eliot, 1910–1950

After about 1910, however, there seems to be a gap of several decades in Hawthorne-George Eliot comparison. It is quite possible that there are references that I have overlooked; there is no Hawthorne bibliography for this period comparable in thoroughness to Nina E. Browne's *A Bibliography of Nathaniel Hawthorne* (Boston and New York, 1905) or Buford Jones's *A Checklist of Hawthorne Criticism 1951–1966, Emerson Society Quarterly*, No. 52, Supplement (III Quarter 1968). The only reference to George Eliot for the period 1905 to 1950 given in *Nathaniel Hawthorne: a Reference Bibliography 1900–1971* (Boston, 1972) is to A.C. Ward's *American Literature 1880–1930*.

Ward, in his opening chapter, entitled "The Incubus", referring to the incubus of European culture which in 1873 Emerson in *The American Scholar* urged the young men of Harvard to cast off, suggested that in Hawthorne, as in Irving, "the European spirit is dominant: this time with something of the effect that might be produced if the imposing high seriousness of George Eliot were made less tense by a touch of Lamb's familiarity and ease", and remarked that "*The Scarlet Letter* itself might be an episode from another *Adam Bede* with outlines more sharply defined."[48]

Critical Comparisons of Hawthorne and George Eliot, 1950–1980

In the period since 1950, Mario Praz was the first critic to point out similarities between George Eliot and Hawthorne. In discussing Tito Melema, in *Romola*, Praz comments:

> The study of the gradual debasement of Tito's soul is reminiscent of similar studies in Hawthorne (*Ethan Brand*, for instance); and indeed the whole atmosphere of *Romola*, and especially the appearance of Baldassarre like a ghost of the past, a Nemesis incarnate, recalls the mysterious apparition that pursues Miriam in *Transformation* (*The Marble Faun*) — which was published in 1860, three years before *Romola*. The comparison might be carried farther, though perhaps not without forcing it, if one sees in the metamorphosis of the fascinating Tito, creature of the Renaissance, into a reprobate,

a reflection of the metamorphosis of the pagan Donatello, in Hawthorne's novel, into a moral man under the stimulus of a crime. The two authors have in common a subtlety in the study of the successive degrees of moral transformation, a faith in the uplifting force of suffering, and a puritan love of allegory of which we shall later see examples in George Eliot.[49]

In further discussing the mixed nature and "the conflicts of conscience" of George Eliot's characters, Praz refers to Gwendolen Harleth.

Gwendolen, in *Deronda*, has criminal tendencies, and her appearance of pale, serpent-like beauty, Lamia-like, and her long narrow eyes (Chap. i) ally her to the type of cold *femme fatale* which was to be met with so often in the Decadents, towards the end of the century. As a child, she had strangled a canary which had exasperated her by interrupting her singing with its shrill warblings. Yet with all this her nature was not ruthless. The consciousness of evil, of having contributed to, if not actually caused, the drowning of the odious Grandcourt, was to act in her as a leaven of redemption, in much the same way as in one of Hawthorne's characters.[50]

Five years later, in 1961, F.R. Leavis, in an essay written as a foreword to the Signet Classics edition of *Adam Bede*, for the first time explicitly suggested that the connections and similarities between the first full-length novels of Hawthorne and George Eliot were more than coincidence. Leavis maintained that, in *Adam Bede*, "George Eliot's distinctive interest focused . . . on Arthur Donnithorne, and the inner drama of conscience in *him* [rather than in Dinah]." Leavis then continued:

Yet, characteristic as the bent of interest is, even here one can see her indebted, at least for stimulus and suggestion . . . to a great predecessor. This time it was not the genial Scott, but the novelist of Puritan New England. George Eliot had read *The Scarlet Letter* when it came out, and (what doesn't surprise us) expressed a great admiration for Hawthorne. The idea that Hawthorne's influence can be discovered in *Adam Bede* was prompted as it came to me, by the name Hetty. Once one thinks of Hester Prynne, the effect of the suggestion has its compelling significance, even if one is at first inclined to dismiss the echo as mere chance. The treatment of the agonized conscience in Arthur Donnithorne convinces one before long that in the treatment of the seduction theme *The Scarlet Letter* has told significantly. This real affinity (for all the differences of temperament and art between the two authors) brings home to one, in fact, that the association of the names was more than a chance clue. One notes, further, that Hawthorne's male sinner is also Arthur — Arthur Dimmesdale for George Eliot's Arthur Donnithorne.

We have here, unmistakably, a case of that profound kind of influence of which the artist in whom it works is unaware. It is of the same order as [the] influence of George Eliot herself on Henry James. . . . The influence of Hawthorne on George Eliot was not so important for her as hers was for James, yet one would be rash to judge it a minor matter, of marginal interest. For a writer in George Eliot's position, with no obvious model to start from, a congenial hint that goes home deeply as a creative impulsion or reinforcement may have a disproportionate momentousness. And . . . Arthur Donnithorne opened for George Eliot a series of intensely characteristic studies: Hawthorne's influence, then, was at the centre and deep down.[51]

Almost simultaneously, and apparently independently (since he does not mention Leavis) Allan Casson, in a brief note, also suggested that "a comparison of *Adam Bede* and *The Scarlet Letter* reveals points of similarity of situation and common ground in technique and theme as well." As well as the similarity of names, Casson points to the situational similarity that both novels "deal with the life of a small, settled rural community"; the similarites of technique in that "both novelists, for the most part, restrict the action of each chapter to a single scene", that both use the forest as an important symbolic setting, and that, in both, "maze" and "labyrinth" are key words; and similarities of theme — "the fortunate fall, the doctrine of consequences, and the humanizing power of sorrow."[52]

As I have mentioned, the most thorough study of the relationship between Hawthorne and George Eliot is Ellin Jane Ringler's dissertation "The problem of evil: a correlative study in the novels of Nathaniel Hawthorne and George Eliot".[53] After an Introduction, the two preliminary chapters ("Biographical and Critical Precedents" and "The Moral Imagination"), Dr Ringer examines in detail the similarities and differences between three pairs of novels — *The Scarlet Letter* and *Adam Bede*; *The House of the Seven Gables* and *Middlemarch*; *The Marble Faun* and *Romola*. Dr Ringler is not concerned to stress Hawthorne's influence on George Eliot, but, inevitably, in quest of evidence of Hawthorne's influence, I have come upon, in the three novels which she treats, many of the same passages.

I have found, subsequent to Ellin Ringler's dissertation, three pieces of criticism, each of which examines, in some detail, relationships between one of Hawthorne's romances and one of George Eliot's novels. One is a chapter of Nicolaus Mills' book, *American and English Fiction in the Nineteenth Century*;[54] Mills' thesis is that the differences between the two bodies of fiction are neither as great nor as clear-cut as critics like Lionel Trilling and

Richard Chase had asserted. His chapter, "Nathaniel Hawthorne and George Eliot", is the fullest (published) comparative treatment of *The Scarlet Letter* and *Adam Bede*. The others are essays: one, by Curtis Dahl,[55] treats another of the pairs of novels examined by Ellin Ringler — the Italian novels, *The Marble Faun* and *Romola*. The second, by Jonathan R. Quick,[56] examines a pair of novels not previously compared — *The Scarlet Letter* and *Silas Marner*. I shall refer to each of these in discussing the particular novel of George Eliot's with which it is concerned.

Romance and Realism: Theories of Fiction of Hawthorne and George Eliot Compared

George Eliot recorded in her journal, in December 1857, under the heading "How I Came to Write Fiction": "September 1856 made a new era in my life, for it was then I began to write Fiction. It had always been a vague dream of mine that some time or other I might write a novel, and my shadowy conception of what the novel was to be, varied, of course, from one epoch of my life to another."[57] Her "conception of what her novel was to be" was, to a considerable extent, formed in the process of reading and reviewing the work (and not only the novels) of others, in the long articles which she wrote for the *Westminster Review* from September 1851 on. George Eliot's theory of fiction has been examined by many critics (among them Weldon Casey,[58] James D. Rust,[59] William J. Hyde,[60] Richard Stang,[61] Ian Milner,[62] Thomas A. Noble,[63] and Darrell Mansell, Jr.[64]). For my present purposes it is sufficient merely to mention a few of her basic beliefs about the proper function, materials and method of the novel.

Most fundamental of all is her belief, explicitly stated in her essay on two books of the German novelist, W.H. Riehl, that art is "the nearest thing to life; it is a mode of amplifying experience and extending our contact with our fellow men beyond the bounds of our personal lot." This is amplified in a famous passage in the same essay: "The greatest benefit we owe to the artist, whether painter, poet, or novelist, is the extension of our sympathies. Appeals founded on generalizations and statistics require a sympathy ready-made, a moral sentiment already in activity; but a picture of human life such as a great artist can give, surprises even the trivial and the selfish into that attention to what is apart from themselves, which may be called the raw material of moral sentiment."[65] As Thomas A. Noble puts it, "The foundation of George Eliot's artistic credo . . . is that art serves morality by widening men's sympathies."[66]

While George Eliot firmly believed in the novelist's function as moral teacher, it is of almost equal importance that she was consistently and vehemently opposed to didacticism in fiction. This attitude was perhaps most clearly expressed much later, in a letter to Frederic Harrison, who urged her to write a Comtean novel: "I think aesthetic teaching is the highest of all teaching because it deals with life in its highest complexity. But if it ceases to be purely aesthetic — if it lapses anywhere from the picture to the diagram — it becomes the most offensive of all teaching."[67] This, however, is a re-statement of, for example, her criticism of Charles Kingsley's *Westward Ho!* a decade before: "If he would confine himself to his true sphere, he might be a teacher in the sense in which every great artist is a teacher — namely, by giving us his higher sensibility as a medium, a delicate acoustic or optical instrument, bringing home to our coarser sense what would otherwise be unperceived by us." But Kingsley, she continued, was unable to shake off his "parsonic habit"; "Mr Kingsley's necessity for strong loves and strong hatreds, and his determination to hold up certain persons as models, is an obstacle to his successful delineation of character. . . . We can no more believe in and love his men and women than we could believe in and love the pattern-boy at school, always cited as a rebuke to our aberrations."[68] As Stang paraphrases, George Eliot's view was that "if art has a moral purpose, that purpose is not to propagate specific doctrines and opinions or to teach a theory of morality."[69]

George Eliot's comment on the incredibility of Kingsley's characters links with the third main article of her theory of the novel — her advocacy of realism. Most explicitly, in her review of Ruskin's *Modern Painters*, she wrote: "The truth of infinite value that he teaches is *realism* — the doctrine that all truth and beauty are to be attained by a humble and faithful study of nature, and not by substituting vague forms, bred by imagination on the mists of feeling, in place of definite, substantial reality.

The thorough acceptance of this doctrine would remould our life."[70]

As Noble points out, George Eliot seldom uses the word "realism"; she usually "suggests the concept by reference to the truthfulness of the presentation or by saying that a faithful picture is given."[71] That she believed that the novel should give a truthful representation of more than the surface, and the outward appearance of things and people, is clear from her comment on Dickens (not named, but obviously intended) in the essay on Riehl: "We have one great novelist who is gifted with the utmost power of rendering the external traits of our town population; and if he could give us their psychological character — their conceptions of life, and their emotions — with the same truth as their idiom and manners, his books would be the greatest contribution Art has ever made to the awakening of social sympathies."[72]

It might, on the face of it, seem highly unlikely that George Eliot, the advocate of realism in the novel, should find anything to admire in, or learn from, Hawthorne, who consistently insisted that his larger fictions were not novels but romances — especially, of course, in the preface to *The House of the Seven Gables*:

> When a writer calls his work a Romance, it need hardly be observed that he wishes to claim a certain latitude, both as to its fashion and material, which he would not have felt himself entitled to assume, had he professed to be writing a Novel. The latter form of composition is presumed to aim at a very minute fidelity, not merely to the possible, but to the probable and ordinary course of man's experience. The former — while as a work of art, it must rigidly subject itself to laws, and while it sins unpardonably, so far as it may swerve aside from the truth of the human heart — has fairly a right to present that truth under circumstances, to a great extent, of the writer's own choosing or creation.

But the parenthetical insistence that it is the romancer's duty to adhere to "the truth of the human heart" clearly indicates that for Hawthorne, no less than for George Eliot, psychological realism was of the greatest importance. And, as with George Eliot, Hawthorne's concern for psychological truth was intimately connected with his pre-occupation with moral questions. As Jesse Bier remarks: "Hawthorne did write seriously with moral purpose aforethought and . . . purposefully considered moral truth as part of the reality he studied."[73]

Like George Eliot, Hawthorne believed in art, including the art of fiction, as an instrument in the service of humanity. But also like her, as another paragraph in the Preface to *The House of the Seven Gables* shows, he deprecated didacticism in fiction. His comment: "The Author has considered it hardly worth his while, therefore, relentlessly to impale the story with its moral, as with an iron rod — or rather, as by sticking a pin through a butterfly — thus at once depriving it of life, and causing it to stiffen in an ungainly and unnatural attitude," is very similar to George Eliot's later criticism that if the "teaching" in a novel "lapses from the picture to the diagram" it becomes offensive — and ineffective. Both would, no doubt, have agreed with Virginia Woolf's formulation of the same view: "When a philosophy is not consumed in a novel, when one can underline this phrase with a pencil, and cut out that exhortation with a pair of scissors and paste the whole into a system, it is safe to say that there is something wrong with the philosophy or with the novel or with both."[74]

The kind of opposition between the two writers, which seems to be implied by Hawthorne's championship of romance, and George Eliot's advocacy of realism, is not by any means as stark as it might at first seem. From Hawthorne's contrasting of "novel" and "romance", it is clear that he is not seeking to distinguish between two forms of fiction, of which one represents reality and the other avoids reality. Both forms engage themselves with reality, but they look at, and present, reality in different ways. As R.K. Gupta elaborates Hawthorne's distinction, "While the novelist fritters away his energy in an exact notation of surface details, the romancer can ignore these details and concentrate on the fundamental facts of human behaviour. While the novelist, tied down, like the historian, to the requirement of a rigid adherence to facts, presents only the particular, the romancer, who, like the poet, can modify facts and fashion them into meaningful patterns, is able to present the universal." Gupta claims that Hawthorne "was more of a realist than many of the so-called realistic novelists, and his realism was of a kind superior to and of more enduring significance than theirs — a realism of theme and character as opposed to a realism of circumstance."[75]

Moreover, Hawthorne's insistence that his own works were

romances, while partly based on a conviction, never explicitly stated, that the romance is a higher form of art than the novel, because of its capacity to present universal human experience, was also partly based on a semi-regretful recognition of his own incapacity to write realistic novels. There is, for example, his well-known comment on his own work and that of Trollope: "It is odd enough that my own individual taste is for quite another class of novels than those which I am myself able to write. If I were to meet with such books as mine by another writer, I don't believe I should be able to get through them. Have you read the novels of Anthony Trollope? They precisely suit my taste; solid and substantial, written on the strength of beef and through the inspiration of ale, and just as real as if some giant had hewn a great lump out of the earth. . . ."[76] This appears to be in line with Hawthorne's comment, in "The Custom-House", that during the period of his custom-house experience,

> It was a folly, with the materiality of this daily life pressing so intrusively upon me, to attempt to fling myself back into another age; or to insist on creating the semblance of a world out of airy matter, when, at every moment, the impalpable beauty of my soap-bubble was broken by the rude contact of some actual circumstance. The wiser effort would have been, to diffuse thought and imagination through the opaque substance of to-day, and thus to make it a bright transparency . . . to seek, resolutely, the true and indestructible value that lay hidden in the petty and wearisome incidents, and ordinary characters, with which I was now conversant.

But it should be stressed that Hawthorne is not, even here, saying that he should have been writing a novel of literal, photographic realism; essentially he is saying, in the second quoted sentence ("to diffuse thought and imagination through the opaque substance of to-day; to seek the true and indestructible value hidden in petty incidents and ordinary characters") that he should have been writing a modern *romance* rather than a romance of the past.

There is the further important point that there is a considerable discrepancy between what Hawthorne says about his work in his prefaces and the books themselves. The prefaces almost invariably suggest a much greater remoteness from reality, a much greater insubstantiality than any reader is likely to find in the romances themselves. For example, *The Scarlet Letter* is no "soap-bubble"; as Gupta remarks, "for all its multiplicity of meaning and complexity of symbolism, [it] has a setting which is both precise and solid. The town and the Puritan society are described in such concrete detail that one finds them completely credible."[77] Similarly in the Preface to *The House of the Seven Gables*, Hawthorne objects to his "fancy-pictures" being brought "into positive contact with the realities of the moment", and asks that "the book may be read strictly as a Romance, having a great deal more to do with the clouds overhead, than with any portion of the actual soil of the County of Essex." But as Dan McCall points out, "The portrait of Matthew Maule's violent end 'a death that blasted with strange horror' his property, does not take place in 'cloud-land'. . . . At the death scene we see 'Clergymen, judges, statesmen — the wisest, calmest, holiest persons of their day — in the inner circle round the gallows, loudest to applaud the work of blood, latest to confess themselves miserably deceived.' All this comes only three paragraphs away from the gently ironic preface . . ."[78] And Henry James, for all his reiterated insistence that "Hawthorne was not a realist", pays tribute to Hawthorne's rendering of the atmosphere of "an elm-shadowed New England town", "the mild provincial quality, the mixture of shabbiness and freshness, the paucity of ingredients."[79]

We can say, then, that Hawthorne's conception and practice of the romance as contrasted with the novel, was not an advocacy of, or indulgence in, a romantic evasion of reality. Northrop Frye's account of the difference between the kind of fiction which Hawthorne was "able to write" and that of Trollope, which "precisely suited his taste", is more accurate and illuminating than Hawthorne's own distinction (which followed Clara Reeve, Scott, Brockden Brown, Cooper and Simms[80]).

> The essential difference between novel and romance lies in the conception of characterization. The romancer does not attempt to create 'real people' so much as stylized figures which expand into psychological archetypes. It is in the romance that we find Jung's libido, anima and shadow reflected in the hero, heroine and villain respectively. That is why the romance so often radiates a flow of subjective intensity that the novel lacks, and why a suggestion of allegory is constantly creeping in around its fringes. . . . The novelist deals with personality, with characters wearing their *personae* or social masks. . . . The romancer deals with individuality, with characters *in vacuo* idealized by revery. . . .[81]

We can say, too, that Hawthorne himself was divided in his attitude towards the kind of fiction he was able to write — divided between a conviction of its superiority, and a sense of dissatisfaction with its insubstantiality. In the mock-preface to "Rappacinni's Daughter" Hawthorne speaks of the "inveterate love of allegory, which is apt to invest his plots and characters with the aspect of scenery and people in the clouds and to steal away the human warmth out of his conceptions", and of M. de L'Aubepine's contenting himself with "the faintest possible counterfeit of real life." This sense that his work was "too remote, too shadowy and insubstantial" led him, especially in *The House of the Seven Gables* and *The Blithedale Romance*, to attempt to deal directly with "the opaque substance of to-day", while still, in his Prefaces, denying that he was doing so.

But if Hawthorne was always a psychologist and moral realist (though one more interested in "individuality" than "personality", to use Frye's terms), and if, in some of his work, he was far more of a physical and social realist than he seemed to want to admit, it remains true that the very centre of his aesthetic creed was the spiritualization and idealization of reality through the imagination. Is not such a theory of the novel totally alien to realism, with its insistence on a minute fidelity to observed reality, to the "solidity of specification" which seemed to Henry James "the supreme virtue of a novel — the merit on which all its other merits . . . helplessly and submissively depend"?[82] And is not, therefore, George Eliot's conception of the novel so completely incompatible with Hawthorne's that, as a practitioner, she could learn nothing from him?

The answer to the first question may be "Yes"; but the answer to the second is "No". As I have said, "realism" is only one, and not the most important, element in George Eliot's theory of the novel; and the notion that George Eliot is a realist must be at least as heavily qualified as the notion that Hawthorne is a romancer.

Even in the few passages that I have quoted from her essays there is evidence that George Eliot did not regard it as the novelist's proper function merely to observe and objectively record what he observed. For example, the comment on Kingsley suggests that the function of the great artist is to give us "his higher sensibility as a medium, a delicate acoustic or optical instrument, bringing home to our coarser senses what would otherwise be unperceived by us." In other words, what the great novelist presents us with is the real world refracted through his individual sensibility and imagination.

In the passage on Ruskin's *Modern Painters* George Eliot defines "realism" as "the doctrine that all truth and beauty are to be obtained by a humble and faithful study of nature"; she does not say that art is, or ought to be, an exact and literal imitation of nature. Certainly Ruskin himself did not say anything of the kind, as George Eliot very well knew. In *Modern Painters, I* (1846) Ruskin had said that the artist uses the real world as "his sources of beauty", but these sources "are not presented by any very great work of art in a form of pure transcript. They invariably receive the reflection of the mind under whose shadow they have passed"; and in *Modern Painters, III* he distinguished between lower art which "merely copies what is set before it", and higher art which "either entirely imagines its subject, or arranges the materials presented to it so as to manifest imaginative power."[83]

George Eliot fully concurred in this view. In an 1855 essay, "Three Months in Weimar", for example, she recognizes "how inevitably subjective art is, even when it professes to be purely imitative — how the most active perception gives us rather a reflex of what we think and feel, than the real sum of objects before us."[84] And, in an 1857 letter, she remarks that in her fiction she tries to exhibit things "seen through such a medium as my own nature gives me."[85]

Similarly, the famous passage in chapter 17 of *Adam Bede*, in which George Eliot praises "the rare precious quality of truthfulness" in Dutch paintings, a passage which has often been taken, by Mario Praz for example, as her "declared programme with regard to realism in art",[86] if read in its context, turns out to be nothing of the kind. It is preceded by George Eliot's assertion that her "strongest effort is . . . to give a faithful account of men and things *as they have mirrored themselves in [her] mind*" (My italics.) She adds: "The mirror is doubtless defective; the outlines will sometimes be disturbed, the reflection faint or confused; but I feel as much bound to tell you precisely what that reflection is, as if I were in the witness-box narrating my experience on oath." What she is arguing for is not a faithful transcription of external reality, but a faithful transcription of the version of reality which exists in the artist's mind and imagination. It is note-worthy that George Eliot's use of the mirror in this passage, not as an indifferently accurate reflector of reality, but as a symbol of the artist's whole temperament — sensibility, emotion and imagination — is very like Hawthorne's use of the mirror in "The Custom House": "So little adapted is the atmosphere of a Custom House to the delicate harvest of fancy and sensibility, that, had I remained there through ten Presidencies . . . I doubt whether the tale of *The Scarlet Letter* would ever have been brought before the public eye. My imagination was a tarnished mirror. It would not reflect, or only with miserable dimness, the figures with which I did my best to people it."

Darrel Mansell effectively sums up George Eliot's conception of the relationship between actuality and art: "Ruskin is not advocating the exact imitation of . . . everyday subjects, and neither is George Eliot. For both, the great artist comes between his subject and the viewer; he changes the subject so that the result is the mirror of his mind. But he must begin by humbly and faithfully studying the everyday life around him; and this everyday life should be the stuff from which a great artist creates imaginative art."[87] "Studying the everyday life around him", as the stuff from which to create imaginative art, is exactly what Hawthorne thought he should have been doing during his years in the Custom House ("The wiser effort would have been, to diffuse thought and imagination through the opaque substance of to-day . . . to seek the true and indestructible value that lay hidden in petty . . . incidents, and ordinary characters . . ."); substantially it is what he actually did in *The House of the Seven Gables*, and, to a degree, in *The Blithedale Romance*.

There are many reasons, then, why Hawthorne should have been a "grand favourite" of George Eliot's. They both believed in the moral (but not didactically moralistic) function of fiction; they were both intensely interested in the inner life; they both recognized the subjective nature of the novel or romance (not as a direct autobiographical self-revelation, but as the product of the interaction between observed reality and the individual temperament, sensibility and imagination of the novelist). Partly because of their similar religious and intellectual backgrounds (Ellin

Ringler describes them both as "Calvinists *manqués*"[88]), they were both pre-occupied by the same themes and problems — egotism and idealism, isolation and estrangement, sympathy and communication, human responsibility and the inexorable law of consequences. There were important differences, but the similarities were far more profound and fundamental.

Hawthorne's Influence in *Scenes of Clerical Life*

"Amos Barton", the first of the *Scenes of Clerical Life*, is, of all George Eliot's work, the most firmly committed to the average, the ordinary, the mediocre in human life. In the opening paragraphs of chapter 5, perhaps the best-known and most often quoted paragraphs in the *Scenes*, George Eliot explicitly insists that "the Rev. Amos Barton . . . was in no respect an ideal or exceptional character", but one who would be regarded as "an utterly uninteresting character" by the "lady reader . . . who prefers the ideal in fiction; to whom tragedy means ermine tippets, adultery and murder . . ."

She goes on to assert that most people are "of this insignificant stamp", are "neither extraordinarily silly, nor extraordinarily wicked, nor extraordinarily wise", but "simply men of complexions more or less muddy, whose conversation is more or less bald and disjointed". Yet, she maintains, "Depend upon it, you would gain unspeakably if you would learn with me to see some of the poetry and the pathos, the tragedy and the comedy, lying in the experience of a human soul that looks out through dull grey eyes, and that speaks in a voice of quite ordinary tones." But anyone who thinks the "homely details" she has to tell beneath his attention will easily find reading more to his taste in "the many remarkable novels, full of striking situations, thrilling incidents, and eloquent writing", which, according to the newspapers, "have appeared only within the last season."

It is not something that can be proved, but I suspect that in writing these paragraphs, and other similar passages in this chapter (as when she describes Barton as "not . . . superlative in anything; unless, indeed, he was superlatively middling, the quintessential extract of mediocrity") and in other chapters (for example, in chapter 7, her claim that "not having a fertile

imagination . . . and being unable to invent thrilling incidents",
her "only merit must lie in the truth with which I represent to
you the humble experience of an ordinary fellow-mortal"),
George Eliot had in mind, as contrast to the anti-idealistic, anti-
romantic, determinedly ordinary and prosaic, fiction which she
was advocating and practising, not merely the ironically-
described "remarkable novels" of "the last season", but a novel
published half a dozen years before, which there is every reason
to believe that she regarded as genuinely remarkable — *The
Scarlet Letter*.

One of the grounds for this suspicion is part of the description,
in chapter 5, of her first clergyman hero, or anti-hero, which I
previously omitted. Amos Barton was a man "very far from
remarkable, — a man whose virtues were not heroic, and who
had no undetected crime within his breast; who had not the
slightest mystery hanging about him, but was palpably and unmistakably commonplace." Barton is, in fact, the obverse of
Hawthorne's Arthur Dimmesdale, who carries the undetected
crime of adultery within his breast, and has an air of mystery
hanging about him which arouses the curiosity of Chillingworth,
even before he suspects that the minister is his wife's former
lover. So far from being "palpably and unmistakably commonplace", Dimmesdale's "eloquence and religious fervour had
already given the earnest of high eminence in his profession"
when we are first introduced to him (*The Scarlet Letter*, chapter
3); so far from looking out "through dull grey eyes" and speaking "in a voice of quite ordinary tones", so far from having "a
narrow face of no particular complexion . . . with features of no
particular expression . . . surmounted by a slope of baldness
gently rising from brow to crown" ("Amos Barton", chapter 2),
Dimmesdale was "a person of very striking aspect, with a white,
lofty and impending brow, large, brown, melancholy eyes, and a
mouth which . . . was apt to be tremulous, expressing . . .
nervous sensibility", whose "voice was tremulously sweet, rich,
deep and broken."

This point-by-point contrast between Barton and Dimmesdale
may be a matter of accident. But Hawthorne's "polluted priest"
(as Dimmesdale describes himself) must have been one of the
best-known fictional clerics in the 1850s; in presenting her utterly commonplace clergyman George Eliot, whether consciously

or not, seems to have insisted on his mediocrity — physical, physiognomical, emotional, psychological, spiritual — through implied contrast with the intellectually gifted, impassioned, sinning and tormented Dimmesdale.

There is at least one passage in "Amos Barton" which seems to have an even closer relationship to *The Scarlet Letter*, a passage concerned with the clergyman's relationship to his parishioners. In Chapter 10, after the death of Milly, and when Amos Barton is on the point of leaving Shepparton, the narrator describes the reactions of his parishioners. "There was general regret among the parishioners at his departure; not that any one of them thought his spiritual gifts pre-eminent, or was conscious of great edification from his ministry. But his recent troubles had called out their better sympathies, and that is always a source of love. Amos failed to touch the spring of goodness by his sermons, but *he touched it effectively by his sorrows; and there was now a real bond between him and his flock*" (my italics).

In this passage, I believe, there is a distinct reference to chapter 11 of *The Scarlet Letter* ("The Interior of a Heart"), which describes the bond between Dimmesdale and his parishioners. There are, of course, great differences; it is through his eloquent preaching that Dimmesdale touches the heart of his flock, who do regard his spiritual gifts as pre-eminent ("They deemed the young clergyman a miracle of holiness. They fancied him the mouth-piece of Heaven's messages of wisdom, and rebuke, and love"). Dimmesdale has not suffered bereavement, and virtual dismissal and banishment; his public self-condemnation from the pulpit is taken by his hearers not as the confession of a specific sin, but as an avowal of man's fallen and corrupted state. But, for all the differences in character and situation, I doubt whether the similarity between the passage quoted from "Amos Barton", and these sentences from *The Scarlet Letter* is purely coincidental.

While thus suffering under bodily disease, and gnawed and tortured by some black trouble of the soul . . . the Reverend Mr. Dimmesdale had achieved a brilliant popularity in his sacred office. *He won it, indeed, in great part by his sorrows. . . .* To . . . high mountain-peaks of faith and sanctity he would have climbed, had not the tendency been thwarted by the burden, whatever it might be, of crime or anguish, beneath which it was his doom to totter. It kept him down, on a level with the lowest. . . . But this very burden it was, that gave him *sympathies so intimate with the sinful brotherhood of mankind*;

so that his heart vibrated in unison with theirs . . . and sent its own throb of pain through a thousand other hearts. . . .

One surely detects, also, in George Eliot's description of the grass-grown grave with its "tombstone telling *in bright letters, on a dark ground,* that beneath were deposited the remains of Amelia, beloved wife of Amos Barton", an echo of the conclusion of *The Scarlet Letter*: "Yet one tombstone served for both. . . . It bore a device, a herald's wording of which might serve for a motto and brief description of our now-concluded legend; so sombre is it, and relieved only by one ever-glowing point of light gloomier than the shadow:- 'ON A FIELD, SABLE, THE LETTER A, GULES.' "

I do not detect much evidence of Hawthorne's influence, in the second of the *Scenes*, "Mr Gilfil's Love Story". Perhaps the brief account of the childhood of "The little black-eyed monkey", Caterina, in Cheverel Manor owes something to Hawthorne's Pearl. "The little southern bird had its northern nest lined with tenderness, and caresses, and pretty things. A loving sensitive nature was too likely, under such nurture, to have its susceptibilities heightened into unfitness for an encounter with any harder experience; all the more because there were gleams of a fierce resistance to any discipline that had a harsh or unloving aspect. For the one thing in which Caterina showed any precocity was a certain ingenuity in vindictiveness" (chapter 4). In the chapter entitled "Pearl" (*The Scarlet Letter*, chapter 6), Hawthorne tells us "Throughout all . . . there was a trait of passion, a certain depth of hue which she never lost. . . ." "The child could not be made amenable to rules"; in Pearl Hester "could recognise her wild, desperate, defiant mood, the flightiness of her temper." Hester "early sought to impose a tender, but strict, control over the infant immortality" but "was ultimately compelled to stand aside. . . . Physical compulsion or restraint was effectual, of course, while it lasted. As to any other kind of discipline . . . little Pearl might or might not be within its reach, in accordance with the caprice that ruled the moment." Pearl has "a certain peculiar look so intelligent, yet inexplicable, so perverse, sometimes so malicious . . . that Hester could not help questioning . . . whether Pearl was a human child." Sometimes "Pearl would frown, and clench her little fist, and harden her small features into a stern, unsympathizing look of discontent"; she has "outbreaks of a fierce temper", in which she requites "the little Puritans" "with the bitterest hatred that can be supposed to rankle in a childish bosom." Hester fancies she sees reflected "in the small black mirror of Pearl's eye . . . a face, fiend-like, full of smiling malice. . . . It was as if an evil spirit possessed the child."

The passionate, rebellious, vengeful, nature of George Eliot's "little southern bird" may owe something to the perverse, malicious, fierceness of Pearl. Caterina's smashing of Lady Cheverell's flower-vase is reminiscent of Pearl's flinging stones at the Puritan children, and wildflowers at Hester's scarlet letter. Her flight from the body of Anthony Wybrow, whom she had wished to stab to death in revenge for his treacherous baseness, is also faintly reminiscent of the flight of Clifford and Hepzibah Pyncheon from the body of their cousin Jaffrey, whom they have had every reason to wish dead, for his cruel framing of Clifford for his uncle's "murder".

There is, I think, another — admittedly trivial — link with *The House of the Seven Gables*. In chapter 20 of "Mr Gilfil's Love-Story", when Caterina is recuperating witl Gilfil's sister at Foxholm Parsonage, her room looks out on to a farm homestead; we are told that "contented speckled hens, industriously scratching for the rarely-found corn, may sometimes do more for a sick heart than a grove of nightingales; there is something irresistibly calming in the unsentimental cheeriness of top-knotted pullets . . ." No doubt this is a discovery that the country-bred George Eliot could have made for herself; but it is a discovery that Hawthorne's Phoebe Pyncheon had previously made in tending her elderly cousin Clifford. "One of the available means of amusement, of which Phoebe made the most, in Clifford's behalf, was that feathered society, the hens. . . . All hens are well-worth studying, for the piquancy and rich variety of their manners. . . . We linger too long, no doubt, beside this paltry rivulet of life that flowed through the garden of the Pyncheon house. But we deem it pardonable to recall these mean incidents, and poor delights, because they proved so greatly to Clifford's benefit. They had the earth-smell in them, and contributed to give him health and substance" (*The House of the Seven Gables*, chapter 10).

As I have mentioned, George Eliot re-read *The Scarlet Letter* shortly before she started to write the third of the *Scenes*. It is therefore not surprising that it is in "Janet's Repentance" that Hawthorne's influence is most clearly discernible. In the first place, it can hardly be doubted that Janet Dempster, in physical appearance, is closely modelled on Hester Prynne. The first descriptions of the two characters are strikingly similar. "The young woman was tall, with a figure of perfect elegance, on a large scale. She had dark and abundant hair, so glossy that it threw off the sunshine with a gleam, and a face which, besides being beautiful from regularity of feature and richness of complexion, had the impressiveness belonging to a marked brow and deep black eyes. She was . . . characterized by a certain state and dignity . . ." (*The Scarlet Letter*, chapter 2). "She had on a light dress which sat loosely about her figure, but did not disguise its liberal, graceful outline. A heavy mass of straight jet-black hair . . . hung over her shoulders. Her grandly-cut features . . . had premature lines about them . . . and the delicately curved nostril . . . seemed made to quiver with the proud consciousness of power and beauty . . . Her wide open black eyes had a strangely fixed, sightless gaze. . . ." ("Janet's Repentance", Chapter 4). Later descriptions of Janet underline the similarity. For example, ". . . the tall, rich figure, looking all the grander for the plainness of the deep mourning dress, and the noble face with its massy folds of black hair, made matronly by a simple white cap. Janet had that enduring beauty which belongs to pure majestic outline and depth of tint" (chapter 14).

Janet Dempster's story is very different from Hester Prynne's; but like Hester's it is a story of sin and sorrow, atonement and dedicated service to others. She is not the adulterous mother of an illegitimate child; to escape from the wretchedness of a life made miserable by the brutality of a boorish and drunken husband, she too takes to drink. When she is turned out of the house by Dempster, in the middle of the night, she sinks into a state of despair, but regains a belief in divine and human goodness through the sympathy of the Evangelical clergyman, Edgar Tryan.

There is something of Arthur Dimmesdale in Edgar Tryan. No doubt the story which he tells Janet of his own sin — his seduction and desertion of a girl, who became a prostitute and committed suicide — was, as Noble remarks, "hackneyed even when it was written"; it has generally been thought no more convincing than Janet's own dipsomania. But, as Noble adds, "the fact that George Eliot could make it a part of her story indicates how important she felt it to be to give some concrete evidence of Mr Tryan's being a fellow-sufferer with Janet . . . He can sympathize fully because he has suffered as deeply. . . . He can . . . make that imaginative identification upon which the fullest sympathy depends."[89]

Tryan tells Janet (chapter 18): "Ten years ago, I felt as wretched as you do. I think my wretchedness was even worse than yours, for I had a heavier sin on my conscience. I had suffered no wrong from others as you have, and I had injured another irreparably in body and soul." Before he confesses the specific nature of his sin, we are told: "Janet's anguish was not strange to Mr Tryan. He had never been in the presence of a sorrow and a self-despair that had sent so strong a thrill through all the recesses of his saddest experience. . . ." He recalls his former "state of mind . . . the state of self-reproach and despair, which enables me to understand to the full what you are suffering . . ." All this, it seems to me, is distinctly reminiscent of Dimmesdale's agony of self-loathing and despair, "the burden . . . of crime or anguish . . . that gave him sympathies so intimate with the sinful brotherhood of mankind; so that his heart vibrated in unison with theirs, and received their pain into itself . . ." (*The Scarlet Letter*, chapter 11).

Tryan's compassionate understanding restores Janet to life and hope, through recognition that selfishness is the root-cause of her misery. There is a surprising similarity, especially in the images of prison and light, between the scene in which Janet attends church, the day after her first interview with Tryan, and the forest-scene between Dimmesdale and Hester Prynne, in which Hester reveals that Chillingworth is her husband and Dimmesdale's mortal enemy, and Dimmesdale agrees to flee with her.

"The decision once made, a glow of strange enjoyment threw its flickering brightness over the trouble of his breast. It was the exhilarating effect — upon a prisoner just escaped from the dungeon of his own heart — of breathing the wild, free atmosphere of an unredeemed, unchristianized, lawless region. His spirit rose, as it were, with a bound, and attained a nearer prospect of the sky, than throughout all the misery which had kept him grovelling on the earth. . . ."

"As if the gloom of the earth and sky had been but the effluence of these two mortal hearts, it vanished with their sorrow. All at once, as with a sudden smile of heaven, forth burst the sunshine. . . . The objects that had made a shadow hitherto, embodied the brightness now. . . ."

"Such was the sympathy of Nature . . . with the bliss of these two spirits! Love, whether newly born, or aroused from a death-like slumber, must always create a sunshine, filling the heart so full of radiance, that it overflows upon the outward world. . . ." (*The Scarlet Letter*, chapter 18).

"There was a liquid brightness in her eyes as they rested on the mere walls, the pews, the weavers and colliers in their Sunday clothes. The commonest things seemed to touch the spring of love within her, just as, when we are suddenly released from an acute absorbing bodily pain, our heart and senses leap out in new freedom. . . . A door had been opened in Janet's cold dark prison of self-despair, and the golden light of morning was pouring in its slanting beams through the blessed opening. There was sunlight in the world; there was a divine love caring for her . . . it had been preparing comfort for her in the very moment when she had thought herself forsaken" ("Janet's Repentance", chapter 21).

The death scene of Edgar Tryan, tenderly nursed by the regenerate Janet (whose recovered peace, calm and faith have, however, been saved from severe testing by the fortuitous death of her drunken husband) is also somewhat reminiscent of the death of Arthur Dimmesdale on the scaffold, after his confession, his head supported on Hester's bosom. Reminiscent, but, of course, very different; for, while Dimmesdale answers Hester's questions " 'Shall we not meet again? Shall we not spend our immortal life together?' " with " 'I fear! I fear! It may be, that, when we forgot our God — when we violated our reverence each for the other's soul, — it was henceforth vain to hope that we could meet hereafter, in an everlasting and pure reunion' " (*The Scarlet Letter*, chapter 23), Tryan tells Janet " 'You will have a long while to live after I have gone. . . . But you will not feel the need of me as you have done. . . . You have a sure trust in God . . . I shall not look for you in vain at the last' " ("Janet's

Repentance", chapter 27). And, as David Lodge comments, George Eliot "Even compromised her disbelief in immortality to the extent of allowing her hero and heroine 'a sacred kiss of promise' at the end of the story."[90]

Actually, it is not quite the end of the story, for "Janet's Repentance", like *The Scarlet Letter*, has an epilogue. An Italian critic of George Eliot, Pietro di Logu (who, as well as quoting, and slightly amplifying, Mario Praz on *Romola*, finds similarities to Hawthorne in "Janet's Repentance" and *Felix Holt*) comments (my translation): Janet Dempster "as a widow, like Hester Prynne in Hawthorne's *The Scarlet Letter*, devotes her life, which she had once wished to discard, to good and charitable works . . . Janet returns, at the end, to the human community, spending herself for her neighbour with dedicated altruism."[91] Just as, "in the lapse of toilsome, thoughtful and self-devoted years that made up [her] life . . . Hester Prynne had no selfish ends, nor lived in any measure for her own profit and enjoyment" (*The Scarlet Letter*, chapter 24), so Janet Dempster "thirsted for no pleasure, she craved no worldly goods. Life to her . . . was a solemn service of gratitude and patient effort" ("Janet's Repentance", chapter 28). The similarity in wording provides the final proof of how strongly *The Scarlet Letter* was present in George Eliot's mind when she wrote the third and longest of the *Scenes*.

Hawthorne's Influence in *Adam Bede*

Joan Bennett has remarked that George Eliot's "entry in the journal for 16 November 1858, when she had just written the last word of [*Adam Bede*], indicates the degree in which the characters of Adam and Dinah were drawn from life, and reveals the problems of composition of which the author was most clearly aware."[92]

"The germ of 'Adam Bede' ", according to George Eliot's journal entry, was the story told to her in 1839 or 1840, by her Methodist aunt Samuel, "of how she had visited a condemned criminal, — a very ignorant girl, who had murdered her child and refused to confess; how she had stayed with her praying, through the night and how the poor creature at last broke out into tears, and confessed her crime." George Eliot goes on to recount that in December 1856 (when she had written "Amos Barton") she told this story to Lewes, who "remarked that the scene in the prison would make a fine element in a story"; she then "began to think of blending this and some other recollections of my aunt in one story, with some points in my father's early life and character. The problem of construction that remained was to make the unhappy girl one of the chief *dramatis personae* and connect her with the hero."

In the following paragraphs George Eliot insists that while "the character of Dinah grew out of my recollections of my aunt . . . Dinah is not at all like my aunt," whom she knew only when she was about sixty years old; and that while "the character of Adam and one or two incidents connected with him were suggested by my father's early life . . . Adam is not my father any more than Dinah is my aunt. Indeed, there is not a single portrait in "Adam Bede"; only the suggestions of experience wrought up into new combinations."

It appears, then, that some months before she began to write her first full-length novel, George Eliot had in her mind two characters, based on, or at least suggested by, two of her own relations; she had an incident, the prison-interview, which was to provide the novel's climax, involving a third character, but one for whom she had only the real-life information that she was "a very ignorant girl." But before she began to write the novel, this character had, apparently, been more fully developed in her mind, and she had also thought of the necessary fourth main character (necessary because there was presumably never any thought of making the character based on her father the girl's seducer), though the journal entry gives no hint of his origin; he suddenly appears, unheralded, in the next sentence. "When I began to write it, the only elements I had determined on besides the character of Dinah were the character of Adam, his relation to Arthur Donnithorne, and their mutual relations to Hetty, — that is, to the girl who commits child-murder . . ."[93]

Where did Arthur Donnithorne come from? And how did the historical child-murderess, Mary Voce, become Hetty Sorrel? No doubt Arthur and Hetty are products of George Eliot's creative imagination. And one remembers George Eliot's comment on fictional characters: "It is invariably the case that when people discover certain points of coincidence in a novel with facts that happen to have come to their knowledge, they believe themselves able to furnish a key to the whole. That is amusing enough to the author, who knows from what widely sundered portions of experience — from what combinations of subtle, shadowy suggestions — his story has been formed. It would be a difficult thing for me to furnish a key to my characters myself." But when one also remembers that George Eliot had re-read *The Scarlet Letter* in March 1857, when she had already begun to think about "the problem of construction" (that is, the problem of making "the unhappy girl" one of the chief characters, and connecting her with the hero), it seems very likely that some suggestions (and not very "shadowy" ones) had come from her "grand favourite"; it may well be that the very names she gave the two characters (for Hetty's real name, as we learn from the judge who pronounces sentence, is Hester) represent a conscious acknowledgment on George Eliot's part that they were, to some extent, derived from Hester Prynne and Arthur Dimmesdale.

Before examining the nature and extent of George Eliot's indebtedness to Hawthorne, I shall quote one passage from *Adam Bede* which seems to me to provide quite incontrovertible evidence that the indebtedness is not imaginary. It occurs at the end of chapter 24, ("The Health Drinking"). At Arthur's coming of age party, after the speeches have been made, Arthur and Mr Irwine visit the table where the wives and children of the chief tenants are sitting; Arthur and Hetty have been meeting secretly in the chase for more than a month, and have, presumably, already become lovers.

> Arthur did not venture to stop near Hetty, but merely bowed to her as he passed along the opposite side. The foolish child felt her heart swelling with discontent, for what woman was ever satisfied with apparent neglect, even when she knows it to be the mark of love? Hetty thought that this was going to be the most miserable day she had had for a long while; a moment of chill daylight and reality came across her dream; Arthur, who had seemed so near to her only a few hours before, was separated from her, as the hero of a great procession is separated from a small outsider in the crowd.

George Eliot may not have been consciously aware of what "great procession" she was remembering, but there can be little doubt that it was the Election Day procession described by Hawthorne, in chapter 22 ("The Procession") of *The Scarlet*

Letter. On this third day after the forest meeting between Hester and Arthur, when, after her revelation of Chillingworth's identity, they decided to return to the Old World, Dimmesdale is to preach the Election Sermon; he has a place of honour, after the magistrates, in the procession through the streets and market-place to the meeting house. He walks with unusual energy, but completely abstracted, seeing and hearing nothing.

> Hester Prynne, gazing steadfastly at the clergyman, felt a dreary influence come over her, but wherefore or whence she knew not; unless that he seemed so remote from her own sphere, and utterly beyond her reach. One glance of recognition, she had imagined, must needs pass between them. She thought of the dim forest, with its little dell of solitude, and love, and anguish, and the mossy tree-trunk, where, sitting hand in hand, they had mingled their sad and passionate talk with the melancholy murmur of the brook. How deeply had they known each other then! And was this the man? She hardly knew him now! He, moving proudly past, enveloped as it were, in the rich music, with the procession of majestic and venerable fathers; he, so unattainable in his worldly position, and still more so in that far vista of his unsympathizing thoughts, through which she now beheld him! Her spirit sank with the idea that all must have been a delusion, and that, vividly as she had dreamed it, there could be no real bond betwixt the clergyman and herself! And thus much of woman was there in Hester, that she could scarce-ly forgive him . . . for being able so completely to withdraw himself from their mutual world, while she groped darkly, and stretched forth her cold hands and found him not.

There are so many similarities between the two passages — the woman's resentment at the man's remoteness from her, and non-recognition of her, after recent, or recently-renewed, intimacy; her sense that the love she had believed in must have been a dream or delusion — that George Eliot's metaphorical use of the actual "procession" situation of *The Scarlet Letter* merely con-firms a conviction of her indebtedness.

At one other point, at least, Hetty strongly reminds one of Hester. When Adam sees Hetty in the dock (chapter 43), he sees the corpse of "the Hetty who had smiled at him in the garden under the apple-tree boughs", but "others thought she looked as if some demon had cast a blighting glance upon her, withered up the woman's soul in her, and left only a hard despairing obstinacy." This is distinctly reminiscent of Hawthorne's account (*The Scarlet Letter*, chapter 13) of "the effect of the symbol — or, rather, of the position in respect to society that was indicated by it — on the mind of Hester Prynne." "All the light and graceful foliage of her character had been withered up by this red-hot brand, and had long ago fallen away, leaving a bare and harsh outline, which might have been repulsive, had she possessed friends or companions to be repelled by it." As Hester gives an impression of "marble coldness", so Hetty is a "pale hard-looking culprit".

Nicolaus Mills points out various other resemblances between the two Hesters[94] especially that "both believe themselves misunderstood", and "both are prepared to ignore the past when it does not suit their purposes". In the forest scene (*The Scarlet Letter*, chapter 18), Hester exhorts Dimmesdale "Let us not look back. . . . The past is gone. Wherefore should we linger upon it now? See! With this symbol, I undo it all, and make it as it had never been." In her bed-room, dreaming of Arthur Donnithorne, and admiring her reflection (*Adam Bede*, chapter 15), "Hetty could have cast all her past life behind her, and never cared to be reminded of it again." Mills remarks that "at times it seems as if the idea of escape is in reality a death-wish." Both have thoughts of suicide. In chapter 13 of *The Scarlet Letter* we are told: "At times, a fearful doubt strove to possess [Hester's] soul, whether it were not better to send Pearl at once to heaven, and go herself to such futurity as Eternal Justice should provide." Twice (*Adam Bede*, chapter 35 and 37) Hetty seeks out pools in which to drown herself, but twice her resolution fails. Mills adds, however, that "usually Hester and Hetty nourish the belief that they can be happy if they can just escape the society that has so cruelly judged them." Hester exhorts Dimmesdale to leave the Puritan settlement — "So brief a journey would bring thee from a world where thou hast been most wretched, to one where thou mayest still be happy. . . . There is happiness to be enjoyed." For Hetty, finding that "she has not courage to jump into that cold watery bed", "the hope that [Arthur] would receive her tenderly . . . was like a sense of lulling warmth, that made her for the moment indifferent to everything else; and she began now to think of nothing but the scheme by which she should get away." But if these parallel passages indicate basic similarities they also suggest the difference between Hester's active strength and Hetty's passive weakness.

In her physical appearance, too, Hetty seems clearly to owe much to Hester — more, indeed, than seems to be aesthetically convincing. George Eliot emphasizes Hetty's dark and exotic beauty — the "large dark eyes", "the dark tendrils of hair", "the long dark lashes" — as constantly as Hawthorne emphasizes Hester's; she equips Hetty with a red-leather case and a red cloak (which she is wearing throughout "The Journey in Hope" and "The Journey in Despair", at the end of which she abandons her new-born infant to death from exposure and starvation) as a realistic counterpart to Hester's constant association with red — the scarlet letter itself, the rose bush at the prison door, the "crimson velvet tunic" in which she dresses Pearl.

For Hester Prynne this colouring seems totally appropriate. As H.H. Waggoner remarks: "Hester's emblem . . . points to a love both good and bad. The ambiguity of her gray robes and dark glistening hair, her black eyes and bright complexion is . . . emphasized by the flower and weed imagery . . . Hester walks her ambiguous way between burdock and rose, neither of which is alone sufficient to define her nature and her position."[95] But in the presentation of Hetty as a physical being there seems to be not ambiguity, but contradiction. Hetty is so often associated with small, helpless, irresponsible creatures — at her first introduction, with "kittens", "small downy ducks", "a young star-browed calf", and later with "foolish lost lambs", a bright-eyed spaniel with a thorn in its foot, a little bird with ruffled feathers — that it is difficult to believe in her dark beauty. Ellin Ringler comments that "through their colouring — the red and the black — the two heroines suggest doomed passion and dangerous sensuality."[96] In Hester's case this suggestion is qualified by other elements in the characterization, but she never fails to live up to the first impresssion of tragic grandeur and heroic scale; in Hetty's case, it seems to me, any such suggestion is smothered by the images of "young frisking things." One hardly associates "doomed passion and dangerous sensuality" with "very small downy ducks making gentle rippling noises with their soft bills, or babies just beginning to toddle." What I am suggesting is that George Eliot was indeed influenced by Hawthorne's Hester in the portrayal of Hetty, but that Hetty is so much smaller a character, in mind and spirit, that it was a mistake to make her, physically, a youthful counterpart of Hester. If it hadn't been for the example of Hester, Hetty would surely have been (more believably) a blonde.

Different as they are in stature, the two Hesters are alike in that they are studies in estrangement and egotism. There is a further similarity, perhaps not completely fortuitous, in the fact that their creators seem distinctly uncertain in their attitudes towards their creations.

None of the characters of *The Scarlet Letter* has caused more critical controversy than Hester Prynne, who has been regarded as everything from "a heroine, almost a goddess" and ancient New England's "most heroic creature"[97] to "a devil", "the grey nurse . . . the Hecate, the hellcat."[98] If critics have had such diametrically opposite views of Hester, it is largely because of Hawthorne's own complex and ambiguous attitude towards her. Occasionally Hawthorne seems to judge her as her contemporaries did, and as D.H. Lawrence, for very different reasons, did — as the real villain of the piece. More often he seems to admire and respect her; nevertheless it is a qualified respect and admiration. An early critic, Lucy Hazard, was, I think, right in saying that "it is impossible to draw a consistent brief for one . . . view [of Hester] without ignoring the other, [or] to reconcile the two without putting a strained interpretation on clear statements."[99]

One of the key passages for an understanding of Hawthorne's conception of Hester is in chapter 18.

> Hester Prynne, with a mind of native courage and activity, and for so long a period not merely estranged, but outlawed, from society, had habituated herself to such latitude of speculation as was altogether foreign to the clergyman. She had wandered, without rule or guidance, in a moral wilderness. . . . Her intellect and heart had their home, as it were, in desert places. . . . For years past she had looked from this estranged point of view at human institutions, and whatever priests or legislators had established; criticising all with hardly more reverence than the Indian would feel for the clerical band, the judicial robe, the pillory, the gallows, the fireside, or the church. The tendency of her fate and fortunes had been to set her free. The scarlet letter was her passport into regions where other women dared not tread. Shame, Despair, Solitude! These had been her teachers, — stern and wild ones, — and they had made her strong, but taught her much amiss.

The last sentence clearly reveals the divided nature of Hawthorne's reaction to Hester's development. Romantic critics have regarded Hester's development in intellect, her development into a rebel against contemporary institutions and creeds, as wholly admirable. (Lloyd Morris, for example, maintained that "Hester's elaboration of the badge of her shame into a beautiful emblem was paralleled, in her life, by the elaboration of her sin into nothing but beauty", and that the novel "justified the self-reliant individual and expressed [Hawthorne's] contempt for the society which hedges that individual about with conventions devoid of spiritual validity.")[100] But clearly Hawthorne himself did not. Chapter 13, "Another View of Hester", is Hawthorne's fullest analysis of her; it actually provides two views of Hester. One is Hester as seen by the community, outwardly submissive, humble and pious, claiming nothing and giving much, ministering to the sick and the needy, so unfailingly helpful and generous and dependable that many "refused to interpret the scarlet A by its original signification. They said it meant Able; so strong was Hester Prynne, with a woman's strength." The other is Hester as she really is — hardened into an austere marble pride and strength, and unrepentant. It is in this chapter that we learn of "the freedom of speculation" which she has assumed about the whole social system, especially the subordinate position of women, and the double moral standard. William Bysshe Stein sees her becoming "the feminine counterpart of Faust, a virtual Puritan Fausta" who "in all her thoughts manifests the blind pride of Lucifer and his most notorious disciple, the ill-fated Faust."[101] Hawthorne himself is never quite so specific, but he is clearly divided in his attitude towards Hester, between admiration for her pride, indomitable will and independent self-reliance of spirit, and a fearful admonitory hostility.

The difference between Hester and Hetty is symbolized by the difference between the scarlet letter (which Hester is condemned to wear, but which she has embroidered with such "fertility and gorgeous luxuriance of fancy" that it becomes a symbol of pride and defiance instead of submission and penitence) and "the little pink silk handkerchief", which Arthur thrusts into the wastepaper basket in the Hermitage, after the fight with Adam, and retrieves after he has managed to secure Hetty's reprieve. A critic in the *Edinburgh Review* a century ago, without actually referring to Hester Prynne, defined the difference when he remarked: "In most cases, when a human soul . . . is brought face to face with the darker passions and calamities, it is of a nature lofty enough to cope with and combat them; but George Eliot was the first to

[show] a helpless, frivolous, childish creature, inadequate even to understand, much less to cope with those gigantic shadows. . . ."[102]

If Hester's is the egotism of pride, intellectual freedom and refusal to "measure . . . ideas of right and wrong by any standard external to herself", Hetty's is the egotism of childish vanity and self-regard. But in her outward demeanour she does, on occasions, behave in a manner reminiscent (and probably not accidentally) of Hester. Her behaviour in the Poyser household, when, pregnant, she has agreed to marry Adam, is not unlike Hester's activity in the Puritan community; "Hetty had to manage everything down-stairs . . . and she seemed to throw herself . . . entirely into her new functions, working with a grave steadiness which was new to her . . ." (chapter 34). And, like Hester on the scaffold, Hetty, after the first shock of the discovery, at Windsor, that Arthur has gone to Ireland with the Loamshire Militia, reappears next month with "a resolute air of self-reliance"; and on the return journey, "after five days of wondering, always avoiding speech or questioning looks", she is still able to "recover her air of proud self-dependence whenever she was under observation" (chapter 37).

It is, I think, only in this later part of the novel that the characterization of Hetty is completely successful — particularly in chapter 36 and 37 — "The Journey in Hope" and "The Journey in Despair". In these chapters authorial commentary is almost completely withdrawn; the narrative is starkly simple, sometimes almost verging on indirect interior monologue, confined to the girl's narrow, dumbly suffering consciousness, gradually descending into despair and animal fear, torn between the instinct to survive and a yearning to escape from shame into death. Here George Eliot suspends all judgments, and submerges herself imaginatively in the experience of her creation; the question of the degree of Hetty's guilt, or responsibility for her own suffering becomes irrelevant.

But up to this point in the novel, the portrayal of Hetty suffers from an uncertainty of attitude on George Eliot's part towards her character, which is not unlike Hawthorne's uncertainty of attitude towards Hester. R.T. Jones suggests, as the probable reason, that the other characters "typify possibilities that were, or had been, or might have been, open to her, but with her intelligence, her ardour, and her strenuous and enquiring mind, she could only guess at the quality of such a life as Hetty's."[103] Whatever the reason, in the treatment of Hetty, there seems to be a hiatus, or even a conflict, between George Eliot the creative artist, and George Eliot the didactic moralist. The creative artist presents Hetty, in chapter 7, in her "spring tide beauty . . . the beauty of young frisking things". The initial impression is of natural, instinctive, a-moral innocence; but even in this paragraph the moralist intrudes to imply that Hetty's is "a false air of innocence", though how or why it is false we are not told.

What strikes one as an inappropriate and unjustified moral censoriousness becomes more apparent in chapter 9, when George Eliot tells us: "I am afraid Hetty was thinking a great deal more of the looks Captain Donnithorne had cast at her than of Adam and his troubles." But, a few pages later, George Eliot asks: "In this state of mind, how could Hetty give any feeling to Adam's troubles, or think about poor old Thias being drowned? Young souls, in such pleasant delirium as hers, are as unsympathetic as butterflies sipping nectar; they are isolated from all appeals by a barrier of dreams. . . ." The two quotations neatly sum up the oscillation in George Eliot's attitude towards Hetty, between an acceptance of Hetty for what she is (and a recognition of the effect that Arthur's tenderness and affection have on her), and a determination to find her culpable.

Similarly in chapter 15, "The Two Bedchambers", in which Hetty's narcissistic, self-adoring vanity, and her indulgence in romantic dreams of herself as the beautiful dairy-maid about to be swept away by a princely lover into a rosy paradise of jewellery, beautiful clothes and luxurious surroundings, are contrasted with Dinah's selfless, outward-looking sympathy and feeling for others, the irony directed against Hetty is harsh and heavy-handed, especially in the paragraph beginning: "Ah, what a prize the man gets who wins a sweet bride like Hetty." What Hetty is explicitly accused of in this chapter is lack of roots, lack of familial devotion, and hardness of heart. But one may well feel that if Hetty, an orphan, has no strong attachment to the family, dominated by sharp-tongued Mrs Poyser, in which she is a poor relation and semi-servant, this is neither surprising nor reprehensible.

Moreover, whatever it is that causes her to succumb to Arthur

Donnithorne, it is not hardness of heart. Nor is it calculating ambition. The coming together of Arthur and Hetty is presented, in R.T. Jones' words, "with a soft, decisionless inevitability, a kind of innocent passivity in the power of natural forces"[104] particularly in the image "Such young unfurrowed souls roll to meet each other like two velvet peaches that touch softly and are at rest" (chapter 12).

In George Eliot's attitude towards Hetty there is some confusion and contradiction. Generally Hetty is presented as a "vain and superficial" (Henry James' adjectives[205]), but uncalculating innocent, craving for and responding to the love and tenderness that her forster-home does not provide. But occasionally George Eliot seems to be implying that she is a calculating female trying to ensnare the wealthy young squire as a means of social advancement. Sometimes George Eliot accepts Hetty, with compassionate sympathy for her limitations, for what she is; occasionally she harshly rebukes Hetty for not being what she isn't. As I have suggested, this conflict between sympathetic understanding and censorious moralism in George Eliot's portrayal of Hetty is distinctly similar to Hawthorne's ambivalent attitude towards his much larger heroine, Hester.

Alan Casson suggests that "Hetty's silence at her trial could be compared with Hester's refusal to reveal Arthur Dimmesdale";[106] and Ellin Ringler draws attention to the "crucial interviews with the two Hesters in prison"[107] — Chillingworth's interview with Hester, and Dinah's interview with Hetty. But since Hetty's silence, and her tearful confession to Dinah in prison, were the essential features of the original real-life story, they can hardly be attributed to the influence or example of Hawthorne. Nevertheless though Hetty is so much smaller in scale and stature than Hester, there are so many resemblances (in name and appearance, in temperament and situation) that it can hardly be doubted that one character contributed to the other.

There can, I think, be even less doubt about the links between the two Arthur D's. There are, of course, great differences between the seventeenth century Puritan minister and the dashing young late eighteenth century squire and soldier, between the phases of their lives which the novels present, and between the ways in which they are presented. As Ellin Ringler sums up:

Donnithorne's background and personality are carefully and complexly developed: we know of his relationship to his grandfather and to his friends; his social status, his milieu, his hopes, his weaknesses, his strengths, his physical beauty — all are described. And, through a series of significant incidents, we witness the slowly developing changes of character that lead to his downfall. Arthur Dimmesdale is enveloped in mystery; we learn only those aspects of his character which are revealed in his reactions to the crime that he has committed — not, as with the more fully drawn Donnithorne, through a series of other events. As a result, one can see Donnithorne is doomed by his character to commit his crime and to work out his redemption. One is left to wonder what it was that made Dimmesdale sin. . . .[108]

I would quality this a little, however. I do not think that we are left completely without clues about "what it was that made Dimmesdale sin"; Chillingworth, early in his association with Dimmesdale detects in him "a strong animal nature" inherited from his parents, and by his persistent probing of Dimmesdale's spiritual malady provokes him to a display of anger which causes Chillingworth to surmise that " 'He hath done a wild thing ere now, this pious Master Dimmesdale, in the hot passion of his heart!' " (*The Scarlet Letter*, chapter 10). But while there are hints at elements in Dimmesdale's temperament which make his sexual sin credible, it is true that Hawthorne concentrates attention mainly on "aspects of Dimmesdale's character which are revealed in his reactions to the crime he has committed"; there is indeed (as Ghulam Ali Chaudhry suggests) some psychological implausibility in the fact that, while the sufferings of Dimmesdale's stricken conscience and his agonized self-torturing are very fully presented, "never has there come, *away from Hester*, even a fleeting suggestion of a latent desire to return to his 'strong animal nature' or 'the hot passion of his heart.' "[109]

This, then, is the difference between the two Arthurs. In Dimmesdale's case we see the writhings of conscience for a sin already committed; it is not for some considerable time that we know that it was the sin of adultery, compounded by the sin of cowardly concealment and hypocrisy. In Donnithorne's case we see rather the winding course of the vacillations and insidious rationalizations, the short lived resolutions to avoid temptation, in conflict with the very real strength of his attraction to Hetty, the partial recognitions of his own folly, and of the damage that his irresponsible self-indulgence may cause, which precede the actual commission of the sin. But what is common to the two Arthurs, as to the two Hesters, is their egotism.

I do not think there is sufficient evidence in the text for one to agree with Ellin Ringler that "Dimmesdale's sexual encounter with Hester Prynne, like Donnithorne's with Hetty, was the result of a fundamental exaltation of self that weakened his moral control."[110] But it is largely egotism that prevents Dimmesdale from publicly confessing his guilt. In conversation with Chillingworth, Dimmesdale (while purporting to be speaking generally) is obviously justifying himself, when he claims: ". . . It may be that [such men] are kept silent", because, "guilty as they may be, retaining, nevertheless a zeal for God's glory and man's welfare, they shrink from displaying [themselves] black and filthy in the view of men; because, thenceforward, no good can be achieved by them; no evil of the past be redeemed by them" (chapter 10). But in this avowal, as in his vague pulpit confessions of his own sinfulness, Dimmesdale is "a subtle but remorseful hypocrite" (chapter 11). Terence Martin comments, justly: "Dimmesdale is afflicted with a devious pride. He cannot surrender an identity which brings him the adulation of his parishioners, the respect and praise of his peers. His contortions in the guise of humility only add to the public admiration, which, in turn, feeds an ego fundamentally intent on itself."[111]

After Dimmesdale has agreed to escape to the Old World with Hester and Pearl, he is pleased to learn that the ship is not to sail for several days.

> Now, why the Reverend Mr Dimmesdale considered it so very fortunate, we hesitate to reveal. Nevertheless, — to hold nothing back from the reader, — it was because, on the third day from the present, he was to preach the Election Sermon, and, as such an occasion formed an honourable epoch in the life of a New England clergyman, he could not have chanced upon a more suitable mode and time of terminating his professional career. 'At least, they shall say of me,' thought this exemplary man, "that I leave no public duty unperformed, nor ill performed!' . . . We have had . . . no evidence, at once so slight and irrefragable, of a subtle disease, that had long since begun to eat into the real substance of his character. No man, for any considerable period, can wear one face to himself, and another to the multitude, without finally getting bewildered as to which may be the true. (chapter 20).

This is perhaps the most explicit comment on Dimmesdale's egotism. It is a passage which, I believe, was particularly influential in George Eliot's portrayal of Arthur Donnithorne. Arthur is an amiable young man, "nothing if not good-natured", well-disposed to everyone, and to himself. "His own approbation was necessary to him; and it was not an approbation to be enjoyed quite gratuitously; it must be won by a fair amount of merit" (*Adam Bede*, chapter 22). The tone of the comment indicates that he is not a severe self-critic; he is too convinced of his own good intentions and good nature to believe that he could do harm to anyone. And he is so imbued with class-psychology that he sees all human relationships in terms of the social hierarchy, and believes that if he should inadvertently harm someone, he can easily make amends by liberal patronage. He lives in a world of fantasy and day dream, in which he is to be the good young squire, the generous and beloved provider for and protector of a prosperous, contented and adoring tenantry; he is dominated by the desire to cut a fine figure, to be universally loved and admired.

Having drifted into the seduction of Hetty, and then into the deception of Adam that his relationship with Hetty is a mere playful flirtation, he manages to convince himself that he has committed only a good-natured peccadillo with no permanent ill-effects for anyone, and that Hetty's marriage to Adam will put everything right. There is a famous passage in chapter 29, which is very characteristically George Eliot's, but is nevertheless very reminiscent of Hawthorne: "There is a terrible coercion in our deeds which may first turn the honest man into a deceiver, and then reconcile him to the change; for this reason — that the second wrong presents itself to him in the guise of the only practicable right." The passage almost applies to the earlier, as to the later, Arthur; Dimmesdale is not really "reconciled to the change" in himself from "honest man" to "deceiver", but, continued deception and concealment seem to him to be the only practicable course, if not the "only practicable right". He tells Hester (chapter 17): "Wretched and sinful as I am, I have had no other thought than to drag on my earthly existence in the sphere where Providence hath placed me.' " It is, it seems, only when he recognizes that he is near death that he is prepared to shatter the image of holy, angelic purity, by his public confession; even in that final action there is an element of histrionic exhibitionism.

There is a well-known entry in Hawthorne's journal: "Character of a man who, in himself and his external circumstances shall be equally and totally false; his fortune resting on baseless credit . . . his domestic affections, his honor and honesty, all a show. His own misery in the midst of it — making the whole universe, heaven and earth alike, an unsubstantial mockery to him."[112] The idea was fully developed in the character and situation of Dimmesdale; one of the most deeply perceptive sections of *The Scarlet Letter* is the examination of the introspective, self-lacerating guilt of Dimmesdale. "The agonized conscience" of Arthur Donnithorne (to borrow Leavis' phrase[113]) is not quite so agonized, but it is the product of a similar process of guilt, self-deception, concealment, and rationalization. As Ellin Ringler remarks: "The guilt experienced by Arthur Dimmesdale and Arthur Donnithorne arises from their untrue relationships to the community. Because the two Arthurs have public responsibilities, their private sins must be masked, and thus their guilt and hypocrisy are born. As minister and landlord, shepherds of their people, they become agonizingly aware of their debt to society; and the profoundest ironies develop from the gap that exists between their private and public lives."[114] There can be little doubt that the example of Hawthorne was a potent factor in ensuring that George Eliot's fourth main character, for which the real-life anecdote furnished no clue, would be more than the conventionally wicked squire's son seducing the village maiden in mere ruthless self-indulgence.

If the English Hetty and Arthur owe much to the American Hester and Arthur, so too, probably, does their trysting-place owe something to the scene of the most important meeting of Hester and Arthur. This, of course, is the forest, which is the setting for chapters 16 to 19, the longest continuous sequence in *The Scarlet Letter*.

The "primeval forest" in which Hester meets Dimmesdale (and in which, it is strong hinted, their original sin was committed) is gloomy, mysterious, sombre, dreary; "to Hester's mind, it imaged not amiss the moral wilderness in which she had so long been wandering". It is an unredeemed, lawless and pagan region, the meeting-place of witches with the Black Man (Hester tells Pearl that she once met the Black Man, and the Scarlet Letter is his mark). As Leo B. Levy remarks, "the dominant visual impression is one of antiquity; as the lovers talk, they sit on 'the mossy trunk of the fallen tree' . . . where the moss 'at some epoch of the preceding century, had been a gigantic pine, with its roots and trunk in the darksome shade, and its head aloft in the upper atmosphere'. This setting, with a brook in the midst, a leaf-strewn bank on either side, and trees impending over it whose fallen branches have choked the current, fixes an impression of time inexorable in its action, ever tending towards decay and death."[115] But if the forest in its dimness and gloom reflects the plight of the lovers, it also reflects the bright, pagan vivacity of their child, who catches "the sportive sunshine", and stands "laughing in the midst of it, all brightened by its splendour". While her parents are speaking together, Pearl wanders through the forest, whose wild creatures "all recognized a kindred wildness in the human child"; she decorates her head and waist with violets, anemones and columbines, and becomes "a nymph-child, or an infant dryad or whatever else was in closest sympathy with the antique wood." When Dimmesdale has agreed to escape with Hester, and she has cast off the scarlet letter,

> her sex, her youth and the whole richness of her beauty come back from what man call the irrevocable past. . . . All at once, as with a sudden smile of heaven, forth burst the sunshine, pouring a very flood into the obscure forest, gladdening each green leaf, transmuting the yellow fallen ones to gold, and gleaming adown the gray trunks of the solemn trees. . . . Such was the sympathy of Nature — that wild, heathen Nature of the forest, never sub-jugated by human law, nor illumined by higher truth — with the bliss of these two spirits (chapter 18).

Ellen Ringler remarks that "the heathen forest setting has been turned, by Hawthorne, into a perfectly appropriate symbol of the illicit love which, in its radiance, blinds Hester and Arthur to Puritan law and allows their sexual passion to 'overflow' all moral restrictions."[116]

In *Adam Bede* there is the important difference that the meeting-place of Arthur and Hetty is described before their first meeting (chapter 12). Fir-tree Grove is a much more Edenic setting than Hawthorne's primeval wilderness. It is very likely that it owes something to *Paradise Lost*, but it probably owes something also to Hawthorne's transformed forest, in which the "wood's heart of mystery" has become "a mystery of joy." Fir-tree Grove is "a delicious labyrinthine grove"; it may be acciden-tal that the second adjective recalls Hester Prynne's wandering "in the dark labyrinth of mind" (which is imaged for her in the forest, before it is transformed by the resurgence of passionate love and her new-found hope of happiness). "It was a wood of beeches and limes . . . just the sort of wood most haunted by the nymphs"; it may be accidental that this recalls the flower-bedecked Pearl, who is like "a nymph-child, or an infant dryad, or whatever else was in closest sympathy with the antique wood." There is no brook in the Grove; it may be accidental that the presence of a brook is suggested by the "soft liquid laughter" of the nymphs who "make you believe that their voice was only a running brooklet" (recalling "the course of the little brook might be traced by its merry gleam"). George Eliot adds that perhaps, in the grove, "the nymphs metamorphose themselves into a tawny squirrel that scampers away and mocks you from the top-most bough." Perhaps it is accidental that this recalls that a squirrel is among "the small denizens of the wilderness" which Pearl encounters: "A squirrel, from the lofty depths of his domestic tree chattered either in anger or merriment . . . and flung down a nut upon her head". When we first see Arthur Donnithorne walking through the grove: "It was a still afternoon — the golden light was lingering languidly among the upper boughs, only glancing down here and there on the purple pathway and its edge of faintly-sprinkled moss." It may be accidental that the description of the sunlight almost exactly reproduces part of a sentence in *The Scarlet Letter*: "Overhead was a grey expanse of cloud, slightly stirred, however, by a breeze, so that a gleam of flickering sunshine might now and then be seen at its solitary play along the path."

George Eliot goes on to say that it is "an afternoon in which destiny disguises her cold awful face behind a hazy radiant veil, encloses us in warm downy wings, and poisons us with violet-scented breath." It is probably accidental that the image of radiance was used by Hawthorne in the sentence following that concerning "the sympathy of nature . . . with the bliss of their two spirits." "Love, whether newly born, or aroused from a deathlike slumber, must always create a sunshine, filling the heart so full of radiance, that it overflows upon the outward world." Hawthorne, in the chapter (18) entitled "A Flood of Sunshine" is not so explicit in forecasting that the sunshine is a "radiant veil" disguising the face of destiny, but it does, of course, prove to be so. Hester's hopes of happiness and a new life are to be destroyed; she sees Dimmesdale only twice more. When she sees him next, he moves past in the procession, unseeing, "remote from her own sphere"; and after preaching the Election Sermon he dies, in her arms, on the scaffold. Leo B. Levy suggests that, even in the forest scene itself, where the flood of sunshine is "synonomous with beauty, warmth and richness" "an undercurrent of qualification may be present: sunlight gleams 'adown the grey trunks of the solemn trees', but the grayness and solemnity are still there, and though the leaves are turned to gold, yellowness — the sign of their decline — is also part of the image."[117]

There are, I think, too many similarities between Hawthorne's primeval forest, particularly as it has been transfigured by the radiant overflow of "love aroused from a death-like slumber", and George Eliot's Fir-tree Grove to be purely coincidental. And, of course, the functions of the two settings in the total structures of the two novels are remarkably similar. Both the forest and the grove are havens of sensual freedom from the moral restrictions and repressions of contemporary society. In the forest Hester casts off the scarlet letter, removes "the formal cap that confined her hair", and "her sex, her youth, and the whole richness of her beauty" return; and Dimmesdale, having made the decision to escape, feels joy again: "A glow of strange enjoyment threw its flickering brightness over the trouble of his breast. . . . His spirit rose, as it were, with a bound. . . ." In the grove, when Arthur meets Hetty, and kisses her, the lovers seem suspended in a timeless world of myth and pre-moral innocence: "for a long moment time has vanished. He may be a shepherd in Arcadia for aught he knows, he may be the first youth kissing the first maiden, he may be Eros himself, sipping the lips of Psyche. . . ."

Not only are the emotions of the two Arthurs in the forest settings, and under the influence of the two Hesters (who like Eve, are both innocent and deadly, desirable and dangerous) similar; so are their emotions and behaviour on leaving the place of amoral enjoyment and freedom from inhibition, as the following passages suggest.

> The excitement of Mr. Dimmesdale's feelings, as he returned from his inter-view with Hester, lent him unaccustomed physical energy, and hurried him townward at a rapid pace. The pathway among the woods seemed wilder,

more uncouth with its rude natural obstacles, and less trodden by the feet of man than he remembered it on his outward journey. But he leaped across the plashy places, thrust himself through the clinging underbrush, climbed the ascent, plunged into the hollow, and overcame, in short, all the difficulties of the track, with an unweariable activity that astonished him.

He returns to the town a different man, "at every step . . . incited to do some strange, wild, wicked thing or other"; after his encounters with the deacon, the pious old dame, the pure maiden, the children and the drunken seaman, to each of whom he is tempted to utter blasphemies and profanities, he demands of himself: " 'Am I mad? or am I given over utterly to the fiend? Did I make a contract with him in the forest, and sign it with my blood?' " (*The Scarlet Letter*, chapter 20).

As for Arthur, he rushed back through the wood, as if he wanted to put a wide space between himself and Hetty. . . . He walked right on into the chase, glad to get out of the Grove, which surely was haunted by his evil genius. Those beeches and smooth limes — there was surely something enervating in the very sight of them; but the strong knotted old oaks had no bending languor in them — the sight of them would give a man some energy. Arthur lost himself among the narrow openings in the fern, winding about without seeking any issue, till the twilight deepened almost to night under the great boughs. . . . (*Adam Bede*, chapter 13).

There are differences, of course. Donnithorne does not return to a human community, and is not tempted by impulses to blasphemy and profanity. (But, in the turmoil of his thoughts, he admits to himself that "there was no knowing what impulse might seize him to-morrow.") But the similarities are greater. Dimmesdale's excitement hurries him at a rapid pace; Donnithorne rushes through the wood. Both recognize the pagan amorality of forest and grove — Dimmesdale wonders if he has made a contract with "the fiend" in the forest; for Donnithorne the Grove surely is "haunted by his evil genius." The sexual imagery (palpable in the "plashy places", "clinging underbrush" and "the hollow" into which Dimmesdale plunges, discreetly attenuated in the "narrow openings in the fern" in which Donnithorne loses himself) clearly suggests the association of forest and grove with the women the two Arthurs have just left, whose sexuality attracts and tempts them into transgression of social, moral and religious laws and responsibilities.

Michael Squires, in a valuable article relating *Adam Bede* to the pastoral tradition, shows how George Eliot's use of the *locus amoenus* or "lovely place" in chapters 12 and 13 "fuses pastoral conventions and Christian morality." Squires points out that "the *locus amoenus* traditionally has had both sensual and moral functions. . . . George Eliot tends to combine both functions in *Adam Bede* by creating a sensual haven and then stressing the moral implications of the meetings between Hetty and Arthur in Fir-tree Grove. Her model for the chapters of the novel appears to be *Paradise Lost*, which also combines both functions of the *locus amoenus*."[118] Very probably *Paradise Lost* was one model; but it seems equally likely that *The Scarlet Letter*, which George Eliot had so recently re-read, was another.

I have previously quoted a comment made by a *North British* critic in 1860 that, in Hawthorne's novels, "The crime of yesterday is curiously interwrought with the retribution of to-day. It follows the present with menacing tenacity, and clings to it with an immitigable grasp", and remarked that it was surprising that the critic did not recognize that this "trait of Mr. Hawthorne's mind" was also a trait of the habit of thought of George Eliot, with whom he had compared Hawthorne.[119] Certainly this doctrine of consequences, of the irrevocable nature of human actions, and their unforseeable effects both on the person performing the action and on others, are themes that are equally important in *The Scarlet Letter* and *Adam Bede*.

In *The Scarlet Letter* these ideas are expressed by the narrator in such passages as: "And be the stern and sad truth spoken, that the breach which guilt has once made into the human soul is never, in this mortal state, repaired. It may be watched and guarded. . . . But there is still the ruined wall, and, near it, the stealthy tread of the foe that would win over again his unforgotten triumph" (chapter 18) and "There was a sense of inevitable doom upon her, as she thus received back this deadly symbol from the hand of fate. . . . So it ever is . . . that an evil deed invests itself with the character of doom" (chapter 19). The first idea is expressed by George Eliot in *Adam Bede* in such passages as "Our deeds determine us, as much as we determine our deeds. . . . There is a terrible coercion in our deeds which may first turn the honest man into a deceiver, and then reconcile himself to the change. . . . No man can escape this vitiating effect of an offence against his own sentiment of right" (chapter 29); the second by Mr Irwine, who can undoubtedly be regarded as

George Eliot's spokesman, at least in such statements as "Consequences are unpitying. Our deeds carry their terrible consequences, quite apart from any fluctuations that went before — consequences that are hardly ever confined to ourselves" (chapter 16), and "There is no sort of wrong deed of which a man can bear the punishment alone; you can't isolate yourself, and say that the evil which is in you shall not spread . . . evil spreads as necessarily as disease . . . so does every sin cause suffering to others besides those who commit it" (chapter 41). It is to be noted too that this doctrine of "the terrible consequences of our deeds" is propounded not only by the narrators and their spokesmen, but, in each novel, by the character most wronged by the Arthurs and the Hesters. Roger Chillingworth and Adam Bede are totally different characters; both men, however — Chillingworth when he discovers that he has been cuckolded, Adam Bede when he discovers that the girl he loves has been enticed into a love affair, and, even more, when he learns that she has been arrested for infanticide — are plunged into vengeful fury. Chillingworth's vengeance takes the form of protracted mental and psychological torture of his wife's lover, under the guise of medical treatment; Adam Bede's the form of violent physical attack, which Irwine fears will be renewed, with fatal effects to Arthur and Adam himself, when Hetty is brought to trial.

Ellin Ringler comments that "Different as they are, however, these characters share the same functions in their respective novels and voice the same truths about sin. One of these is that evil is irrevocable. Both Hawthorne and Eliot rejected the easy optimism of men like Emerson, who could find 'compensation' in the darkest deed."[120] Actually "the truths about sin" which the two characters voice are not quite the same. Important parallel scenes in the two novels are chapter 14 ("Hester and the Physician") in *The Scarlet Letter* and chapter 41 ("The Eve of the Trial") in *Adam Bede*. In the former Hester informs Chillingworth of her determination to reveal his identity to Dimmesdale, and pleads with him to purge himself of "the hatred that has transformed a wise and just man into a fiend", to "leave [Dimmesdale's] further retribution to the Power that claims it"; she exhorts him, for his own sake, if not for Dimmesdale's, not to reject the "privilege" and "priceless

benefit" of pardon. Chillingworth replies, "with gloomy stern-
ness. 'It is not granted to me to pardon. . . . My old faith long
forgotten, comes back to me, and explains all that we do, and all
we suffer. By thy first step away, thou didst plant the germ of
evil; but, since that moment, it has all been a dark necessity. Ye
that have wronged me are not sinful . . . neither am I fiend-like,
who have snatched a fiend's office from his hands. It is our fate.
Let the black flower blossom as it may!' " I do not think that
Hawthorne endorses Chillingsworth's words, which virtually
assert, not merely that human actions are irrevocable, but that
the commission of one "small sin" (and he has previously admitted to Hester, in Chapter 4, " 'Mine was the first wrong, when I
betrayed thy budding youth into a false and unnatural relation
with my decay' "), leads inexorably and inevitably to the commission of worse and worse sins by others — from mis-marriage,
to adultery, to hypocritical and cowardly concealment, to sadistic
"violation in cold blood of the sanctity of a human heart."
Chillingworth did not *have* to become "a fiend". As he himself
says, he has "*snatched* a fiend's office from his hands"; and, as
Hawthorne says, "Chillingworth was a striking evidence of
man's faculty *of transforming himself* into a devil, if he will only,
for a reasonable space of time, undertake a devil's office." The
"truth about sin", in fact, which Chillingworth illustrates, as
distinct from the doctrine that he enunciates, is that "Our deeds
determine us"; his ascription of his own behaviour, his
monomaniacal pursuit of vengeance, to "fate" and "dark
necessity" is a rationalization, a denial of his own moral responsibility and capacity for moral choice.

In chapter 41 of *Adam Bede*, what Adam feels most bitterly, as
"the deepest curse of all" is that "*it can never be undone*. My poor
Hetty . . . she can never be my sweet Hetty again. . . ." But
Irwine is able to persuade him, as Hester was not able to persuade Chillingworth, that an act of vengeance against Arthur
would simply be an added evil, "that would leave all the present
evils as they were, and add worse evils to them." In his interview
with Arthur, in chapter 48, Adam has forsworn vengeance
against Arthur, but is still bitterly indignant when he thinks he
perceives in Arthur's words "that notion of compensation for ir-
retrievable wrong, that self-soothing attempt to make evil bear
the same fruits as good", and he makes Arthur "feel more in-

tensely the irrevocableness of his own wrong-doing" ("There's a sort o' damage, sir, that can't be made up for"). But when Adam is convinced that Arthur does recognize that his wrong is ir-retrievable, that he had not meant to injure Hetty, that he bitter-ly repents and will continue to endure "the inward suffering which is the worst form of Nemesis", he forgives him. ("I've no right to be hard towards them as have done wrong and repent.")

If Chillingworth (but not Hawthorne) asserts that one wrong leads inevitably to greater wrongs, what Adam Bede (and George Eliot) asserts, reduced to proverbial banality, is "What's done cannot be undone", but "Two wrongs do not make a right." One could argue that this must have been the view that Chillingworth himself came to, when "by his last will and testament . . . he bequeathed a very considerable amount of property . . . to little Pearl, the daughter of Hester Prynne" (*The Scarlet Letter*, chapter 24). The "moral" of *The Scarlet Letter*, as of *Adam Bede*, is that wrong-doing is irrevocable, and that every sin causes suf-fering to others besides those who commit it; but neither novel suggests that the consequences of a single evil deed must be infinitely extended.

In investigating the influence of Hawthorne on *Adam Bede*, one should remember that George Eliot had almost certainly read *The House of the Seven Gables* as well as *The Scarlet Letter*. In some way *Adam Bede* is closer to Hawthorne's second, "more genial" romance. As in *The House of the Seven Gables* the ancient feud between Maules and Pyncheons is finally resolved by the marriage of Holgrave-Maule and Phoebe Pyncheon, so *Adam Bede* ends with the marriage of Adam and Dinah. But in neither novel is the "happy ending" allowed to annul or unequivocally compensate for the previous wrongs. Almost the last utterance in *Adam Bede* is Arthur's remorseful admission to Adam: " 'I could never do anything for her, Adam — she lived long enough for all the suffering — and I'd thought so of the time when I might do something for her. But you told me the truth when you said to me once, "There's a sort of wrong that can never be made up for" ' " ("Epilogue"). The words are a paraphrase (whether George Eliot was aware of it or not) of Hawthorne's comments about Clifford Pyncheon in the final chapter of *The House of the Seven Gables*: "After such wrong as he had suffered there is no reparation. . . . It is a truth . . . that no great mistake, whether actual or endured, in our mortal sphere, is ever really set right" (chapter 21).

Finally, among the themes which Allan Casson notes as common to *The Scarlet Letter* and *Adam Bede* is "the humanizing power of sorrow."[121] The theme is embodied in two very different characters — Pearl and Adam Bede — but there are some surprisingly similar passages, which provide further corroborative evidence of Hawthorne's influence.

There are actually only a couple of passages in *The Scarlet Letter* concerned with the "humanization" of Pearl. The first occurs in Chapter 16 in which Hawthorne remarks that Pearl's "never-failing vivacity of spirits ... was certainly a doubtful charm, imparting a hard, metallic lustre to the child's character. She wanted — what some people want throughout life — a grief that would deeply touch her, and thus humanize and make her capable of sympathy." The other occurs in chapter 23. When Dimmesdale has made his dying confession on the scaffold, he asks his daughter to kiss him: "Pearl kissed his lips. A spell was broken. The great scene of grief, in which the wild infant bore a part, had developed all her sympathies; and as her tears fell upon her father's cheek, they were the pledge that she would grow up amid human joy and sorrow, nor for ever do battle with the world, but be a woman in it."

What in *The Scarlet Letter* is a subordinate theme, elliptically treated, in *Adam Bede* becomes a dominant theme, treated very fully. Adam Bede's "hardness", first recognized by himself at his father's funeral, is very different from Pearl's; it is the hardness of proud, self-reliant and self-righteous rectitude, of impatience with the weaknesses and follies of others. George Eliot comments (chapter 19): "Perhaps here lay the secret of the hardness he had accused himself of: he had too little fellow-feeling with the weakness that errs in spite of foreseen consequences. Without this fellow-feeling, how are we to get enough patience and charity towards our stumbling, falling companions in the long and changeful journey? And there is but one way in which a strong determined soul can learn it — by getting his heart-strings bound round the weak and erring, so that he must share not only the outward consequences of their error, but their inward suffering."

Through "getting his heart-strings bound round the weak and

erring" Hetty, and being compelled to share in her suffering, Adam undergoes what George Eliot specifically describes as "a baptism, a regeneration, the initiation into a new state". He attains this new state when the passion for revenge gives way to pity, and pity for Hetty and for himself is absorbed into compassionate sympathy for the sufferings of humanity. George Eliot's comment (in chapter 42), "Doubtless a great anguish may do the work of years, and we may come out from that baptism with a soul full of new awe and pity", is very like Hawthorne's previously quoted comment on Pearl.

Adam Bede, with its ample rendering of the life of a rural community, with its host of vividly realized subsidiary characters (some of whom, especially Mrs Poyser, actually figure more prominently than either Dinah or Arthur) is a very different novel from the spare and unremittingly intense and sombre *The Scarlet Letter*. But in view of the many similarities that I have mentioned, it can hardly be doubted that Hawthorne contributed significantly to George Eliot's first full-length novel.

Hawthorne's Influence in *The Mill on the Floss*

In George Eliot's second novel, *The Mill on the Floss* (1860), there is less evidence of Hawthorne's influence than in *Scenes of Clerical Life* or *Adam Bede*; but I believe that there is some, though, so far as I know, no one else shares the belief.

I have come across only two passing references to Hawthorne in criticism of *The Mill on the Floss*. Bernard Paris remarks that "Maggie's situation is approximately the same as that of Hawthorne's more fanciful creation, Donatello, in *The Marble Faun* (both novels, incidentally, were published in the same year, 1860). Both novelists were writing with the developmental hypothesis in mind. An anomalous organism must either adapt itself to its environment or perish. Maggie, as Donatello, must either bring herself into harmony with her environment or perish."[122] Paris, presumably, intends only to draw attention to a coincidental similarity, not to imply that either novel influenced the other; they were written simultaneously and published within a month or so of one another.

The other reference occurs in Alexander Welsh's essay,

"George Eliot and the Romance."[123] In order to make a case for Hawthorne's influence on *The Mill on the Floss*, which Welsh himself does not do, it will be necessary to outline the development of Welsh's illuminating article.

Welsh begins by remarking on the general dissatisfaction with the ending of *The Mill on the Floss*, on the divergent interpretations of George Eliot's purposes and methods, and on some of the various explanations of her alleged failure. He then suggests that "the usefulness — and the contradictions — of these suggestions needs to be submitted to a broader understanding of the genre of fiction to which this novel relates";[124] his eventual conclusion is that "if the ending of *The Mill on the Floss* seems artificial, it is not so much because George Eliot has failed to work it out thoroughly in realistic terms, as that we are no longer experienced readers of the highly stylized genre with which this novel engages."[125]

The "highly stylized genre", Welsh maintains, is the romance. "More than any other novel of George Eliot, *The Mill on the Floss* adheres closely to the typical plot, and the typical dark-haired heroine of the romance — predominantly that of Sir Walter Scott. *The Mill on the Floss* ends with a triangular affair and the death of Maggie primarily because that is what always happens in the romance."[126] Welsh points out that George Eliot, on two occasions, makes her heroine's literary relationships quite explicit — Maggie's implied association of herself with Minna Troil, the dark heroine of Scott's *The Pirate* (in book 5, chapter 2), and her refusal to finish reading Mme de Staël's *Corinne* (in book 5, chapter 4). She tells Philip Wakem:

"I didn't finish the book. . . . As soon as I came to the blond-haired young lady reading in the park, I shut it up, and determined to read no further. I foresaw that that light-complexioned girl would win away all the love from Corinne and make her miserable. I'm determined to read no more books where the blond-haired women carry away all the happiness. I should begin to have a prejudice against them. If you could give me some story, now, where the dark woman triumphs, it would restore the balance. I want to avenge Rebecca and Flora MacIvor, and Minna, and all the rest of the dark unhappy ones.' " Philip replies: " 'Well, perhaps you will avenge the dark women in your own person, and carry away all the love from your cousin Lucy.

She is sure to have some handsome young man of St. Ogg's at her feet now: and you have only to shine upon him — your fair little cousin will be quite quenched in your beams.' "

This, of course, is what does happen in Book 6, in which Stephen Guest, who is at least half-engaged to Lucy Deane, is irresistibly attracted to Maggie, who has promised Philip Wakem that she will marry no one else. Maggie has usually been thought to be a character with a high autobiographical content, or at least a character in which there is a strong element of self-idealization and self-pity — in Leavis' well-known phrases, "the direct (and sometimes embarrassing) presence of the author's own personal need."[127] To digress from Welsh's argument, this "personal need" is most strongly felt in the final scene, when Maggie and her brother Tom drown in one another's arms: "The boat reappeared — but brother and sister had gone down in an embrace never to be parted: living through again in one supreme moment, the days when they had clasped the little hands in love, and roamed the daisied fields together" (book 6, chapter 5).

It is difficult not to see the estrangement of Tom and Maggie, when he pharisaically disowns her after her involuntary elopement with Stephen Guest, as a reflection of Isaac Evans' disowning of his sister after she went to live with George Henry Lewes; and equally difficult not to see the last-moment reconciliation of Tom and Maggie, and his belated recognition of his sister's worth (when "pale with a certain awe and humiliation" he utters "the old childish — 'Magsie'!" and she can "make no answer but a long deep sob of that mysterious wondrous happiness that is one with pain") as George Eliot's vicarious achievement of an ardently-desired reconciliation with her brother which life denied her.

Maggie has also been generally recognized, in her ardour and idealism, as very similar to Dorothea Brooke, the heroine of *Middlemarch*. In the "Prelude" to *Middlemarch*, George Eliot, of course, describes Dorothea as a latter-day St. Theresa, whose "passionate ideal nature", "helped by no coherent social faith and order" found "no epic life wherein there was a constant unfolding of far-resonant action." One can assume that she regarded Maggie as belonging to the same sisterhood. It is Alexander Welsh's contention, however, that "Dorothea Brooke, and Maggie, owe at least as much to [Scott's] Minna, Flora,

Rebecca, and [Mme de Stael's] Corinne as they do to St. Theresa or to autobiography."[128] Welsh points out, in support of his argument that *The Mill on the Floss* adheres closely to the formulas of romance, not only that Maggie resembles the earlier dark-haired heroines in her passionate sensibility, vivid imagination, her intellectual aspirations and yearning for "masculine wisdom", but that she, like her predecessors, is "paired against a more happily constituted light-haired beauty,"[129] her cousin Lucy Deane (who even has the same Christian name as Corinne's rival and half-sister, Lucy Edgermonde), for whom Maggie, again like her predecessors, "must somehow gracefully leave the stage", after "a reconciliation between light and dark complexions."[130]

Welsh points out another important resemblance between *The Mill on the Floss* and the romance of Scott and Mme de Stael — that "characterization in the romance persistently draws on the heredity of its principals. . . . Minna and Brenda Troil are carefully distinguished, the one inheriting her mother's aspect and the other her father's"; in just the same way Maggie is very much a Tulliver, while her brother is essentially a Dodson. Welsh adds, in passing, that "Corinne had set the style of a more special case of hereditary influence (the pattern of Hawthorne's *The Blithedale Romance*, for example) by which the older, brunette half sister was indelibly inked by an earlier and slightly exotic marriage, or affair, of the father, and the younger, blond half sister the product of a more conventional marriage."[131]

It is not my intention to question the validity of Welsh's argument; the case that he makes for the influence of Scott and Mme de Stael in *The Mill on the Floss* — seen in the dark-haired, ardent, dynamic heroine, her pairing with her blond, conformist, passive cousin, her involvement in a triangle situation with her cousin's near-betrothed, her renunciation of personal happiness through duty and loyalty to her beloved cousin and her own lover, her sacrificial death — seems unassailable. By her references to *The Pirate*, *Waverley*, *Ivanhoe* and *Corinne*, indeed, George Eliot herself seems gracefully to acknowledge her indebtedness. But I suggest that there was also some indebtedness to the romance which Welsh mentions only in passing, Hawthorne's *The Blithedale Romance*. George Eliot could hardly acknowledge indebtedness to Hawthorne in the same way as she does to Scott and Mme de Stael, since Maggie, who seems to be an almost exact contemporary of her own, reads and discusses *Corinne* and Scott's novels when she is sixteen — that is in the mid-1830s — fifteen years or so before *The Blithedale Romance* was published.

The question of influence is complicated further by the fact that Scott was one of Hawthorne's own favourite authors (with his wife he re-read "the complete shelf of Sir Walter Scott's romances"[132]), and Mme de Stael was also among the "sources of a more substantial nature" listed by Arlin Turner.[133] But there seem to be sufficient resemblances between the later part of *The Mill on the Floss* and *The Blithedale Romance* to make it likely that, if Maggie had been born twenty years later, she would have added the name of Zenobia to her list of "dark unhappy ones" whom she wants to avenge.

One basic similarity is that both books are essentially four-person novels, presenting the complicated love-relationships of two contrasted women and two contrasted men. In *The Blithedale Romance* both women, the dark, exotically beautiful, passionate Zenobia and the fair, gentle parasite Priscilla (who unknown to Zenobia, but not to Priscilla, is Zenobia's half-sister), love the rugged, aggressively-masculine, ex-blacksmith philanthropist, Hollingsworth; while the narrator, Coverdale, who appears throughout to be a half-concerned, half-detached observer of the triangle drama, makes a last-line, shame-faced confession that "I — I myself — was in love — with — PRISCILLA!" In *The Mill on the Floss* both women, the dark, radiantly beautiful Maggie and her fair, gentle, unobtrusive cousin Lucy, love St Ogg's' most eligible bachelor, Stephen Guest; while Philip Wakem, the deformed artistic son of Maggie's father's enemy, loves Maggie, who has promised to marry no one else. There are the further complications, making the quadrilaterals pentagons, that in *The Blithedale Romance*, Westervelt has some relationship (secret husband or former lover?) with Zenobia, and is also the hypnotic controller of Priscilla in her "Veiled Lady" role; and, in *The Mill on the Floss*, Tom Tulliver has a repressed love of his cousin, Lucy, which more or less corresponds with Coverdale's unspoken love of Priscilla.

One could hardly contend that there is any similarity between

Hollingsworth and Stephen Guest, beyond the fact that they are both egotists (but of very different kinds — the one a monomaniac, prepared to sacrifice all human ties and responsibilities to one altruistic obsession; the other a self-satisfied, conceited provincial dandy), and that both end as husbands of the fair maidens. We learn nothing of Stephen's final spiritual condition, but when Coverdale last sees Hollingsworth he has "a depressed and melancholy look", "a self-distrustful weakness" and a childish dependence on Priscilla; he is haunted by remorse for her part in driving Zenobia to suicide.

There are rather closer similarities between the other male characters. Philip Wakem, the amateur dabbler in several arts, doomed to a solitary half-life by his deformity, is not unlike Miles Coverdale, the minor poet who recognizes in his final chapter that he has "made but a poor and dim figure in my own narrative . . . suffering my colorless life to take its hue from other lives". Coverdale, confessing, in his last chapter, that want of purpose "has rendered my own life all an emptiness" that "life . . . has come to rather an idle pass with me", implies that his "foolish little secret", his love of Priscilla, "may have had something to do with these inactive years of meridian manhood, with my bachelorship, with the unsatisfied retrospect that I fling back on life, and my listless glance towards the future"; more romantically, we learn of Philip Wakem that, after the death of Maggie, he "was always solitary. His great companionship was among the trees of the Red Deeps, where the buried joy seemed still to hover — like a revisiting spirit."

There is some similarity too between the fair-haired maidens of the two novels. Neither Priscilla nor Lucy is a blue-eyed blonde. Both have brown hair — Priscilla's "brown hair fell down from beneath a hood, not in curls but with only a slight wave" (*The Blithedale Romance*, chapter 4); Lucy has "light-brown ringlets" (*The Mill on the Floss*, book 6, chapter 1). Priscilla has "large, brown, melancholy eyes", Lucy "soft hazel eyes." Neither has any strongly marked character; they are quiet, gentle, passive, dependent little creatures. When Priscilla first appears at Blithedale, having somehow escaped from Westervelt and her "Veiled Lady" role, her face has a wan, almost sickly hue; she is a sad and depressed figure. After a few months at Blithedale, she has budded and blossomed; "her animal spirits waxed high" and she has a "simple, careless, childish flow of spirits . . . like a butterfly at play in a flickering bit of sunshine." She is, however, totally incompetent: "she let the poultry into the garden; she generally spoilt whatever part of the dinner she took in charge; she broke crockery. She dropt our biggest pitcher into the well; and — except with her needle . . . — was as unserviceable a member of society as any young lady in the land" (Chapter 9). Virginie Ogden Birdsall comments: "Hawthorne seems to have intended that Priscilla's spirituality should supply the overintellectual and egotistical inhabitants of Blithedale with a necessary balance and that Blithedale in turn should provide Priscilla with a 'decided place among creatures of flesh and blood.' But because she seems to be more of a theory than a reality for Hawthorne, she never achieves flesh and blood and in fact comes close to evaporating into a mere symbol."[134] A symbol, presumably, of purity and uncontaminated innocence; but she is also a symbol of pure will-less passivity. She says, explicitly (chapter 20): " 'I am blown about like a leaf . . . I never have any free will.' " One is likely to agree with Zenobia's contemptuous dismissal of Priscilla, after Hollingsworth has cast Zenobia off for her (mainly, it is implied, because Zenobia has been disinherited in favour of Priscilla) as a "poor, pale flower", who will only be able to "tend towards him with a pale, instinctive love, and hang her little puny weakness for a clog upon his arm!" (chapter 26).

Lucy is not quite such a passive and parasitic "pale flower" as Priscilla. She stays very much in the background, overshadowed, like Priscilla, by her dynamic, dark-haired relative; but she seems to have something of the flesh-and-blood reality of Hawthorne's first brown-haired maiden, Phoebe Pyncheon, who, like her, is "so small as to be almost childlike" and, like her, has "brown ringlets." It would be no surprise to be told of Lucy's gracefulness, "the ripeness of her lips, the virginal development of her bosom." (*The House of the Seven Gables*, chapter 9). We do see "her little womanly ways", in her after-dinner manipulation of her father (*The House of the Seven Gables*, book 6, chapter 8).

It is the dark ladies, however, who are most alike, in appearance and fate, if not in temperament. Like Maggie, but unlike the others mentioned by Alexander Welsh as contributors to Maggie, Zenobia suffers death by water. Zenobia's suicide, admittedly, is very different from Maggie's accidental death, in her brother's embrace. Zenobia wilfully terminates the life in which, in Coverdale's words, "everything had failed her; prosperity, in the world's sense, for her opulence was gone, — the heart's prosperity, in love. . . . Young as she was, she had tried life fully, had no more to hope, and something, perhaps, to fear" (*The Blithedale Romance* chapter 28). Maggie does not actively seek, but desires, death. Just before she feels the flood water about her feet and knees she thinks: " 'I will bear it, and bear it till death. . . . But how long it will be before death comes! I am so young, so healthy. How shall I have patience and strength?' " (*The Mill on the Floss*, book 7, chapter 5). For her, death is a welcome release from the insoluble dilemma of the conflict between passion and duty. That George Eliot intended, even before she began writing, that Maggie should drown, is clear from the first reference in her journal to the conception of the novel: "We went into town today, and looked in the Annual Register for cases of *inundation*."[135] Her choice of a watery grave for the end of Maggie's troubles and struggles — an end which, one critic has claimed, "is so heavily foreshadowed throughout the novel that it seems almost artistically impossible for the book to end in any other way"[136] — may well have been influenced by Zenobia's example. There is, incidentally, an extraordinary similarity between Coverdale's comment, immediately following that just quoted — "Had Providence taken her away in its holy hand, I should have thought it the kindest dispensation that could be awarded to one so wrecked" — and the comment of John Blackwood, the first reader, apart from Lewes, of *The Mill on the Floss* — "the greatest lovers of all ending happily must admit that Providence was kind in removing Maggie. She could not have been happy here and she will not be forgotten by others besides Lucy, Philip, and Stephen."[137] If George Eliot had not let Providence intervene, but allowed Maggie to determine her own end (and the flood would have provided the perfect opportunity to make suicide look like accident) most readers would have been happier.

Maggie's physical appearance, it seems certain, owes something to Zenobia's. Coverdale's descriptions of Zenobia emphasize the vitality and mature sexuality which he finds not a little disturbing. At their first meeting (chapter 3):

She was dressed as simply as possible, in an American print . . . but with a silken kerchief, between which and her gown there was one glimpse of a white shoulder. It struck me as a great piece of good fortune that there should be just that glimpse. Her hair, which was dark, glossy, and of singular abundance, was put up rather severely and primly, without curls, or other ornament, except a single flower. . . . Her hand, though very soft, was larger than most women would like to have, or than they could afford to have, though not a whit too large in proportion with the spacious plan of Zenobia's entire development. . . . She was, indeed, an admirable figure of a woman, just on the hither verge of her rich maturity, with a combination of features which it is safe to call remarkably beautiful, even if some fastidious persons might pronounce them a little deficient in softness and delicacy. But we find enough of those attributes everywhere. Preferable — by way of variety, at least — was Zenobia's bloom, health and vigor, which she possessed in such overflow that a man might well have fallen in love with her for their sake only. In her quiet moods, she seemed rather indolent; but when really in earnest . . . she grew all alive, to her finger-tips.

Later in the same chapter Coverdale has a vision of "that fine perfectly developed figure, in Eve's earliest garment" and adds

we seldom meet with women nowadays, and in this country, who impress us as being women at all, — their sex fades away, and goes for nothing, in ordinary intercourse. Not so with Zenobia. One felt an influence breathing out of her such as we might suppose to come from Eve, when she was just made, and her Creator brought her to Adam, saying 'Behold! here is a woman!' Not that I would convey the idea of essential grace, modesty, and shyness, but of a certain warm and rich characteristic, which seems, for the most part, to have been refined away out of the feminine system.

When Coverdale is ill, and Zenobia plays nurse (feeding him with gruel "with almost invariably the smell of pine smoke upon it"), Coverdale again pays tribute to her disquieting femininity.

Zenobia was truly a magnificent woman. The homely simplicity of her dress could not conceal, nor scarcely diminish, the queenliness of her presence . . . she should have made it a point of duty . . . to sit endlessly to painters and sculptors and preferably the latter; because the cold decorum of the marble would consist with the utmost scantiness of drapery, so that the eye might chastely be gladdened with her material perfection in its entireness. I know not well how to express, that the native glow of colouring in her cheeks, and even the flesh warmth over her round arms and what was visible of her full bust, — in a word, her womanliness incarnated, — compelled me sometimes to close my eyes, as if it were not quite the privilege of modesty to gaze at her" (chapter 6).

Maggie Tulliver, as a child, is an ugly duckling whose "brown skin as makes her look like a mulatter" and "heavy dark locks" of

hair, are her mother's despair. But when, in her seventeenth
year, she first meets Philip Wakem in the Red Deeps, she is
already becoming distinctly Zenobia-like. "One would certainly
suppose her to be farther on in life than her seventeenth year . . .
perhaps because her broad-chested figure has the mould of early
womanhood. . . . The eyes are liquid, the brown cheek is firm
and rounded, the full lips are red. With her dark colouring and
jet crown surmounting her tall figure, she seems to have a sort of
affinity with the grand Scotch firs. . . ." (book 5, chapter 1).
Three years later, when she comes to stay with Lucy, the homely
simplicity of *her* dress does not diminish the queenliness of her
presence either. Lucy almost paraphrases Coverdale's comment
about Zenobia when she remarks (book 6, chapter 2): " 'I can't
think what witchery it is in you, Maggie, that makes you look
best in shabby clothes. . . . I wonder if Marie Antoinette looked
all the grander when her gown was darned at the elbows.' "
Stephen, who has been expecting "a fat, blonde girl, with round
blue eyes" cannot "conceal his astonishment at the sight of this
tall dark-eyed nymph with her jet-black coronet of hair" and his
first thought is " 'An alarming amount of devil there."
(Coverdale, incidentally, described Zenobia as "an
enchantress.") At the church bazaar (book 6, chapter 9),
Maggie's "simple noble beauty, clad in a white muslin of some
soft-floating kind, appeared with marked distinction among the
more adorned and conventional woman around her"; but
"Maggie's conspicuous position, for the first time, made evident
certain characteristics which were subsequently felt to have an
explanatory bearing. There was something bold in Miss
Tulliver's direct gaze, and something undefinably coarse in the
style of her beauty. . . ." In the following chapter, when Maggie
consents to dance at Park House, "her eyes and cheeks had that
fire of young joy in them which will flame out if it can find the
least breath to fan it; and her simple black dress, with its bit of
black lace, seemed like the dim setting of a jewel." It is in the
conservatory during the dance that Stephen is seized by the
"mad impulse" to shower kisses on Maggie's arm; in a passage
again recalling Coverdale's celebrations of Zenobia's physical
beauty, George Eliot waxes lyrical about this tempting limb: "A
woman's arm touched the soul of a great sculptor two thousand
years ago, so that he wrought an image of it for the Parthenon

which moves us still as it clasps lovingly the time-worn marble of a headless trunk. Maggie's was such an arm as that — and it had the warm tints of life." I suppose that the bringing together in one passage of "the cold decorum of the marble" and "the flesh-warmth of the round arms", and in the other "the time-worn marble" and the "warm tints of life", could be accidental, but, added to the other parallel passages I have cited, I think it unlikely.

Maggie and Zenobia are alike, then, not only in their darkness, but in their physical grandeur, amplitude, glowing warmth and vitality. They are not greatly alike in temperament, or in the manner of their presentation. Zenobia is, of course, much more aggressive, self-willed, opinionated and ruthlessly egotistic. Except for his celebration of her beauty, Hawthorne–Coverdale's treatment of her is often coolly satiric, as when he remarks that "she was made . . . for a stump-oratress. I recognized no severe culture in Zenobia; her mind was full of weeds" (chapter 6); but he does attribute to her qualities which she can hardly be said to demonstrate — "a fine intellect", "noble courage", "the sweet, liberal, but womanly frankness of a noble and generous disposition" — but which, whether by coincidence or not, are also qualities of Maggie Tulliver.

It hardly needs to be said (or to quote passages already quoted in other contexts to demonstrate) that, if Maggie, physically, is like Zenobia, she is also like Hester Prynne. And it is of Hester's, rather than of Zenobia's, that Maggie's experiences and emotions sometimes remind one. In particular, Maggie's life in adolescence, when the Tullivers are reduced to poverty following Tulliver's bankruptcy and illness, and her experiences after she returns to St Ogg's, after the involuntary elopement with Stephen, have certain similarities to Hester's years of outcast loneliness.

The opening paragraphs of the second chapter of book 4 (which is called "The Valley of Humiliation") are a good example:

> There is something sustaining in the very agitation that accompanies the first shocks of trouble, just as an acute pain is often a stimulus, and produces an excitement which is transient strength. It is in the slow, changed life that follows — in the time when sorrow has become stale, and has no longer an emotive intensity that counteracts its pain — in the time when day follows

day in dull unexpectant sameness . . . — it is then that despair threatens. . . .
And now her lot was beginning to have a still, sad monotony, which threw
her more than ever on her inward self.

One remembers Hawthorne's comments, after Hester's release
from prison (*The Scarlet Letter*, chapter 5):

Perhaps there was a more real torture in her first unattended footsteps from
the threshold of the prison, than even in the procession and spectacle that
have been described, when she was made the common infamy. . . . Then,
she was supported by an unnatural tension of the nerves, and by all the com-
bative energy of her character, which enabled her to convert the scene into a
kind of lurid triumph. It was, moreover, a separate and insulated event, to
occur but once in her lifetime, and to meet which, therefore, reckless of
economy, she might call up the vital strength that would have sufficed for
many quiet years. . . . But now . . . began the daily custom, and she must
either sustain it and carry it forward by the ordinary resources of her nature,
or sink beneath it. . . . To-morrow would bring its own trial, and yet the very
same that was now so unutterably grievous to be borne. The days of the far-
off future would toil onward, still with the same burden for her to take
up. . . .

In the next chapter of *The Mill on the Floss* we are told of
Maggie's deepening "sense of loneliness, and utter privation of
joy", "the oppressive emptiness" of her life; of the yearning for
learning and wisdom that would "enable her to understand, and
in understanding, endure, the heavy weight that had fallen on
her heart", of her rebellion against her lot, her "fits of anger and
hatred towards her mother and father", and her eventual
discovery of Thomas a Kempis' *The Imitation of Christ*, in which
she finds an answer to the fundamental need of the human heart
— that of finding inward peace through self-knowledge, self-
discipline and generous love. "It was by being brought within
the long lingering vibrations of such a voice that Maggie . . .
found an effort and a hope that helped her through years of
loneliness, making out a faith for herself without the aid of
established authorities and appointed guides." One remembers
how Hester's loneliness, and complete estrangement from the
community, her rebellion against her lot, drive her into
"freedom of speculation", to a questioning of all "human institutions, and whatever priests or legislators had established". She
does not find "a voice from the past" to counsel and direct her;
and she comes to have "hardly more reverence than the Indian
would feel for the clerical band, the judicial robe, or the church".

But despite her bold speculation, she conforms "with the most perfect quietude to the external regulations of society."

There are differences, of course, but Maggie is basically similar to Hester in living "an intense inward life", with "some volcanic upheavings of imprisoned passions" while outwardly "submissive and backward to assert her own will." The similarity is underlined by the fact that as Hester lives by her needle and employs much of her time "in making coarse garments for the poor" (and "there was an idea of penance in this mode of occupation"), Maggie also works at "plain sewing", and "in her zeal of self-mortification" obtains her supplies in a linen-shop in St Ogg's.

In book 7, Maggie's ostracism after she returns to St Ogg's, when old acquaintances turn aside without speaking, and young Torry bows to her "with that air of nonchalance which he might have bestowed on a friendly bar-maid", is reminiscent of Hester's ostracism ("even the silence of those with whom she came in contact, implied, and often expressed, that she was banished. . ."). So is her determination to remain in St Ogg's reminiscent of Hester's determination to remain in the Puritan settlement, and her return to it, and resumption of the scarlet letter in the final chapter of *The Scarlet Letter*. In chapter 5 Hawthorne tells us: "But there is a fatality, a feeling so irresistible and inevitable that it almost compels human beings to linger round and haunt, ghost-like, the spot where some great and marked event has given the colour to their lifetime. . . . All other scenes of earth . . . were foreign to her in comparison." And "What she compelled herself to believe . . . was half a truth, and half a self-delusion. Here, she said to herself, had been the scene of her guilt, and here should be the scene of her earthly punishment; and so, perchance, the torture of her daily shame would at length purge her soul . . ." But the scarlet letter does not do its office, and there is no genuine penitence. But when Hester returns, years after Dimmesdale's death, we are told: "Here had been her sin; here, her sorrow; and here yet was to be her penitence."

Maggie's statement of her reasons for wanting to stay in St Ogg's virtually provides a summary of most of Hester's reasons: " 'O, if I could but stop here! I have no heart to begin a strange life again. I should have no stay. I should feel like a lonely wanderer — cut off from the past. . . . If I remained here, I could perhaps atone in some way to Lucy — to others: I could convince them that I'm sorry. . . . The only thing I want is some occupation that will enable me to get my bread and be independent. . . . I shall not want much."

The Mill on the Floss is an unusual novel in the way that it combines a large-scale, realistic creation of a provincial society with a love-story owing much to the established conventions of romance. Much of its strength and originality lies in areas and aspects to which I have not had to refer — in its beautifully vivid and completely convincing account of Maggie's childhood and adolescence; and in the abundant impression of life that it conveys through the presentation of the Tulliver family and the Dodson aunts. My concern has been only to show that, in the romance side of the novel, while George Eliot undoubtedly owed a good deal to Scott and Mme de Stael, as Alexander Welsh has convincingly demonstrated, she also found many hints, in character, situation and theme, in her "grand favourite", Hawthorne.

Hawthorne's Influence in *Silas Marner*

In maintaining Hawthorne's influence on George Eliot's third novel, *Silas Marner* (1861), I have at least one ally, Jonathan R. Quick, whose essay, "*Silas Marner* as Romance: The Example of Hawthorne", I have previously mentioned.[138]

In 1968 Quick presented as a Yale Ph.D. dissertation a critical edition of *Silas Marner*, which included a substantial and useful introduction, comprising sections on the novel's composition and publication, its contemporary reception, the revisions made by George Eliot (in the manuscript; the proofs of the first edition; the revised cheap edition — also 1861; and the 1878 Cabinet edition); and a thirty-five page "Commentary". In detailing and discussing the revisions made by George Eliot, Quick argues that some of them "imply that in *Silas Marner* George Eliot wished to avoid the thoroughness of descriptive detail which she had achieved to such great effect in her previous novels", and maintains that "the 'blurred', 'indistinct' or 'shadowy' image which the story left' in the minds of some reviewers, and which they "considered a flaw, was deliberate on George Eliot's part."[139] At the end of his "Commentary" Quick suggests that "the important role of preternatural events in *Silas Marner* is associated with George Eliot's idea of the story as 'a sort of legendary tale'. In its traditional inclusion of miraculous episodes, the legendary tale, or romance, allowed her to deal with dark and complex truths beyond the scope of more strictly realistic fictional forms."[140] Although Quick here introduces the term "romance", he does not suggest any analogy with, or influence of, the romances of Hawthorne; the only example of "the romance form" which he invokes for comparison is *The Tempest*.

In 1970, R.T. Jones, in his chapter on *Silas Marner*, remarks: "What impresses the reader who turns to *Silas Marner* immediately after *The Mill on the Floss* is not, I think, that it is a better novel, but that it is very different from it — almost a different form of art, so that it seems unsatisfactory to call both books simply 'novels'. Perhaps the word 'tale' could be used of the later work, to suggest its conciseness, impersonality and singleness. . . ."[141] After noting the impersonality, the "disengaged" intelligence of *Silas Marner*, Jones remarks: "Nathaniel Hawthorne called his *The House of the Seven Gables* a 'romance', and the term as he uses it might also be applied to *Silas Marner*." After quoting the opening paragraph of Hawthorne's preface, Jones suggests: "If we have in mind the distinctions that Hawthorne makes between a 'Romance' and a 'Novel' we may recognize more clearly the difference between *Silas Marner* and George Eliot's other works of fiction."[142]

So far as I know, Jones' reference to Hawthorne's well-known distinction between "novel" and "romance", as a means of suggesting the nature of *Silas Marner*, was the first introduction of Hawthorne's name into criticism of this particular novel. Jones does not himself suggest that Hawthorne's own romances influenced *Silas Marner*; but perhaps his comments prompted Jonathan Quick's recognition of George Eliot's indebtedness to "the example of Hawthorne."

Quick begins his 1974 essay by mentioning some of the evidence for George Eliot's interest in Hawthorne — an interest, which he, rather surprisingly, suggests was "somewhat eccentric." He contends that "while George Eliot was so eagerly intent on reading Hawthorne, most English readers remained hostile or indifferent to him"[143] — a contention that hardly squares with the fact, reported, for example, by Clarence Gohdes, that "*The Scarlet Letter* had a larger sale in the British Isles within the first year or two of publication than in the United States",[144] or Gohdes' summary of the evidence that "after 1850, approval of Hawthorne was all but universal in British critical circles"[145] — an estimate based on such comments as one made, in 1860, by a critic in the *Illustrated London News* (quoted by Gohdes[146]) to the effect that Hawthorne had "established so complete a reputation in this country as well as in his own that the only introduction a new tale from his pen needs is a congratulation."[147]

Quick goes on to assert, however, that more interesting than George Eliot's "somewhat eccentric interest in Hawthorne . . . is the evidence suggesting that the example of Hawthorne's experiments in the romance . . . helped to shape the conception and writing of *Silas Marner* (1861)." He suggests that terms like " 'moral fable' containing features of the 'fairy tale' ", used repeatedly by Leavis and others to describe *Silas Marner*, "are not really very useful, because they apply clumsily, at best, to Silas' story and barely at all to the story of Godfrey Cass", and that Leavis' comments fall "a single step short of invoking Hawthorne's notion of the prose romance as a solution to the problem of reconciling poetic treatment and novelistic form."[148]

In quoting in his turn from Hawthorne's Preface, Quick refers particularly to Hawthorne's view that "the characters and action must retain their footing in daily experience, acquiring their romantic character primarily through the 'atmospherical medium' with which the author seeks to 'deepen and enrich the shadows of the picture'."[149] He remarks that if George Eliot had not observed Hawthorne's "chiaroscuro effects" for herself, they were pointed out in the 1860 *North British Review* essay, "The Author of *Adam Bede* and Nathaniel Hawthorne", to which I have previously referred.[150] The article, Quick contends, "correctly points to the indistinctness and shading effects of Hawthorne's style as a major difference between him and the author of *Adam Bede*. In *Silas Marner*, however, this stylistic contrast is greatly diminished, strongly implying that George Eliot wished to find a way to use Hawthorne's 'shadows' for her own purpose of creating a fictive twilight where the commonplace and the mysterious could meet.''[151] Quick now maintains, in fact, that the "intentional blurring effects", which he had noted in the introduction to his critical edition of *Silas Marner* — for example, in the description of the interior of Silas' cottage, of the Red House; and in the account of Silas' trial and conviction in Lantern Yard — owe much to the example of Hawthorne, in *The Scarlet Letter*.

> In both cases, it is the indistinct atmosphere shading the event that accents its fundamental mysteriousness. For in the art of the romance the rigorous logic and clarity of realism is commonly abandoned in deference to a 'poetic' reality that resists rational understanding in order to admit the mysterious into the 'real'. In *Silas Marner* and *The Scarlet Letter* the authors' final ambition is not the novelist's desire to analyze objectified social dilemmas but to record individual psychological struggles with the imperfectly soluble riddles of guilt and expiation.[152]

Quick maintains also that "*Silas Marner* is George Eliot's only novel in which important events in the main character's history remain obscure to the end";[153] that "virtually all of the main shaping events of Silas's career ... occur amid mysterious or seemingly causeless circumstances never wholly understood" and that "equally, the plot of *The Scarlet Letter* turns on such unaccountable or ill-explained events as the early relationship of Hester and Dimmesdale, the birth of Pearl, Chillingworth's startling arrival at Salem [sic], and Dimmesdale's strange illness and death.''[154]

Quick then argues that "to further substantiate this relationship between *Silas Marner* and *The Scarlet Letter* we can identify correspondences of structure, characterization and style which appear so regularly that it is difficult to think of them as wholly accidental."[155] I fully agree with this contention, but I would add that there is, again in *Silas Marner* as in *Adam Bede* and *The Mill on the Floss*, evidence of George Eliot's indebtedness to other romances of Hawthorne, besides *The Scarlet Letter*, especially, in this case, *The House of the Seven Gables*. Rather than continuing to follow Quick's article (the appearance of which has made necessary the re-writing of this section), I propose to cite a number of passages of *Silas Marner* (some also noted by Quick) in the order in which they appear, together with passages from Hawthorne to which they appear to relate more or less directly.

The second paragraph of *Silas Marner* seems to me to be full of echoes of *The Scarlet Letter* (most of which Quick has also noticed). The action of the novel is placed "in the early years of this century", as in the second chapter of *The Scarlet Letter*, the action is placed in the more remote past of "not less than two centuries ago." We are told that "a linen-weaver, named Silas Marner, worked at his vocation in a stone cottage that stood among the nutty hedgerows near the village of Raveloe, and not far from the edge of a deserted stone-pit", and may be reminded how Hester Prynne, after her release from prison, went to live in a "little, lonesome dwelling", "a small thatched cottage . . . built by an earlier settler, and abandoned, because the soil about it was too sterile for cultivation." In their isolated cottages, Hester and Silas support themselves by the related trades of needlework and weaving; they are visited — or, more accurately, spied on — by the village children, who regard them with a superstitious awe and suspicion. The passage in *The Scarlet Letter* (chapter 5): "A mystic shadow of suspicion immediately attached itself to the spot. Children, too young to comprehend wherefore this woman should be shut out from the sphere of human charities, would creep nigh enough to behold her plying her needle at the cottage-window, or standing at the doorway . . . and discerning the scarlet letter on her breast, would scamper off with a strange contagious fear," seems to have inspired the passage in *Silas Marner*:

> The questionable sound of Silas's loom . . . had a half-fearful fascination for the Raveloe boys, who would often leave off their nutting or bird's-nesting to peep in at the window of the stone cottage, counterbalancing a certain awe at the mysterious action of the loom, by a pleasant sense of scornful superiority. . . . But sometimes it happened that Marner . . . became aware of the small scoundrels and . . . he liked their intrusion so ill that he would descend from his loom, and, opening the door, would fix on them a gaze that was always enough to make them take to their legs in terror.

Also in the opening chapter of *Silas Marner*, we are told that, after fifteen years of solitary work, in almost total solitude, regarded with suspicion and "vague fear" by the villagers, "while opinion concerning him had remained nearly stationary, and his daily habits had presented scarcely any visible change, Marner's inner life had been a history and a metamorphosis, as that of every fervid nature must be when it has fled, *or been condemned* to solitude" (my italics). Silas, of course, has fled to solitude, after his unjust condemnation by his co-religionists of Lantern Yard; but George Eliot's interpolation of the phrase I have italicized suggests that she again had in mind Hawthorne's "fervid nature", Hester Prynne, the "metamorphosis" of whose "inner life" is fully presented, especially in chapters 5 and 13 of *The Scarlet Letter* (while her outer demeanour has remained unchanged).

Perhaps George Eliot had also in mind another of Hawthorne's "fervid natures", Clifford Pyncheon, who is reduced to near-lunacy by being wrongly condemned to life-imprisonment, for the murder of his uncle. Certainly there seems to be a striking similarity between the two cases of wrongful condemnation. In *The House of the Seven Gables*, as Holgrave re-constructs the "supposed murder, thirty or forty years ago, of the Judge Pyncheon's uncle" (chapter 21), Jaffrey Pyncheon, who had alienated his uncle (also Jaffrey), by his wild dissipation, reckless spending, and addiction to "low pleasures", was searching his uncle's "private drawers", at night, when he was surprised by his uncle, who, in his horrified agitation, died of the hereditary disorder. Jaffrey with "cool hardihood" continued his search, found and destroyed old Jaffrey's most recent will, in favour of Clifford, and apparently left behind evidence (the nature of which is not specified) which pointed to Clifford as his uncle's robber. Clifford, in the event, was charged with murder; Jaffrey, knowing that their uncle had died a natural death, kept silence, and Clifford was sentenced to life-imprisonment. In *Silas Marner*, Silas's close friend, William Dane, comes to relieve Silas at two in the morning, at the bedside of the dangerously ill senior deacon; he finds the deacon dead and Silas in a cataleptic fit (which Dane had previously insinuated was "a visitation of Satan"). Dane plants Silas's pocket-knife in the bedside bureau, steals from it the little bag of church money, and plants the empty bag in Silas's room. Silas is not accused of murder; but, in the "trial" by his brethren, the lots declare him guilty of the robbery. He is expelled from church-membership; Sarah breaks off their engagement; and, in bitterness and despair, Silas goes into self-imposed exile and fifteen years of solitude.

Silas's case, the condemnation of a "framed" innocent, is much more like Clifford's than Hester's; though the sentencing of Hester to public exposure on the scaffold, and the perpetual

wearing of the scarlet letter may seem excessively harsh, she had
committed adultery, and might have been executed, branded or
flogged (as some of the "iron beldames" insist she should have
been). But Silas's situation in his fifteen years of solitude, on the
edge of, but completely estranged from, a village community, is
obviously very like Hester's. As for Hester, "In all her intercourse with society . . . there was nothing that made her feel as if
she belonged to it. Every gesture, every word, and even the
silence of those with whom she came in contact, implied, and
often expressed, that she was banished, and as much alone as if
she inhabited another sphere. . . ." (*The Scarlet Letter*, chapter
5), so for Silas, in the Raveloe which was so totally different from
all that he had known, "there was nothing that called out his love
and fellowship towards the strangers he had come amongst", and
"so, year after year, [he] had lived in this solitude . . . his life nar-
rowing and hardening itself into a mere pulsation of desire and
satisfaction that had no relation to any other being" (*Silas
Marner*, chapter 2).

I am not contending, of course, that Hester and Silas are alike
in temperament: they are alike only in their situation of estrangement from the community near which they have chosen to live —
or, in Hester's case, to continue to live. For Hester, in remaining
in the Puritan settlement, has in fact chosen a form of exile, no
less than has Silas in choosing to leave Lantern Yard, where all
his life has been spent. And there is a crucial difference: Hester's
life is never totally without "relation to any other being", since
she always has her daughter Pearl, who, as Quick remarks, is
"not only the manifestation and sustainer of Hester's life-giving
vitality, but also a visible reminder of the community's verdict
against her."[156] But Silas's only companionship, in his "insect-
like existence" of "weaving and hoarding", is with the mounting
pile of guineas, crowns and half-crowns. George Eliot's comment
(chapter 2): "The same sort of process has perhaps been
undergone by wiser men, when they have been cut off from faith
and love — only, instead of a loom and a heap of guineas, they
had some erudite research, some ingenious project, or some well-
knit theory" is strongly reminiscent of Hawthorne's
monomaniacs — notably Hollingsworth, in *The Blithedale
Romance*, whose whole being is dedicated to the ingenious
project of the reform of "our criminal brethren." Hawthorne
comments (chapter 7):

But, by and by, you missed the tenderness of yesterday, and grew drearily conscious that Hollingsworth had a closer friend than you could even be; and this friend was the cold spectral monster which he had himself conjured up, and on which he was wasting all the warmth of his heart, and of which, at last . . . he had grown to be the bond-slave. . . . This was a result exceedingly sad to contemplate, considering that it had been mainly brought about by the very ardor and exuberance of his philanthropy. Sad, indeed, but by no means unusual: he had taught his benevolence to pour its warm tide exclusively through one channel; so that there was nothing to spare for other great manifestations of love to man, nor scarcely for the nutriment of individual attachments, unless they could minister in some way to the terrible egotism which he mistook for an angel of God.

Dunstan Cass' theft of Silas's hoard leaves him "groping in darkness, with his prop utterly gone." In a very Hawthornesque image George Eliot comments: "Formerly his heart had been as a locked casket with its treasure inside; but now the casket was empty, and the lock was broken" (chapter 10). It is while he is in this state of grief and despair, and "arrested by the invisible wand of catalepsy", that Godfrey Cass's unacknowledged child wanders into Marner's cottage out of the snow, where her mother has died in drugged unconsciousness, and Silas's redemption begins.

There are very strong resemblances (surely too strong to be accidental) between Eppie and Hawthorne's Pearl, and between the Silas–Eppie and Hester–Pearl relationships. Both children are given "Bible names". Hester "named the infant 'Pearl', as being of great price, — purchased with all she had, — her mother's only treasure!" (*The Scarlet Letter*, chapter 6). (The reference, of course, is to Matthew 13: 45–46: "Again, the kingdom of heaven is like unto a merchant man, seeking goodly pearls: who, when he had found one pearl of great price, went out and sold all that he had, and bought it.") Silas gives the providentially sent infant the name of his mother and sister, Hephzibah (*Silas Marner*, chapter 14); the source of the name (Isaiah 62:4) has a clear reference to Silas's own changed spiritual state ("Thou shalt no more be termed Forsaken; neither shalt thy land any more be termed Desolate, but thou shalt be called Hephzibah, and thy land Beulah: for the Lord delighteth in thee. . . "). George Eliot must have known, too, that one of the main characters of *The House of the Seven Gables* is called Hepzibah.

When Eppie wakes in the arms of her mother, lying dead in the snow, her "eyes were caught by a bright glancing light on the white ground" and she "was immediately absorbed in watching the bright living thing running towards it, yet never arriving. That bright living thing must be caught, and in an instant the child slipped on all fours, and held out one little hand to catch the gleam. But the gleam would not be caught in that way, and now the head was held up to see where the cunning gleam came from". (*Silas Marner*, chapter 12). It seems likely that the idea for this little episode, of a child attracted by elusive light, came from chapter 16 of *The Scarlet Letter*, in which Hester and Pearl walk through the forest; the fitful sunlight withdraws as they approach, until at Hester's bidding, Pearl runs ahead alone. "Pearl set forth, at a great pace, and . . . did actually catch the sunshine, and stood laughing in the midst of it. . . . The light lingered about the lonely child . . . until her mother had drawn almost nigh enough to step into the magic circle too.

'It will go now!' said Pearl, shaking her head.

'See!' answered Hester, smiling. 'Now I can stretch out my hand, and grasp some of it.'

As she attempted to do so, the sunshine vanished."

When Silas carries Eppie to the Red House (chapter 13) in quest of the doctor, Mrs Kimble tells him to leave the child.

"No — no — I can't part with it, I can't let it go,' said Silas abruptly. 'It's come to me — I've a right to keep it.'

The proposition to take the child from him had come to Silas, quite unexpectedly, and his speech uttered under a strong sudden impulse, was almost like a revelation to himself; a minute before, he had no distinct intention about the child."

Later, when Godfrey Cass, the child's real, but unadmitted, father asks Silas: " 'Why, you shouldn't like to keep her, should you — an old bachelor like you?'

'Till anybody shows they've a right to take her away from me,' said Marner. 'The mother's dead, and I reckon it's got no father; it's a lone thing — and I'm a lone thing. My money's gone, I don't know where — and this is come from I don't know where.' "

One can hardly fail to be reminded of the scene in *The Scarlet Letter* in which Hester has come to Governor Bellingham's house, "full of concern" that "there was a design on the part of

some of the leading inhabitants ... to deprive her of her child
(chapter 7). When the three-year old Pearl perversely refuses to
answer Mr Wilson's catechism, the Governor, aghast that "she
cannot tell who made her," is confirmed in his resolve to remove
Pearl from Hester's charge.

> Hester caught hold of Pearl, and drew her forcibly into her arms, confron-
> ting the old Puritan magistrate with almost a fierce expression. Alone in the
> world, cast off by it, and with this sole treasure to keep her heart alive, she
> felt that she possessed indefeasible rights against the world, and was ready to
> defend them to the death.
>
> "God gave me the child!" cried she. "He gave her in requital of all things
> else, which ye had taken from me. She is my happiness — she is my torture
> too, none the less! Pearl keeps me here in life! ... Ye shall not take her! I will
> die first!"
>
> "My poor woman," said the not unkind old minister, "the child shall be
> well cared for — far better than thou canst do it."
>
> "God gave her into my keeping," repeated Hester Prynne, raising her
> voice almost to a shriek. "I will not give her up" (chapter 8).

Eppie has none of the impish perversity, the apparent
maliciousness, the "stern, unsympathizing look of discontent",
the fierce temper, which Hester sees with alarm in Pearl. Eppie
is a much softened version; but still, I feel sure, she is a version of
Pearl. Hawthorne emphasizes Pearl's creative vitality, and her
"never-failing vivacity of spirits", as well as the "unquiet
elements" and "fitful caprice" in her nature. "The spell of life
went forth from her ever creative spirit, and communicated itself
to a thousand objects, as a torch kindles a flame wherever it may
be applied. ... It was wonderful, the vast variety of forms into
which she threw her intellect ... always in a state of preternatural activity. ..." Pearl, as soon as she is "big enough to run
about", amuses herself "with gathering handfuls of
wild-flowers" (though with her usual precocity she uses them as
missiles to throw at the scarlet letter); later, alone in the forest,
she decks herself with violets, anemones and columbines, and is
accepted without alarm by the partridges and the pigeons. All of
this seems to be reflected (somewhat palely) in a paragraph of
Silas Marner (chapter 14).

> And when the sunshine grew strong and lasting, so that the buttercups were
> thick in the meadows, Silas might be seen ... strolling out ... to carry
> Eppie beyond the stone-pits to where the flowers grew, till they reached
> some favourite bank where he could sit down, while Eppie toddled to pluck

the flowers, and make remarks to the winged things that murmured happily above the bright petals, calling 'Dad-dad's' attention continually by bringing him the flowers. Then she would turn her ear to some sudden bird-note . . . when it came, she set up her small back and laughed with gurgling triumph.

Eppie soon develops "a fine capacity for mischief". When she cuts the broad strip of linen and escapes, Silas finds her playing in the mud beside a pond. "Overcome with convulsive joy at finding his treasure again, [he] could do nothing but snatch her up, and cover her with half-sobbing kisses." One can hardly fail to be reminded again of *The Scarlet Letter* (chapter 6): "Hester was constrained to rush towards the child, — to pursue the little elf in the flight which she invariably began, — to snatch her to her bosom, with a close pressure and earnest kisses. . . ." Silas, like Hester, tries "to impose a tender, but strict, control over the infant immortality" committed to his charge. But as Hester "after trying both smiles and frowns, and proving that neither mode of treatment possessed any calculable influence . . . was ultimately compelled to stand aside, and permit the child to be swayed by her own impulses" (chapter 6) (though, annoyed by Pearl's questions about the scarlet letter, she does later (chapter 15) threaten to shut Pearl "into the dark closet"); so Silas's "belief in the efficacy of punishment" is destroyed by the "total failure of the coal-hole discipline." "So Eppie was reared without punishment, the burden of her misdeeds being borne vicariously by father Silas" (chapter 14).

There is, of course, one great difference between the situations of Pearl and Eppie. Pearl, from birth, stands with her mother "in the same circle of seclusion from human society"; she instinctively recognizes "the destiny that had drawn an inviolable circle around her." But for Eppie not only is "the stone hut . . . made a soft nest for her, lined with downy patience: also in the world that lay beyond the stone hut she knew nothing of frowns and denials."

Despite the important differences (Pearl is Hester's only companion in her banishment from the human community — her very existence indeed the cause of Hester's banisment; Eppie not only provides Silas with a new purpose in living, "reawakening his senses with her fresh life", but "the little child had come to link him once more with the whole world") the correspondences are sufficiently striking to suggest, as Jonathan Quick claims,

"that George Eliot found a model for her story of spiritual sur-
vival and recovery in Hawthorne's development of a sustaining
relationship between parent and child."[157] Pearl is "the sole
treasure to keep [Hester's] heart alive"; "Pearl keeps me in here
in life", as she tells Bellingham. In a later passage, Hawthorne
suggests that Hester's passionate assertion is truer than she
knew:

> It is remarkable, that persons who speculate the most boldly often conform
> with the most perfect quietude to the external regulations of society. The
> thought suffices them, without investing itself in the flesh and blood of
> action. So it seemed to be with Hester. Yet, had little Pearl never come to her
> from the spiritual world, it might have been far otherwise. . . . She might,
> and not improbably would, have suffered death from the stern tribunals of
> the period, for attempting to undermine the foundations of the Puritan
> establishment. But, in the education of her child, the mother's enthusiasm of
> thought had something to wreak itself upon (chapter 13).

If Pearl keep Hester in life, Eppie restores Silas to life: "The
child created fresh and fresh links between his life and the lives
from which he had hitherto shrunk continually into narrower
isolation" (chapter 14).

The eighteen-year old Eppie of Part Two, the "blonde,
dimpled girl", with her "curly auburn hair", and her merry
laughter, whose ties of love and loyalty to Silas are so strong that
the life of privileged ease belatedly offered by her real father,
Godfrey Cass, provides no real temptation, has, it seems to me,
distinct similarities to Hawthorne's Phoebe Pyncheon.

Hawthorne's influence is also, I believe, discernible in other
characters and situations — even in Nancy Lammeter who marries Godfrey Cass. Nancy, after fifteen years of marriage, spends
her Sundays "living inwardly again and again, through all her
remembered experience . . . asking herself continuously whether
she had been in any respect blamable." The sentence that follows
— not so much in what it says (though the word "morbid"
occurs in both passages) as in the tone and contour of the
sentence seems to echo a comment of Hawthorne's on Hester's
abjuring of the joys of needlework.

"This excessive rumination and self-questioning is perhaps a
morbid habit inevitable to a mind of much moral sensibility
when shut out from its due share of outward activity and of practical claims on its affections. . . ." (*Silas Marner*, chapter 17).

"This morbid meddling of conscience with an immaterial matter betokened, it is to be feared, no genuine and steadfast penitence, but something doubtful, something that might be deeply wrong, beneath." (*The Scarlet Letter*, chapter 5).

There are, however, clearer echoes of Hawthorne in the portrayal of Godfrey Cass. Does not the opening paragraph of chapter 12 ("While Godfrey Cass was taking draughts of forgetfulness from the sweet presence of Nancy, willingly losing all sense of *that hidden bond which at other moments galled and fretted him* so as to mingle irritation with the very sunshine. . . .") recall part of Hawthorne's account (chapter 5) of the reasons for Hester's decision to remain in the Puritan settlement ("The chain that bound her here was of iron links, and galling to her inmost soul, but never could be broken.")? Is not a passage in chapter 13 even more reminiscent of the tortured introspection of Arthur Dimmesdale, whose situation of unadmitted paternity is so similar? ("Deeper down, and half-smothered by passionate desire and dread, there was the sense that he ought not to be waiting for these alternatives; that he ought to accept the consequences of his deeds, own the miserable wife, and fulfil the claims of the helpless child. But he had not moral courage enough to contemplate that active renunciation of Nancy as possible for him: he had only conscience and heart enough to make him forever uneasy under the weakness that forbade the renunciation.")

In the same chapter occurs this passage, describing Godfrey's reaction, when Silas enters the White Parlour, carrying Godfrey's own child: "But when Godfrey was lifting his eyes from one of those long glances, they encountered an object as startling to him as if it had been an apparition from the dead. It *was* an apparition from that hidden life which lives, like a dark by-street, behind the goodly ornamented facade that meets the sunlight and the gaze of respectable admirers." The second sentence, I have no doubt, is a brief version of a long and lurid passage, using similar architectural imagery, to describe the reality behind the "genial benevolence", the beaming public mask of Jaffrey Pyncheon. To quote a few sentences (*The House of the Seven Gables*, chapter 15). "Hidden from mankind, — forgotten by himself, or buried so deeply under a sculptured and ornamented pile of ostentatious deeds that his daily life could take no note of it, — there may have lurked some evil and unsightly thing."

"With these materials, and with deeds of goodly aspect, done in the public eye, an individual of this class builds up, as it were, a tall and stately edifice, which, in the view of other people, and ultimately in his own view, is no other than the man's character, or the man himself. . . . Ah! but in some low and obscure nook . . . may lie a corpse, half decayed, and still decaying, and diffusing its death-scent all through the palace!"

"We might say . . . that there was enough of splendid rubbish in his life to cover up and paralyze a more active and subtle conscience than the Judge was ever troubled with."

I do not contend that George Eliot, in *Silas Marner*, was consciously imitating Hawthorne. There is no reason to doubt her claim, in a letter to John Blackwood, that the book had its origin in a sudden flash of inspiration. "It came to me first of all, quite suddenly, as a sort of legendary tale, suggested by my recollection of having once, in early childhood, seen a linen-weaver with a bag on his back."[158] But there seems to be some analogy between this account, and Hawthorne's (fictitious) account, in "The Custom House", of the origin of *The Scarlet Letter* in his discovery of the package containing the "worn and faded rag" of scarlet cloth, and his recognition of "some deep meaning . . . which streamed forth from the mystic symbol, subtly communicating itself to my sensibilities, but evading the analysis of my mind."

In the same letter George Eliot remarked, "I have felt all through as if the story would have lent itself best to metrical rather than prose fiction, especially in all that relates to the psychology of Silas. . . ." It is probable that the idea of "metrical fiction" was suggested by Wordsworth's "Michael", from which she took the epigraph of *Silas Marner*. (George Eliot had just mentioned Wordsworth — "I should not have believed that anyone would have been interested in it but myself (since William Wordsworth is dead). . . ." And Lilian Haddakin has shown that "had she decided upon a multiple epigraph . . . she could have chosen several other passages from Wordsworth", for the novel has many strong Wordsworthian affinities.)[159] But, so George Eliot also told Blackwood, as her "mind dwelt on the subject, [she] became inclined to a more realistic treatment." I think it very probable that the process of reflection, which led to the decision to adopt a treatment more realistic than would be expected in a "legendary tale", included her awareness that Hawthorne had both written and defined the kind of fiction that she now felt impelled to write — a kind of fiction which scrupulously adheres to "the truth of the human heart", but, not content with reflecting "the probable and the ordinary" with "minute fidelity," "mellows the lights, deepens and enriches the shadows", and "mingles the Marvellous . . . as a slight, delicate and evanescent flavour."

It is also worth mentioning that George Eliot, in conversation with Blackwood, gave a somewhat different (or at least fuller) account of the origin of the book. Apparently it wasn't only the bag on the linen-weaver's back that she remembered: " 'Silas Marner' sprang from her childish recollection of a man with a stoop and expression of face that led her to think he was an alien from his fellows."[160] Despite the "fairy-tale" "happy-ever-after" ending of his story, Silas Marner is, as Fred C. Thompson has remarked, George Eliot's "first full study of alienation",[161] and the parts of the book "describing Silas' exile, loneliness, and deprivation are dark-hued indeed", with "a sustained somber tonality oddly different from almost anything in her previous novels."[162] George Eliot, with her strong admiration for Hawthorne, could hardly have failed to be influenced by *The Scarlet Letter* in her portrayal of the plight of Silas Marner, deprived in shattering succession of friendship, religious fellowship, love, belief in human and divine justice, native environment. It is, as I have tried to demonstrate, in this early part of the novel that one hears most clearly the echoes of Hawthorne.

Hawthorne's Influence in *Romola*

I have previously mentioned that in a letter from Florence, in May 1860, in which George Eliot gave the first hint of an "ambitious project" to write an historical novel set in Italy, she also remarked that "Hawthorne's book [i.e. the recently published *The Marble Faun*] is not to be found here yet." George Eliot was diverted from the Italian project to write *Silas Marner*. There seems to be no doubt that she read *The Marble Faun* before she began the actual writing of *Romola* on New Year's Day 1862,[163] having spent much of 1861 researching the background of her subject in contemporary records and histories of fifteenth century Italy.

I have also previously quoted the earliest comment that I have discovered which brings together Hawthorne's book (which he subtitled, "The Romance of Monte Beni") and George Eliot's (which, in a letter in August 1860, she had described, prospectively, as "a historical romance"[164]). This is H.S. Salt's verdict in 1887 that both books, though based on "earnest study", are "slight and artificial", compared with their authors' other work, "inspired by the natural objects . . . known from childhood."[165] This verdict has been almost unanimously endorsed by subsequent critics, whether they have been referring to only one of the novels, or to both together. It is virtually paraphrased (probably quite unconsciously) by the most recent critic to compare the two novels, Curtis Dahl — "Both books are 'rootless' in the sense that neither is set in a place or society which the author deeply, instinctively, unselfconsciously feels and knows. All the Baedeker facts of Hawthorne and all the arduous, wearying research of Eliot cannot make Rome or fifteenth-century Florence have the living meaning that the farms of Warwickshire have in *Adam Bede* or the Puritan village of Boston has in *The Scarlet Letter*."[166]

I have also referred to three post-1950 comparisons of the two books — a brief comment by Mario Praz in *The Hero in Eclipse*;[167] a chapter of Ellin Jane Ringler's unpublished dissertation, "The Problem of Evil. . . .";[168] and Curtis Dahl's essay, "When the Deity Returns. . . ." from which I have just quoted. Neither of these two most recent critics is primarily concerned to assert, or demonstrate, George Eliot's indebtedness to Hawthorne; but both have examined the similarities and differences between the two novels so thoroughly that they have noted virtually every aspect and passage of *Romola* which I would regard as evidence of the possible or probable influence of *The Marble Faun*. I would suggest, however, that *Romola* was not influenced only by *The Marble Faun*; I shall point to what seem to me to be echoes — some faint, but some quite distinct — of each of Hawthorne's three American romances.

Let me begin, however, by saying that I do not think there is any reason to believe that George Eliot was (in her own words, in August 1860, when she had probably read *The Marble Faun*) "fired with the idea of writing a historical romance — scene Florence; period, the close of the fifteenth century, which was marked by Savonarola's career and martyrdom",[169] by a passing reference in *The Marble Faun* (chapter 28) to "a certain famous monk" who was confined in a cell in Donatello's tower "about five hundred years ago . . . and afterwards burned at the stake in the Grand-Ducal square at Firenze." It is doubtful whether Hawthorne intended a reference to Savonarola, as Curtis Dahl suggests;[170] Savonarola had been hanged, and his body burnt, only about three hundred and a half centuries before. Nor do I imagine that George Eliot's choice of 1492 for the beginning of the action of *Romola* is a cryptographic clue to an American influence.

I wonder, however, whether the links between names of characters in the two books are purely coincidental. Hawthorne gave his modern faun the name of Donatello, the Florentine sculptor who was one of the chief initiators of Renaissance art in Italy; is it mere accident, I wonder, that the first of the many works of art mentioned in *Romola* (book 1, chapter 1) is "Donatello's stone statue of Plenty"? Furthermore the historical Donatello's real name was Donato di Niccolo de Betto Bardi; is it purely by chance that George Eliot's eponymous heroine is also a Bardi? Romola's father is Bardo de Bardi; it seems unlikely that the blind old scholar, descendant of an ancient grandee family of soldiers, merchants and usurers was related to Niccolo di Betto Bardi, the wool-carder and labour agitator who sired the great sculptor, was exiled and dragged at an ass's tail for manslaughter. But perhaps Niccolo was one of the black sheep of the family, whose history, George Eliot remarks, (book 1, chapter 5) "included even more vicissitudes and contrasts of dignity and disgrace, of wealth and poverty, than are usually seen on the background of wide kinship."

More important, it seems possible that one source of Bardo de Bardi may have been the "English signore" who is Donatello's informant about his own family history and traditions (who was based on Seymour Kirkup, whom Hawthorne visited in 1858[171]). When Donatello mentions him, Kenyon remarks (*The Marble Faun*, chapter 28): " 'Ah, I have seen him in Florence. . . . he is a

necromancer, as you say, and dwells in an old mansion . . . close
by the Ponte Vecchio, with a great many ghostly books, pictures
and antiquities, to make the house gloomy, and one bright-eyed
little girl to keep it cheerful!' " The house in which George
Eliot's "moneyless blind old scholar" lives is "one of those large
sombre masses of stone buildings" with "small windows" and
"grim doors"; the room where Tito first meets Romola and her
father is "surrounded with shelves, on which books and antiquities were arranged in scrupulous order." Among the "pale or
sombre" objects — the carpet "worn to dimness", "the dark
bronzes" and "the dark pottery", the "only spot of bright
colour"is the reddish gold hair of Romola (*Romola*, book 1,
chapter 5). Perhaps another source for the Bardo-Romola relationship is the relationship between the prison-sheltered elderly
aesthete, Clifford Pyncheon, and his sunny young cousin,
Phoebe, in *The House of the Seven Gables*.

For Romola herself, probably a more important Hawthorne
source than either "the bright-eyed little girl" or Phoebe is, as
both Ellin Ringler and Curtis Dahl have argued, the "dove" of
The Marble Faun, Hilda (who, Marius Bewley has maintained,
was virtually taken over by James as his dove, Minnie Theale[172]).
There are certainly some strong similarities. Hilda, the
"daughter of the Puritans", lives in her tower, alone and aloof
from the corrupt atmosphere of nineteenth century Rome, as fair
and pure as the dove that she feeds, or the Virgin whose lamp she
tends. Similarly Romola, though a native Florentine, lives alone
with her elderly father, insulated from life. Hilda is a copyist, an
artist who has relinquished all personal ambition to produce
original work and dedicated herself to the reproduction of the
work of the Renaissance masters — a role which Hawthorne suggests is "something far higher and nobler", "the better and
loftier and more unselfish part, laying her individual hopes, her
fame, her prospects of enduring remembrance, at the feet of
those great departed ones, whom she so loved and venerated"
(chapter 6). Similarly Romola sacrifices her own individuality in
the devoted service of the father whom she loves and venerates,
acting as his eyes in his scholarly researches in the work of the
great immortal dead; before Tito comes, hers has been a "self-
repressing colourless young life, which had thrown all its passion
into sympathy with aged sorrows, aged ambition, aged pride and
indignation" (book 1, chapter 12).

Hilda's unstained innocence is, so Miriam tells her (chapter 6) "like a sharp steel sword." When she repudiates Miriam after witnessing the murder of the model, Miriam tells her: "You have no sin, nor any conception of what it is; and therefore you are so terribly severe! As an angel you are not amiss; but, as a human creature, and a woman among earthly men and women, you need a sin to soften you" (chapter 23). Similarly Romola, before her marriage to Tito, is "in a state of girlish simplicity and ignorance concerning the world outside her father's books" (book 1, chapter 5); her ignorance makes her self-righteous and rigid in her moral judgments. Within the novel there is scarcely a hint of criticism of her, but there is a good deal of justification for such comments as Jerome Thale's: "Tito receives all the blame for the failure of the marriage, yet, for all her high intentions — or perhaps because of them — Romola makes no effort to understand and help him and is in fact a very difficult wife."[173] Romola's reaction to Tito's announcement that he has sold her dead father's library — a betrayal of trust which she regards as being as bad as murder — is, like Hilda's to Miriam, one of complete repudiation, which leads to her abortive attempt to flee from Florence and her marriage.

For both heroines the revelation of the sinful proclivities of those they love is a shattering experience, from which their first impulse is to escape. Hilda is eventually driven to ease the burden of vicarious guilt by "confession" in St Peters. After Kenyon has repeated Miriam's charge that she is "a terribly severe judge", who "needs no mercy, and therefore knows not how to show any" (chapter 42), Hilda begins to have doubts whether she has not committed a wrong "towards the friend once so beloved." She asks herself "whether a close bond of friendship, in which we once voluntarily engage, ought to be severed on account of any unworthiness, which we subsequently detect in our friend. For, in these unions of hearts, — call them marriage, or whatever else, — we take each other for better or worse." When she has remorsefully recognized " 'Miriam loved me well ... and I failed her at her sorest need' ", Hilda remembers and carries out Miriam's commission to deliver the sealed packet at the Palazzo Cenci, after which she mysteriously disappears. After her release from captivity, though she repudiates with horror Kenyon's speculation that sin may be "merely an element of human education, through which we struggle to a higher and purer state than we could otherwise have obtained" she admits that she is "a poor weak girl, [with] no such wisdom as you fancy in me", and consents to marry Kenyon (chapter 50).

Romola's flight from Florence, disguised as a nun, is checked by Savonarola himself, who tells her (in words very reminiscent of Hilda's situation) " 'You have lived with those who sit on a hill aloof, and look down on the life of their fellow-men' " and " 'You have been as one unborn to the true life of man' " (book 2, chapter 20). As Ellin Ringler remarks, "the Frate persuades Romola to return to Tito by appealing to her social conscience, to her duty to serve the city of Florence and, primarily to her obligation as a wife."[174] He reminds her, as Hilda reminded herself, that she took Tito "for better or worse"; and tells her that if her husband " 'were a malefactor, your place would be in the prison beside him.' " Romola returns to Florence, becomes an adherent of Savonarola's, and during the famine (like Hester, rather than like Hilda) devotes herself to service of the sick and suffering. Like Hester "she had no innate taste for tending the sick and clothing the ragged. . . . But they had come to be the one unshaken resting-place of her mind, the one narrow pathway on which the light fell clear" (book 3, chapter 3).

The revelation that the old man, Baldassare, is the foster-father whom Tito has grossly betrayed, by selling the gems which should have ransomed Baldassare from Turkish slavery, affects Romola in a manner that is even more similar than her previous repudiation of him to Hilda's horrified revulsion from Miriam after she witnesses the murder of the model: "Her horror of his conduct towards Baldassarre projected itself over every conception of his acts; it was as if she had seen him committing a murder, and had had a diseased impression ever after that his hands were covered with fresh blood" (book 3, chapter 7). The transformation of the actual murder of *The Marble Faun* into simile can hardly be any more accidental than George Eliot's transformation of the actual procession of *The Scarlet Letter* into simile in *Adam Bede*. When to this horror of her husband is added the execution of her god-father, Bernardo del Nero, on whose behalf Savonarola refuses to intervene, Romola again flees from Florence: "The bonds of all strong affection were snapped", and her "best support under that supreme woman's sorrow had slipped away from her." Like Maggie Tulliver, "she wished she could pass from sleep into death"; but the sea to which she commits herself brings her to shore in the plague-stricken village, where, even more Hester-like, she spends months as a "self-ordained Sister of Mercy" (George Eliot does not use Hawthorne's phrase, but Romola is mistaken for the Madonna), before returning to Florence, where Tito has just been murdered, and Savonarola has been arrested, tried and tortured, and is soon afterwards executed. The novel ends with Romola, in her mid-thirties in 1509, devoting her life to the Hetty-like Tessa and her illegitimate children.

There are obviously many difference between Hilda and Romola, and their respective experiences of life. Curtis Dahl comments, quite justly: "But how much more active, practical and social is Romola's final life than even Hilda's!" (But, as I have suggested, there is much in Romola's life, especially its last recorded phases, that reminds of Hester rather than of Hilda.) But Dahl is also right in stressing the essential similarity of theme. "Though the result may differ, both women must leave their lofty towers and descend into the hurly-burly of active life. Hilda for good or evil . . . must painfully leave her figurative as well as her stone-and-mortar tower before she can become wife to Kenyon . . . Romola . . . must leave the realms of classical scholarship and even of religious enthusiasm before she can take up her life of living service. For good or ill — she must see her love betrayed and her ideals thwarted and her hopes destroyed."[175]

An important point of similarity which I have not sufficiently emphasized is their transformation, quite explicit in both cases, from Virgin to Madonna. The first chapter (6) devoted mainly to Hilda in *The Marble Faun* is called "The Virgin's Shrine"; the shrine is as much that of the virgin Hilda, as of the Virgin Mary. In chapter 40 Kenyon tells her: " 'Do not say you are no saint! You will still be Saint Hilda whatever church may canonize you.' " At the end of the chapter, Kenyon, looking up at Hilda in her tower, thinks " 'How like a spirit she looks, aloft there, with the evening glory round her head, and those winged creatures claiming her as akin to them. . . . How far above me! How unattainable!" But, in the final chapter, Hilda comes "down from her old tower, to be herself enshrined and worshipped as a household saint, in the light of her husband's fireside."

Romola is more especially associated with virgins of classical legend — especially Ariadne, the daughter of Minos, King of Crete, who fell in love with Theseus, and gave him a thread to guide him through the labyrinth, which enabled him to slay the Minotaur. She was carried off, and deserted, by the cunning and unscrupulous Greek hero (as, of course, Romola is by Tito), but survived to marry Dionysius. (It is as Bacchus — or Dionysius — and Ariadne, not as Theseus and Ariadne, that Tito Melema commissions Piero di Cosimo to paint himself and Romola.) But Piero di Cosimo tells Romola (book 2, chapter 8), in a speech that also mentions "the most holy Virgin herself" that she is "fit to be a model for a wise St Catherine of Egypt" (i.e. St Catherine of Alexandria, the fourth century young virgin martyr, patroness of Christian philosophers, who was tortured and beheaded). A few chapters before, in her ministrations to the famine-stricken poor, she has become "The Visible Madonna" (the title of book 2, chapter 2). In the plague-stricken village, she is mistaken for "the Holy Mother", and "many legends were afterwards told in that valley about the blessed lady who came over the sea" (book 2, chapter 27).

There is no character in *The Marble Faun* who has any resemblance to Savonarola, who has such an important role in *Romola*. Curtis Dahl expresses a commonly-held view when he remarks that "Savonarola is depicted more like a nineteenth-century Protestant engaged in social and political reform than like a Renaissance enthusiast given to devotion and contemplation."[176] I don't think anyone has suggested, however, that Savonarola has certain resemblances to Hawthorne's nineteenth-century Protestant reformer — Hollingsworth in *The Blithedale Romance*; but there seems to me to be a remarkable parallel between the following passages.

> Savonarola had that readily roused resentment towards opposition hardly separable from a power-loving and powerful nature, accustomed to seek great ends that cast a reflected grandeur on the means by which they are sought. . . . Such feelings were nullified by that hard struggle which made half the tragedy of his life, — the struggle of a mind possessed by a never-silent hunger after purity and simplicity, yet caught in a tangle of egoistic demand, false ideas, and difficult outward conditions, that made simplicity impossible (*Romola*, book 3, chapter 8).

It was inevitable that she should judge the Frate unfairly on a question of individual suffering, at which *she* looked with the eyes of personal tenderness, and *he* with the eyes of theoretic conviction. In that declaration of his, that the cause of his party was the cause of God's kingdom, she heard only the ring of egoism. Perhaps such words have rarely been uttered without that meaner ring in them; yet they are the implicit formula of all energetic belief. And . . . such energetic belief, pursuing a grand and remote end, is often in danger of becoming a demon-worship, in which the votary lets his son and daughter pass through the fire with a readiness that hardly looks like sacrifice. . . . (*Romola*, book 3, chapter 20).

[Hollingsworth] had taught his benevolence to pour its warm tide exclusively through one channel; so that there was nothing to spare for other great manifestations of love to man, nor scarcely for the nutriment of individual attachments, unless they could minister, in some way, to the terrible egotism which he mistook for an angel of God (*The Blithedale Romance*, chapter 7).

He was not altogether human. . . . This is always true of those men who have surrendered themselves to an overruling purpose. It does not so much impel them from without, nor even operate as a motive power within, but grows incorporate with all that they think and feel, and finally converts them into little else save that one principle. . . . They have no heart, no sympathy, no reason, no conscience. They will keep no friend, unless he makes himself the mirror of their purpose; they will smite and slay you, and trample your dead corpse under foot, all the more readily if you take the first step with them, and cannot take the second, and the third, and every other step of their terribly strait path. They have an idol to which they consecrate themselves high-priest, and deem it holy work to offer sacrifices of whatever is most precious; and never once seem to suspect — so cunning has the Devil been with them — that this false deity, in whose iron features . . . they see only benignity and love, is but a spectrum of the very priest himself, projected upon the surrounding darkness. And the higher and purer the original object, and the more unselfishly it may have been taken up, the slighter is the probability that they can be led to recognize the process by which godlike benevolence has been debased into an all-devouring egotism (*The Blithedale Romance*, chapter 9).

It seem unnecessary to underline the similarities, not only between the particular passages, but between the basic conceptions of the two characters — as men of powerfully dominant personality, with genuinely noble and lofty purposes, to which they are so totally dedicated that their humanity is destroyed, and their reforming mission becomes a monstrous form of self-worship.

Mario Praz, in a comment on Tito Melema, which I have previously quoted, remarked that "the study of the gradual debasement of Tito's soul is reminiscent of similar studies in

Hawthorne (*Ethan Brand*, for instance)", and added: "The comparison might be carried farther, though perhaps not without forcing it, if one sees in the metamorphosis of the fascinating Tito, creature of the Renaissance, into a reprobate, a reflection of the metamorphosis of the pagan Donatello, in Hawthorne's novel, into a moral man under the stimulus of a crime."[177] It is quite true, as Praz suggests, that the degeneration of Tito is the obverse of the "fortunate fall", the "education through sin" of Donatello, but (as both Ellin Ringler and Curtis Dahl have shown) the two characters are initially so alike that it seems very probable that one is, to a large extent, derived from the other. I suspect that, in at least two places, George Eliot may have subtly acknowledged her indebtedness.

In book 1, chapter 3 of *Romola*, the barber Nello, shows Tito a sketch of Piero di Cosimo's which "represented three masks — one a drunken, laughing Satyr, another a sorrowing Magdalen, and the third, which lay between them, the rigid cold face of a Stoic; the masks rested obliquely on the lap of a little child, whose cherub features rose above them with something of the supernal promise in the gaze which painters had by that time learned to give to the Divine Infant.

'A symbolic picture, I see', said the young Greek. . . .' The child perhaps, is the Golden Age, wanting neither worship nor philosophy. . . . Or the child may mean the wise philosophy of Epicurus, removed alike from the gross, the sad, and the severe.' " The description of the sketch, and Tito's interpretation of its meaning have a clear application to himself; but they are also reminiscent of the speculations about the faun in chapter 2 of *The Marble Faun*, especially Miriam's speech: " 'Imagine, now, a real being, similar to this mythic Faun; how happy, how genial, how satisfactory would be his life, enjoying the warm, sensuous, earthy side of nature; revelling in the merriment of woods and streams, living as our four-footed kindred do, — as mankind did in its innocent childhood; before sin, sorrow or morality itself had ever been thought of. . . . For I suppose the Faun had no conscience, no remorse, no burden on the heart, no troublesome recollections of any sort; no dark future either." They recall also the comment on Miriam and Donatello frolicking in the woods: "It was a glimpse far backward into Arcadian life, or, further still, into the Golden Age, before mankind was burdened with sin and sorrow, and before pleasure had been darkened with those shadows that bring it into high relief, and make it happiness" (chapter 9).

The other occurs in book 1, chapter 5, when Romola reads from Politian's "Miscellanea" the story of the blinding of Teiresias, because he "inadvertently beheld Minerva unveiled" when she was "bathing her disrobed limbs in the Heliconian Hippocrene." The story has an obvious ironical reference to the blind old pedant, Bardo. But it is also faintly reminiscent of the legend (*The Marble Faun*, chapter 27) of the love of Donatello's ancestor (himself descended from a sylvan creature of the Golden Age) for the nymph of the fountain, who disappeared when he polluted the pure water by trying to wash a blood-stain from his hand.

Even if the suggestion that the artist's sketch and the ancient legend have, or are meant to have, an oblique reference to *The Marble Faun*, is dismissed as fanciful speculation, they will serve to illustrate one important similarity between Donatello and Tito — the aura of legendary and mythical association in which they exist. Dahl contends, indeed, that "the most striking similarity of method is the use in both novels of the idea of a classical deity who returns to later times."[178]

Donatello is, of course, associated from the beginning with the Faun of Praxiteles. He seems, like the statue, to be "neither man nor animal, and yet no monster, but a being in whom both races meet on friendly ground", "not supernatural, but just on the verge of nature, and yet within it." "So full of animal life as he was, so joyous in his deportment, so handsome, so physically well-developed, he made no impression of incompleteness, or maimed or stinted nature. And yet, in social intercourse, these familiar friends of his habitually and instinctively allowed for him, as for a child or some other lawless being. . . . There was an indefinable characteristic about Donatello that set him outside of rules." When he refuses to shake aside his brown curls to reveal whether he has pointed ears like the faun, his "mute, helpless gesture of entreaty" is like "the aspect of a hound when he thinks himself in fault or disgrace"; Miriam bestows on him "a little careless caress, singularly like what one would give to a pet dog" (*The Marble Faun*, chapter 2).

Tito too has "long dark-brown curls"; there is "something ir-

resistibly propitiating in his bright young smile." The barber
Nello thinks that "this youth might be taken to have come
straight from Olympus" (*Romola*, book 1, chapter 2). In a
retrospect we learn (book 1, chapter 9) that "he had been . . . a
very bright, lovely boy; a youth of ever splendid graces, who
seemed quite without vices, as if that beautiful form represented
a vitality so exquisitely poised and balanced that it could know
no uneasy desires, no unrest — a radiant presence . . . the curves
of Tito's mouth had ineffable good humour in them." When he
first meets Romola and her father, "Tito's bright face showed its
rich-tinted beauty without any rivalry of colour. . . . It seemed
like a wreath of spring, dropped suddenly in Romola's young
and wintry life" (book 1, chapter 6).

Two passages in this scene of the first meeting of Tito and
Romola seem to be especially clear echoes of *The Marble Faun*.
George Eliot's remark that "Romola's astonishment could
hardly have been greater if the stranger had worn a panther-skin
and carried a thyrsus . . ." almost inevitably recalls Hawthorne's
comment: '. . . if a lion's skin could have been substituted for his
modern talma, and a rustic pipe for his stick, Donatello might
have figured perfectly as the marble faun . . ." (chapter 1). The
passage: "Tito's glance . . . had that gentle, beseeching admiration in it which is the most propitiating of appeals to a proud,
shy woman. . . . The finished fascination of his air came chiefly
from the absence of demand and assumption. It was that of a
fleet, soft-coated, dark-eyed animal that delights you by not
bounding away in indifference from you, and unexpectedly
pillows its chin on your palm, and looks up at you desiring to be
stroked — as if it loved you" recalls several in *The Marble Faun*
(some already cited): "He now came close to Miriam's side, gaz-
ing at her with an appealing air, as if to solicit forgiveness [like] a
hound when he thinks himself in fault . . ." (chapter 2). "He
appeared only to know that Miriam was beautiful, and that she
smiled graciously upon him . . . It was delightful to see the trust
which he reposed in Miriam, and his pure joy in her pro-
pinquity; he asked nothing, sought nothing, save to be near the
beloved object." "He gave Miriam the idea of a being not
precisely man, nor yet a child, but, in a high and beautiful sense,
an animal. . . ." " 'He perplexes me, — yes, and bewitches me,
— wild, gentle, beautiful creature that he is! It is like playing
with a young greyhound!' " (chapter 9).

The constant emphasis, in the early portrayal of both Donatello and Tito, is on their beauty, vitality, gentleness, spontaneity, naturalness and apparently eternal freshness of youth; it is these qualities which impress all they encounter, but especially Miriam and Romola. Ellin Ringler has astutely suggested that one passage in *Romola*, describing the overwhelming effect of Tito on Romola, in her sadness after her brother's death (which, incidentally, recalls Miriam's "delight . . . in feeling the zephyr of a new affection, with its untainted freshness, blow over her weary, stifled heart"), gathers up several passages in *The Marble Faun*, describing Donatello's close connection with all natural things.[179]

As he passed among the sunny shadows, his spirit seemed to acquire new elasticity. The flicker of the sunshine, the sparkle of the fountain's gush, the dance of the leaf upon the bough, the woodland fragrance, the green freshness, the old sylvan peace and freedom were all intermingled in those long breaths which he drew (*The Marble Faun*, chapter 7).

A bird happening to sing cheerily, Donatello gave a peculiar call, and the little feathered creature came fluttering about his head, as if it had known him through many summers.

"How close he stands to nature!" said Miriam, observing this pleasant familiarity between her companion and the bird. "He shall make me as natural as himself for this one hour." (*The Marble Faun*, chapter 9).

Without interrupting his brisk, though measured movement, Donatello snatched away the unmelodious contrivance, and flourishing it above his head, produced music of indescribable potency, still dancing with frisky step, and striking the tambourine, and ringing its little bells, all in one jovial act (*The Marble Faun*, chapter 10).

Tito's touch and beseeching voice recalled her; and now in the warm sunlight she saw that rich dark beauty which seemed to gather round it all images of joy, — purple vines festooned between the elms, the strong corn perfecting itself under the vibrating heat, bright-winged creatures hurrying and resting among the flowers, round limbs beating the earth in gladness with cymbals held aloft, light melodies chanted to the thrilling rhythms of strings, — all objects and all sounds that tell of Nature revelling in her force. Strange bewildering transition from those pale images of death to this bright youthfulness, as of a sun-god who knew nothing of night! (*Romola*, book 1, chapter 17).

To this I would add another passage in the same chapter. Tito tells Romola: " 'I wish we lived in Southern Italy, where thought is broken, not by weariness, but by delicious languors. . . . I should like to see you under the southern sun, lying among the flowers, subdued into mere enjoyment, while I bent over you and touched the lute and sang to you some little unconscious strain that seemed all one with the light and the warmth.' "

When one adds the further similarities that both Donatello and Tito are orphans, both are of somewhat mysterious origin, both are constantly associated with figures of classical, pagan myth and legend (Donatello not only with fauns and satyrs, dryads and water-nymphs, but with Bacchus and Apollo; Tito repeatedly with Bacchus and Apollo), both are outsiders in the city, which is alien and antipathetic to their nature (Miriam tells Donatello " 'You are getting spoilt in this dreary Rome' ", and " 'This melancholy and sickly Rome is stealing away the rich, joyous life that belongs to you' ", chapter 16; Tito says " 'There is something grim and grave to me always in Florence . . . and even in its merriment there is something shrill and hard' ", (book 1, chapter 17), one can hardly doubt that Donatello served as a model for Tito.

This is not to maintain, however, that the characters are identical, even at the beginnings of the novels. There is the important difference that, while in Donatello appearance and reality are one, and his innocence and gaiety are genuine and natural, Tito's beauty and disarming brightness are not exactly a mask, but they are half-consciously exploited for his own advantage; his is a "finished fascination". And from being apparently very similar, they develop in opposite ways. As Curtis Dahl efficiently summarizes:

> Hawthorne's Donatello is a naturally good, pagan faun who comes from his age-old tower in the Apennines to Rome, where through love of the mysterious Miriam he repeats the Biblical Fall: sins in the murder of Miriam's ghostly follower, learns bitterly of the mortality of the men of later times, and . . . perhaps rises through his love and his sin to a higher level of moral being. He loses his close, familiar Edenic relationship to nature; he turns from a dancing faun filled with unclouded joy in life, a companion of Bacchus in "an unsophisticated Arcadia", to a desolate and repentant man; but he comes down from his isolated tower to live and love and suffer in the city of men. He becomes a human being. His pagan faunlike nature is darkened but, Hawthorne hints, ennobled.[180]

Donatello's single crime is impulsive and unselfish, an altruistic attempt to destroy the evil that torments his beloved. Tito commits not a single crime, but a series of betrayals of trust which gradually convert the apparent "sun-god", but actual self-indulgent aesthetic hedonist, into a monster of calculating treachery and ruthless selfishness. If Donatello becomes a human being, Tito is dehumanized; he is reduced, when Baldassarre strangles him, to a "startling object in the grass" (book 3, chapter 26). If Donatello finds his soul, Tito loses his. These two passages epitomize the difference between them.

"From some mysterious source . . . a soul had been inspired into the young Count's simplicity, since their intercourse in Roma. He now showed a far deeper sense, and an intelligence that began to deal with high subjects, though in a feeble and childish way. He evinced too a more definite and nobler individuality, but developed out of grief and pain, and fearfully conscious of the pangs that had given it birth" (*The Marble Faun*, chapter 29).

"Only a very keen eye bent on studying him would have marked a certain amount of change in him which was not to be accounted for by the lapse of eighteen months. It was that change which comes from the final departure of moral youthfulness, — from the distinct self-conscious adoption of a part in life. The lines of the face were as soft as ever, the eyes as pellucid; but something was gone, — something as indefinable as the changes in the morning twilight" (*Romola*, book 2, chapter 2).

The main specific resemblance which Mario Praz noticed between *Romola* and *The Marble Faun* was that "the appearance of Baldassarre like a ghost of the past, a Nemesis incarnate, recalls the mysterious apparition that pursues Miriam in . . . *The Marble Faun*." The mysterious avenger is, no doubt, a fairly common figure in literature, particularly in the Gothic romance, which certainly influenced Hawthorne; but it is, I think, a safe assumption that the appearance of this figure in *Romola* owed something to its appearance, so soon before, in *The Marble Faun*. But it should also be said that the differences between the two versions of the archetypal figure effectively illustrate the differences between the two novels. The nameless spectre that dogs Miriam remains almost totally mysterious. He is an embodiment of guilt, an emanation of evil, a figure of allegory representing the sins of the past (far more so than even Chillingworth or Westervelt) rather than a psychologically motivated human being. We do eventually learn (chapter 47) that he was Miriam's destined husband, a marchese whom she refused to marry because his character "betrayed traits so evil, so treacherous, so vile, and yet so strangely subtle, as could only be accounted for by . . . insanity. . . ." But it is not for Miriam's repudiation of the marriage contract that he pursues her; it is for some other crime, with "frightful and mysterious circumstances", in which Miriam (whose own real identity is never divulged) is wrongly suspected of being an accomplice; it is not even clear whether her rejected suitor was himself involved in this crime, as either perpetrator or victim. The only hold he has over Miriam, it appears, is that he knows her real identity, and "could have blasted [her] in the belief of all the world." He has, it appears, already become a monk, whose "severe and self-inflicted penance had acquired him the reputation of unusual sanctity" when he accidentally encounters Miriam in the catacombs, and follows her forth "with fresh impulses to crime." "The spectral figure which she encountered there was the evil fate that had haunted her through life."

In contrast, there is really no mystery about Baldassarre or his motives. He is an elderly scholar, who adopted, educated and loved as his own son a young Greek boy, and was driven by his foster's son's treachery to insane vengeance. Reduced to semi-imbecility by illness and the hardships of his capacity, all that his clouded mind retains is the determination to destroy the "fair slippery viper" who had so basely betrayed him. In the one brief period in which his intelligence is restored to him, he is somewhat reminiscent of Chillingworth: "Baldassarre felt the indestructible independent force of a supreme emotion, which knows no terror, and asks for no motive, which is itself an ever-burning motive, consuming all other desire" (book 2, chapter 18). But he remains a man, and quite understandable; a Nemesis only to his betrayer, not an abstract symbol of "evil fate". As Curtis Dahl remarks: "Eliot's novel follows surprisingly closely the elements of Hawthorne's, but brings the American's lofty, nearly theological abstractions down to a more precise human level."[181]

Ellin Ringler and Curtis Dahl have both catalogued and illustrated various other resemblances between the two novels — the guidebook or textbook quality, the dependence on research and documentation (which in both cases is sometimes tediously over-detailed); the similar divided and ambiguous attitudes towards Italy and Catholicism; the use of the particular Italian locales to prevent universal human problems; the use of works of art as moral symbols. These, I think, are not chance resemblances; but they are evidence of a similar cast of mind, similar basic attitudes and beliefs, rather than of specific indebtedness. It is, I think, in the portrayal of the main characters of *Romola* — Tito, Romola, Savonarola, Baldassarre — that the influence of Hawthorne (and not only of *The Marble Faun*) is virtually undeniable.

Hawthorne's Influence in *Felix Holt*

George Eliot did not begin to write her fifth novel, *Felix Holt, The Radical*, until late in March 1865, almost a year after Hawthorne's death, and five years after the publication of his last completed novel, *The Marble Faun* (1860). In *Felix Holt* (1866), and her two longest novels, *Middlemarch* (1871–72) and *Daniel Deronda* (1876), both of which were originally published in parts, I find much less evidence of Hawthorne influence than in *Scenes of Clerical Life* and the first four full-length novels. But in them, as in Dickens' later novels, there are, I believe, at least some indications of how thoroughly George Eliot had assimilated the work of the American romancer.

So far as I know, only one recent critic has drawn attention to certain similarities between *Felix Holt* and *The Scarlet Letter*. Pietro di Logu, in discussing Mrs Transome, comments (my translation):

> Mrs Transome, depicted with exemplary objectivity, has committed a grave sin, adultery, and expiates her youthful error with loneliness. One thinks immediately of the heroine of *The Scarlet Letter*, Hester Prynne, condemned to live exiled from the world, with the glittering symbol burning on her breast. In *Felix Holt*, as in *The Scarlet Letter*, sin provides the antecedent to the story, but while Hawthorne's heroine find consolation in the presence of Pearl, the product of sin, Mrs Transome reaches the climax of her anguish precisely when her son Harold returns after an absence of fifteen years. The old lady had hoped that her son's affection would have filled the void in her life, but, finding him changed in both appearance and spirit, she has the bitter feeling of meeting a stranger.[182]

The differences between Hester and her situation, and Mrs

Transome and her situation, are so great, however, that it seems to me very probable that M.H. Dodds was right in the speculation, made in 1946, that Mrs Transome's story is, to some extent, "intentionally a re-handling of a theme from *Bleak House*"[183] (which, I have tried to show, was itself a re-handling of the story of Hester Prynne) rather than having a direct connection with *The Scarlet Letter*. I believe that Dodds was mistaken in the comment: "I do not think that she can have been consciously rationalizing it, as she called her heroine Esther, which is also the name of the heroine of *Bleak House*. If she had been aware of a connection between the two, I do not think she would have called attention to it."[184] There is, as I have previously suggested, a good deal of evidence that when George Eliot was aware of a literary indebtedness, she did deliberately call attention to it (e.g. the naming of Hetty (Hester) Sorrel and Arthur Donnithorne in *Adam Bede*; the explicit references to Corinne and the heroines of Scott in *The Mill on the Floss*). I think it extremely likely that George Eliot, in naming her heroine, was thoroughly aware of her antecedents — Esther Summerson, Hester Prynne and the Old Testament Esther. I have previously pointed out links between the biblical Esther and Hester Prynne, and between the biblical Esther and Esther Summerson. David R. Carroll has similarly remarked that

> Esther's [i.e. Esther Lyon's] choice is not merely a personal choice of Felix but also a social commitment to the working-class. This aspect is underlined by the parallel with the biblical Esther. Even before her elevation of rank, she is seen "in this small dingy house of the minister in Malthouse Yard" as "a light-footed, sweet-voiced Queen Esther" (6). Later at Transome Court, Harold assures her that she is "empress" of her fortune. . . . The biblical parallel is further developed by Lyon. . . . His interpretation is wrong, but Esther does continue her biblical role at the trial when she uses her new position to appeal for Felix, identifying herself with the people among whom she has been brought up.[185]

Mrs Transome's situation is certainly much closer to Lady Dedlock's than to Hester Prynne's; there is a good deal of justification for Dodds' suggestion that "George Eliot seems to be going over the same story point by point and bringing it into relation with normal life."[186] There is little similarity in character between Mrs Transome and Hester Prynne, except their aristocratic pride. But there is some resemblance in appearance; Mrs Transome looks much as Hester must have looked when she returned, after many years of absence, to the Puritan settlement. "She walked lightly, for her figure was slim and finely formed, though she was between fifty and sixty. She was a tall, proud-looking woman, with abundant grey hair, dark eyes and eyebrows, and a somewhat eagle-like yet not unfeminine face" (*Felix Holt*, chapter 1). There is, too, a frequent emphasis on Mrs Transome's "marble aspect" that is reminiscent of Hester. "Denner . . . found her mistress seated with more than ever of that marble aspect of self-absorbed suffering" (chapter 39). "Mrs Transome heard with a changeless face. She had for some time been watching, and had taken on her marble look of immobility" (chapter 46). One remembers such passages in *The Scarlet Letter* as "Much of the marble coldness of Hester's impression was to be attributed to the circumstance that her life had turned, in a great measure, from passion and feeling to thought" (chapter 13).

Some of the other characters of *Felix Holt* are somewhat reminiscent of characters of Hawthorne; only in one case, however, are the similarities strong enough for one to feel sure of Hawthorne's influence. Perhaps it is fanciful to be reminded of Arthur Dimmesdale by the following passage about Rufus Lyon?

> A terrible crisis had come upon him; a moment in which religious doubt and newly-awakened passion had rushed together in a common flood, and had paralysed his ministerial gifts. His life of thirty-six years had been a story of purely religious and studious fervour; his passion had been for doctrines, for argumentative conquest on the side of right; the sins he had chiefly to pray against had been those of personal ambition . . . those of a too restless intellect, ceaseless urging questions concerning the mystery of that which was assuredly revealed. . . . (chapter 6).

Another passage in the same chapter, describing Lyon's conflict of feelings when he has rescued Annette Ledru and her infant-daughter from starvation, and has fallen in love with Annette, seems like something that is not actually in *The Scarlet Letter*, but something that Hawthorne might have written if he had chosen to analyze Dimmesdale's emotions when he fell in love with Hester Prynne.

> He never went to bed himself that night. He spent it in misery, enduring a horrible assault of Satan. He thought a frenzy had seized him. Wild visions of an impossible future thrust themselves upon him. He dreaded lest the

woman had a husband; he wished that he might call her his own, that he might worship her beauty, that she might love and caress him. And what to the mass of men would have been only one of many allowable follies . . . was to him a spiritual convulsion. He was as one who raved, and knew that he raved. These mad wishes were irreconcilable with what he was, and must be, as a Christian minister; nay, penetrating his soul as tropic heat penetrates the frame, and changes for it all aspects and all favours, they were irreconcilable with that conception of the world which made his faith. All the busy doubts which had before been mere impish shadows flitting around a belief that was strong with the strength of an unswerving moral bias, had now gathered blood and substance. The questioning spirit had become suddenly bold and blasphemous; it no longer insinuated scepticism — it prompted defiance; it no longer expressed cool inquisitive thought, but was the voice of a passionate mood. Yet he never ceased to regard it as the voice of the tempter; the conviction which had been the law of his better life remained within him as a conscience.

If the passage as a whole seems like George Eliot's attempt to account for and explain what Jonathan Quick describes as one of the "unaccountable or ill-explained events" of *The Scarlet Letter* ("the early relationship of Hester and Dimmesdale"), the last sentences are more directly reminiscent of what is actually in *The Scarlet Letter*. So too is a paragraph a few pages later:

He dreaded, with a violence of feeling which surmounted all struggles, lest anything should take her away. . . . Yet he saw with perfect clearness that unless he tore up this mad passion by the roots, his ministerial usefulness would be frustrated, and the repose of his soul would be destroyed. . . . It was already a fall that he had wished there was no high purpose to which he owed an allegiance — that he had longed to fly to some backwoods where there was no church to reproach him, and when he might have this sweet woman to wife, and know the joys of tenderness.

Surely, it is not fanciful to be reminded of several passages from *The Scarlet Letter*? For example, of Hester's exhortation to Dimmesdale (chapter 17): " 'Whither leads yonder forest-track? Backward to the settlement, thou sayest! Yes; but onward, too? Deeper it goes, and deeper, into the wilderness . . . until, some miles hence, the yellow leaves will show no vestige of the white man's tread. There thou art free! So brief a journey would bring thee from a world where thou hast been most wretched, to one where thou mayst still be happy!' " Or Dimmesdale's reflection (chapter 18): " 'But now, — since I am irrevocably doomed, — wherefore should I not snatch the solace allowed to the condemned culprit before his execution? . . . Neither can I any longer live without her companionship; so powerful is she to sustain, — so tender to soothe!' " And most of all, several passages of chapter 20, "The Minister in a Maze". "Before Mr Dimmesdale reached home, his inner man gave him other evidences of a revolution in the sphere of thought and feeling. In truth, nothing short of a total change of dynasty and moral code, in that interior kingdom, was adequate to account for the impulses now communicated to the unfortunate and startled minister." " 'What is it that haunts and tempts me thus?' cried the minister to himself . . .' Am I mad? or am I given over utterly to the fiend?' " "The wretched minister! . . . Tempted by a dream of happiness, he had yielded himself with deliberate choice, as he had never done before, to what he knew was deadly sin. And the infectious poison of that sin had been thus rapidly diffused throughout his moral system."

Rufus Lyon is, of course, a totally different character from Arthur Dimmesdale. I suggest only that George Eliot may have taken some hints for Lyon's somewhat incongruously romantic past from the relationship between Dimmesdale and Hester, and the spiritual turmoil it causes in Dimmesdale.

Similarly, Felix Holt is a very different character from Hawthorne's Hollingsworth; but it seems possible that George Eliot's character owes something to Hawthorne's, especially in appearance. When Mr Lyon first meets Felix, he "felt a slight shock as his glasses made perfectly clear to him the shaggy-headed, large-eyed, strong-limbed person of this questionable young man, without waist coat or cravat" (chapter 5). When Felix appears in court, charged with manslaughter, Esther for the first time feels "pride in him on the ground simply of his appearance"; but to most observers "there was something dangerous and perhaps unprincipled in his bare throat and great Gothic head; and his somewhat massive person would doubtless have come out very oddly from the hands of a fashionable tailor of that time" (chapter 46). Compare the first description of Hollingsworth (*The Blithedale Romance*, chapter 4): "Hollingsworth's appearance was very striking at this moment. He was then about thirty years old, but looked several years older, with his great shaggy head, his heavy brow, his dark complexion, his abundant beard, and the rude strength with which his features seemed to have been hammered out of iron, rather than chiselled or moulded from any finer or softer material. His figure was not tall, but massive and brawny, and well befitting his original occupation . . . of a blacksmith."

The resemblances go beyond their "massive" and "shaggy" exteriors. Both are radicals and reformers, dedicated to causes — Hollingsworth to the reformation of criminals, Holt to the education of the working-classes. Both are generally brusque and abrupt in speech, but not insensitive or inhumane. Coverdale's comment about Hollingsworth, which follows the physical description, applies equally to Holt (whom Esther at first finds "coarse and rude") as he shows in his behaviour to his mother, and to Job Tudge: "As for external polish, or mere courtesy of manner, he never possessed more than a tolerably educated bear; although, in his gentler moods, there was a tenderness in his voice, eyes, mouth, in his gesture, and in every indescribable manifestation, which few men could resist. . . ." And again, like Hollingsworth, Felix Holt is "endowed with a great spirit of benevolence, deep enough and warm enough to be the source of . . . much disinterested good" (*The Blithedale Romance*, chapter 7). Lyon says of Felix, after their first meeting: " 'This is a singular young man. . . . I discover in him a love for whatsoever things are honest and true, which I would fain believe to be an earnest of further endowment with the wisdom that is from on high" (*Felix Holt*, chapter 5).

Hollingsworth is dehumanized by his devotion to the "cold, spectral monster", of which he has become "the bond-slave" — his "philanthropic theory." Quite similarly, Felix Holt rejects personal commitments, as dangerous to his chosen role of social reformer. He says to Esther (chapter 10): " 'That's what makes women a curse; all life is stunted to suit their littleness. That's why I'll never love, if I can help it; and if I love, I'll bear it and never marry.' " But before the riot, in which he accidentally kills a constable, he recognizes the danger of his own dehumanization. He tells Esther: " 'I know you think I am a man without feeling — at least without strong affections. You think I love nothing but my own resolutions' " (chapter 32). One is reminded of Zenobia's bitter accusation of Hollingsworth: " 'Are you a man? No; but a monster! A cold, heartless, self-beginning and self-ending piece of mechanism! . . . You have embodied yourself in a project' " (*The Blithedale Romance*, chapter 25).

It is, however, another character of *Felix Holt* who is most strongly reminiscent of one of Hawthorne's characters — Matthew Jermyn, Harold Transome's real father. To show how much Jermyn owes to Jaffrey Pyncheon it will be necessary only to quote a few passages.

> He was grey, but still remarkably handsome; fat, but tall enough to bear that trial to man's dignity. There was as strong a suggestion of toilette about him as if he had been five-and-twenty instead of nearly sixty. He chose always to dress in black, and was especially addicted to black satin waistcoats, which carried out the general sleekness of his appearance. . . . (*Felix Holt*, chapter 2).
>
> Mr. Jermyn had a copious supply of words, which often led him into periphrase, but he cultivated a hesitating stammer, which, with a handsome impassiveness of face, except when he was smiling at a woman, or when the latent savageness of his nature was thoroughly roused, he had found useful in many relations . . . (chapter 2).
>
> Jermyn had turned round his savage side, and the blandness was out of sight . . . there was a possibility of fierce insolence in this man (chapter 9).
>
> Jermyn was able and politic enough to have commanded a great deal of success in his life, but he could not help being handsome, arrogant, fond of being heard, indisposed to any kind of comradeship, amorous and bland towards women, cold and self-contained towards men (chapter 29).
>
> On the attorney's handsome face there was a black cloud of defiant determination. . . . No one was ever prepared before-hand for this expression of Jermyn's face, which seemed as strongly contrasted with the cold impenetrableness which he preserved under the ordinary annoyances of business as with the bland radiance of his lighter moments (chapter 35).

Compare with these passages from chapter 8 of *The House of the Seven Gables*.

> It was the portly, and, had it possessed the advantage of a little more height, would have been the stately figure of a man considerably in the decline of life, dressed in a black suit of some thin black stuff. . . . His dark, square countenance, with its almost shaggy depth of eyebrows, was naturally impressive, and would, perhaps, have been rather stern, had not the gentleman considerately taken upon himself to mitigate the harsh effect by a look of exceeding good humour and benevolence.
>
> On raising her eyes, Phoebe was startled by the change in Judge Pyncheon's face. It was quite as striking . . . as that betwixt a landscape under a broad sunshine, and just before a thunder-storm; not that it had the passionate intensity of the latter aspect, but was cold, hard, immitigable, like a day-long brooding cloud.

Like his Puritan ancestor, the Judge was "bold, imperious, relentless, crafty; laying his purposes deep, and following them out with an inveteracy of pursuit that knew neither rest nor conscience. ..."

> It was not pity that restrained him; for, at the first sound of the enfeebled voice, a red fire kindled in his eyes; and he made a quick pace forward, with something inexpressibly fierce and grim darkening forth, as it were, out of the whole man. To know Judge Pyncheon, was to see him at that moment. After such a revelation, let him smile with what sultriness he would, he could much sooner turn grapes purple, or pumpkins yellow, than melt the iron-branded impression out of the beholder's memory.

Jermyn is a slightly less formidable villain, but in his unscrupulousness, his rapacity, his gross materialism, his insensitivity, his "latent savageness" hidden by his "bland radiance", he seems like a modified version of the same essential character — as, indeed, his name seems to be a re-arrangement of the names of Jaffrey Pyncheon.

As well as these resemblances between characters of *Felix Holt* and characters of Hawthorne's romances, there are other aspects of George Eliot's novel which seem distinctly Hawthornesque — notably the constant use of mirrors as vehicles conveying the truth behind outer appearances. Mrs Transome standing "before a tall mirror, going close to it and looking at her face with hard scrutiny" (chapter 1), or "seated before the mirror apparently looking at herself, her brow knit in one deep furrow" in the fine clothes that are "only a smart shroud" (chapter 39), reminds one of Dimmesdale's vigils, "sometimes viewing his own face in a looking-glass, by the most powerful light which he could throw upon it" (*The Scarlet Letter*, chapter 11), or of Hilda seeing in her reflected image the expression of Beatrice di Cenci in her copy of Guido's painting (*The Marble Faun*, chapter 23).

Other images seem like echoes of Hawthorne. For example, Mrs Transome's "hungry desire that her first, rickety, ugly imbecile child should die" is "like a black poisonous plant feeding in the sunlight" (chapter 1), reminding of the prevalent weed imagery of *The Scarlet Letter* — of the weeds with dark flabby leaves which Chillingworth collects in the grave-yard (chapter 10), and of Chillingworth himself, who, after Dimmesdale's death "shrivelled away ... like an uprooted weed that lies wilting in the sun" (chapter 24). Also very reminiscent of Hawthorne is the image describing Mrs Transome's bondage to Harold (chapter 8): "The finest threads, such as no eye sees, if bound cunningly about the sensitive flesh, so that the movement to break them would bring torture, may make a worse bondage than any fetters." (Compare "The bands that were silken once are apt to become iron fetters when we desire to shake them off", *The Blithedale Romance*, chapter 23). Similar poetic images, not quite so directly traceable to Hawthorne, but still with "the scent of the Hawthorne bough", abound. Mrs Transome has "a woman's keen sensibility and dread, which lay screened behind all her petty habits and narrow notions, as some quivering thing with eyes and throbbing heart may lie crouching behind withered rubbish" (chapter 1). "She felt as if she were lighting a torch to flare on her own past folly and misery" (chapter 9). "All around her, where there had once been brightness and warmth, there were white ashes, and the sunshine looked dreary as it fell on them" (chapter 9).

I have suggested that George Eliot, when she was aware of a literary indebtedness, often made some kind of acknowledgment — often by the use of epigraphs. A little surprisingly she did not use Hawthorne as a source of epigraphs. But I wonder whether Felix's rather awkwardly introduced reference to the pilgrim fathers (chapter 5) was a covert acknowledgment of some indebtedness to Hawthorne? When Felix, at their first meeting, says to Esther: " 'Ask your father what those old persecuted emigrant Puritans would have done with fine-lady wives and daughters' ", was she remembering, and expecting some of her readers to remember, what the Puritans did to Hester Prynne, and what Colonel Pyncheon did to his three wives?

Hawthorne's Influence in *Middlemarch* and *Deronda*

From "Amos Barton" to *Romola* George Eliot's fictional works followed one another in rapid succession — five books in half-a-dozen years. But after the exhausting effort of writing *Romola*, it was two years before George Eliot could begin her next novel, *Felix Holt*, which was completed in mid-1866; there was then a longer gap of about three years before she began work on what was to be her greatest novel, *Middlemarch*, which was completed in October, 1872. It was another three years before she started to write her last novel, *Daniel Deronda*, which is usually considered to contain the best and the worst of George Eliot. I have suggested that the Hawthorne influence is less apparent in *Felix Holt*, the first novel written after Hawthorne's death, than in the preceding novels; in *Middlemarch* and *Daniel Deronda* the Hawthornean recollections became even fainter, but do not entirely disappear.

I have mentioned that *Middlemarch* is one of the three novels of George Eliot selected by Ellin Jane Ringler for comparative treatment with three of Hawthorne's romances; but it seems to me that there are much closer and more direct connections between the members of the other pairs — *The Scarlet Letter* and *Adam Bede; The Marble Faun* and *Romola* — than between *The House of the Seven Gables* and *Middlemarch*. Dr Ringler does not claim that *Middlemarch* was influenced by *The House of the Seven Gables*. What she does claim is that

> for both artists the problem of evil is inextricably connected with man's struggle to free himself from time; from his own immediate past, from the more indirect influences of his ancestry, or from the determinants of his social history. No novel that Hawthorne wrote ever treated this theme more insistently than *The House of the Seven Gables*. None that Elliot composed dealt with it so fully or so unsparingly as *Middlemarch*." She maintains further that "a comparison of these two books, as they treat man's past, reveals with new clarity the underlying similarities between Hawthorne and Eliot — their parallel concerns and comparable approaches to certain themes. . . .[187]

These claims, I think, are justified.

It could be argued that *Middlemarch* is, to a large extent, whether George Eliot was aware of it or not (as I have previously argued that *Our Mutual Friend* is, to a large extent, whether Dickens was aware of it or not) an elaborate working out of ideas about the paralyzing and distorting effects of the past expressed by Holgrave in *The House of the Seven Gables* (chapter 12): " 'Just think, a moment; and it will startle you to see what slaves we are to by-gone times — to Death, if we give the matter the right word! . . . a Dead Man, if he happens to have made a will, disposes of wealth no longer his own. . . . Whatever we seek to do, of our own free motion, a Dead Man's icy hand obstructs us!' " The will of Peter Featherstone, which denies Fred Vincy the affluence he has been encouraged to expect, and the codicil to the will of Edward Casaubon, which disinherits his wife, Dorothea, if she marries Will Ladislaw, are, of course, of great importance in *Middlemarch*; but it would be going altogether too far to suggest that Dorothea is obstructed by the icy hand of her dead husband, *because of* the passage in Hawthorne. But it is, I think, legitimate to wonder whether the passage quoted contributed at all to George Eliot's titling book 5 "The Dead Hand", or to her comment about Peter Featherstone "chuckling over the vexations he could inflict by the rigid clutch of his dead hand" (chapter 24).

More important is the question of whether Holgrave, the rebellious fulminator against the past, the radical who is converted to conservatism when he marries Phoebe Pyncheon, contributed anything to Will Ladislaw. I think that there are enough similarities between the two young men to make it likely. The similarities have been fully catalogued by Ellin Ringler, whose lengthy discussion I briefly summarize.

Both are "free spirits", without roots, who try to deny or escape from their family past — restless aliens without home, vocation, or established place in the social order. Throughout most of *The House of the Seven Gables* Holgrave's origins are mysterious; it is only in the last chapter that he reveals that he is the last descendant of Matthew Maule, the dispossessed owner of the land on which his virtual murderer, the first New England Pyncheon, built the house of the seven gables. Will Ladislaw's origins are scarcely less so; it is only gradually that we learn that his grandmother (Casaubon's mother's sister — name unknown) made an "unfortunate marriage", presumably with Dunkirk, a wealthy pawn-broker and receiver of stolen goods, that their daughter, Sarah Dunkirk, ran away from home, went on the stage and married a Pole named Ladislaw (and that subsequently Will's grandmother, Casaubon's aunt, married Nicholas Bulstrode — who, after his first wife's death, married Harriet Vincy). Holgrave cuts himself off from his family past by adopting an assumed name; all he inherits from the Maules is knowledge of the secret spring which moves the Colonel's portrait to reveal the hidden recess containing the ancient deed to a vast tract of Maine land. Will Ladislaw repudiates his family connections by terminating the allowance he has received from Casaubon, and by refusing Bulstrode's proffered reparation.

Holgrave, though not yet twenty-two, has already been a country schoolmaster, a store salesman, political editor of a country-newspaper, a dentist, a European traveller, a member of a Fourierist community, a lecturer on mesmerism, and is now a daguerrotypist. Ladislaw, supported financially by his second cousin, Casaubon, is educated at Rugby, but refuses to go to an English university, and takes what Casaubon regards as "the anomalous course of studying at Heidelberg", and then goes abroad again, declining to choose a profession, "without any special object, save the vague purpose of what he calls culture" (*Middlemarch*, chapter 9). When he refuses further support from Casaubon, he becomes Mr Brooke's general assistant, mainly as editor of the Middlemarch *Pioneer*, in which he takes "very high ground on reform" (chapter 37).

As Will is a rather dilettantish dabbler in various arts — poetry and painting — so Holgrave has tried his hand at writing stories for the magazines. Both are, as Ellin Ringler remarks, "rather vaguely involved in liberal and progressive political movements"; "struggling against the restrictions of time, class, wealth and position" they "seem to embody the principles of liberty and progress".[188]

Perhaps the resemblance between the two (and the suggestion of partial derivation of one from the other) is strongest in the imagery of sunshine and brightness and youth which is associated with both. Holgrave, of course, uses sunshine to make his pictures. And despite his premature experience of life he has not lost "that beautiful spirit of youth, which, gushing forth from one small heart and fancy, may diffuse itself over the universe, making it all as bright as on the first day of creation. . . . He had that sense, or inward prophecy . . . that, this very hour, there are the harbingers abroad of a golden era." He has, and would retain "faith in man's brightening destiny" (*The House of the Seven Gables*, chapter 12). Will Ladislaw's smile was "a gush of inward light illuminating the transparent skin as well as the eyes as if some Ariel were touching them with a new charm" (*Middlemarch*, chapter 21). After his marriage to Dorothea he becomes "an ardent public man, working well in those times when reforms were begun with a young hopefulness of immediate good. . . ." ("Finale").

Despite the difficulties of their lives, and the distorting pressures from the past, both have preserved their identity and integrity. But in both cases there is the danger that their gipsy-like quality, their scornful, iconoclastic attitudes towards obsolete and decaying social institutions, could sputter out in futile meaninglessness. Of Holgrave, Hawthorne remarks: "His career it would be difficult to prefigure. There appeared to be qualities in Holgrave such as . . . could hardly fail to put some of the world's prizes within his reach. But . . . at almost every step in life, we meet with young men . . . for whom we anticipate wonderful things, but of whom . . . we never happen to hear another word. The effervescence of youth and passion, and the fresh gloss of the intellect and the imagination, endow them with a false brilliancy, which makes fools of themselves and other people" (chapter 12). George Eliot expresses similar doubts about Will Ladislaw's future, in a long paragraph concerned with "Will's generous reliance on the intentions of the universe with regard to himself"; she remarks that "the world is full of hopeful analogies and handsome dubious eggs called possibilities"; and despatches him to the continent "without . . . pronouncing on his future. Among all forms of mistake, prophecy is the most gratuitous" (chapter 10).

What the future holds for both is marriage; and the two marriages — Holgrave to Phoebe; Will to Dorothea — have a very similar representative significance. H.H. Waggoner's comment on the marriage of Holgrave and Phoebe, as Ellin Ringer suggests, applies almost equally to the marriage of Will and Dorothea. "The marriage of Phoebe and Holgrave . . . is a marriage of conservative and radical, of heart and head. Woman is the conserver and the conservative, man the speculator whose thoughts may undermine even that which is most sacred, even the hearth and altar. The marriage of Phoebe and Holgrave . . . at least theoretically, preserves some sort of balance between the two attitudes".[189]

There seem to be sufficiently striking similarities between Holgrave and Ladislaw in temperament, attitudes, situation, and life-pattern — and in their creators' ironically qualified admiration of their heroes — to make it likely that one is to some degree — derived from the other. I am less convinced by Ellin Ringler's pairing of other characters. She detects a strong similarity between Bulstrode and Jaffrey Pyncheon. She is, no doubt, right in remarking that "Both men are elderly philanthropists whose benevolent actions hide past evils and whose destinies . . . portray the implacable working-out of Nemesis".[190] But beyond this very general resemblance, I see no similarity between the coarse-grained materialist Jaffrey, whose beamingly radiant smile is such a transparent mask to his arrogance and ruthless egotism, and the sickly Bulstrode, who is no simple, conscienceless hypocrite; and George Eliot's compassionate understanding of Bulstrode is very different from Hawthorne's contemptuous hatred of Jaffrey. If any of George Eliot's characters closely resembles Jaffrey it is, as I have previously argued, not Bulstrode, but Matthew Jermyn, in *Felix Holt*.

Nor do I detect much real likeness between Mary Garth and Phoebe Pyncheon. True, they are both "nice little housewives", and have both been schoolmistresses. But Mary Garth's most attractive quality is the teasing sharpness of wit, directed mainly against her lover, Fred Vincy, which (like her plainness) is far more reminiscent of Jane Eyre than of Phoebe.

The character and the relationship in *Middlemarch* which seem to me to have most certainly been suggested by Hawthorne are Casaubon and his relationship with Dorothea; the source, of course, is not *The House of the Seven Gables*, but *The Scarlet Letter*.

It is worth recalling that George Eliot began work on *Middlemarch* on August 2, 1869, but six weeks later she was not feeling confident she could "make anything satisfactory of *Middlemarch*". The next thing we know of George Eliot's fiction is her note on December 2, 1870: "I am experimenting in a story ("Miss Brooke") which I began without any intention of carrying it out lengthily. It is a subject which has been recorded among my possible themes ever since I began to write fiction".[191] It was not until several months later that she decided to combine the two in one long novel.

Robert K. Wallace has recently detected "one probable literary ingredient in the imaginative process that resulted in Dorothea and Casaubon which has not previously been noted: the early relationship between Hester and Roger Prynne in Hawthorne's *The Scarlet Letter*.[192] Wallace quotes George Eliot's note, points out that George Eliot did not spell out this "subject", but contends that it was "very probably the relationship between Dorothea and Casaubon". He suggests that the fact that it was a subject recorded as a possible theme at the beginning of George

Eliot's fictional career "points to the very months of 1857 when she was re-reading Hawthorne's sketch of the relationship between the young Hester and her scholar-husband", and maintains that "if her subject was not influenced by Hawthorne's the coincidence is a stunning one".[193]

In his brief essay Wallace presents some, but by no means all, of the evidence that the Dorothea–Casaubon relationship is an elaborated re-treatment of the Hester–Chillingworth relationship. There is, indeed, so much evidence of George Eliot's indebtedness that it is extraordinary that it remained unnoticed (or at least unnoted) for more than a century. When, in the paragraph introducing Casaubon, we learn that he has "the spare form and the pale complexion which became a student", and when, in his first utterance in the novel, he remarks: " 'I have been using up my eyesight on old characters lately . . . I find it necessary to use the utmost caution about my eyesight' " (*Middlemarch*, chapter 2), we may be immediately reminded of Hester Prynne's recollection, as she stands on the scaffold, of the "countenance, of a man well stricken in years, a pale, thin, scholar-like visage, with eyes dim and bleared by the lamp-light that had served them to pore over many ponderous books" (*The Scarlet Letter*, chapter 1). If not, then perhaps recollections of Chillingworth may begin to stir when Casaubon, walking with Dorothea, mentions "to her that he felt the disadvantage of loneliness, the need of that cheerful companionship with which the presence of youth can lighten or vary the serious toils of maturity" (*Middlemarch*, chapter 3), or when having proposed, in his excruciatingly ponderous letter, and been accepted by Dorothea, he tells her (chapter 5) " 'You have all — nay, more than all — those qualities which I have ever regarded as the characteristic excellences of womanhood. The great charm of your sex is its capability of an ardent self-sacrificing affection, and hence we see its fitness to round and complete the existence of our own. Hitherto I have known few pleasures save of the severer kind: my satisfactions have been those of the solitary student. I have been little disposed to gather flowers that would wither in my hand, but now I shall pluck them with eagerness, to place them in your bosom' ", or when George Eliot tells us (chapter 7) that Casaubon had "made up his mind that it was now time for him to adorn his life with the graces of female companionship, to irradiate the gloom which fatigue was apt to hang over the intervals of studious labour with the play of female fancy, and to secure in this, his culminating age, the solace of female tendance for his declining years. Hence he determined to abandon himself to the stream of feelings, and perhaps was surprised to find what an exceedingly shallow rill it was."

In *The Scarlet Letter*, of course, there is no account of Chillingworth's courtship of Hester, or of Hester's motives in agreeing to marry him (though, unlike Dorothea, Hester, as she reminds Chillingworth, "felt no love, nor feigned any"). All we are given is Chillingworth's account of what manner of man he was, and of what he hoped for from his marriage with Hester (an account to which Hester assents): " 'All my life had been made up of earnest, studious, thoughtful, quiet years, bestowed faithfully for the increase of mine own knowledge, and, faithfully, too, though this latter object was but casual to the other, — faithfully for the advancement of human welfare . . . was I not, though you might deem me cold, nevertheless a man thoughtful for others, craving little for himself, — kind, true, just, and of constant, if not warm affections?' " (chapter 14). " 'But up to that epoch of my life, I had lived in vain. The world had been so cheerless! My heart was a habitation large enough for many guests, but lonely and chill, and without a household fire. I longed to kindle one! It seemed not so wild a dream . . . that the simple bliss, which is scattered far and wide, for all mankind to gather up, might yet be mine" (chapter 4).

One may feel that Chillingworth considerably magnifies his own capacity for affection. But otherwise the account of his own nature and pre-marital state is obviously very similar to the view of Casaubon that emerges in *Middlemarch*. Though Hester assents to his version of his former self, in the prison interview (chapter 4), seven years later, after the interview on the sea-shore, she recognizes that the reality of their marriage was very different, that Chillingworth had not "drawn her into his heart, into its innermost chamber." Upbraiding herself for hatred that she now feels for Chillingworth for his diabolical torturing of Dimmesdale, she attempts to overcome the sentiment by thinking of their life together; her recollections are very like a summary of the married life of the Casaubons: "She thought of those long-past days, in a distant land, when he used to emerge at eventide from the seclusion of his study, and sit down in the fire-light of their home, and in the light of her nuptial smile. He needed to bask himself in that smile, he said, in order that the chill of so many lonely hours among his books might be taken off the scholar's heart" (chapter 15). George Eliot almost reproduces the last sentence in the already-quoted comment that Casaubon felt it was "time for him to adorn his life with the graces of female companionship, to irradiate the gloom which was apt to hang over the intervals of studious labour with the play of female fancy" and also in Casaubon's own remark, during the ghastly honeymoon in Rome: " 'The task . . . has been a somewhat laborious one, but your society has happily prevented me from that too continuous prosecution of thought beyond the hours of study which has been the snare of my solitary life' " (chapter 20). Surely the similarity is too great to be merely coincidental?

It is only after Hester has come to hate Chillingworth that her married life with him, which seemed happy enough at the time, seems in retrospect utterly repugnant. To Dorothea, in contrast, shortly before Casaubon's death, her marriage has come to seem utterly repugnant — a tomb or a prison; and, momentarily at least, she comes very close to hating Casaubon, for his repeated repulsion and exclusion of her.

> And just as clearly in the miserable light she saw her own and her husband's solitude — how they walked apart so that she was obliged to survey him. If he had drawn her towards him, she would never have surveyed him — never have said, "Is he worth living for?" but would have felt him simply a part of her own life. Now she said bitterly, "It is his own fault, not mine." In the jar of her whole being, Pity was overthrown. Was it her fault that she had believed in him — had believed in his worthiness? — And what, exactly, was he? — She was able enough to estimate him — she who waited on his glances with trembling, and shut her best soul in prison, paying it only hidden visits, that she might be petty enough to please him. In such a crisis as this, some women begin to hate. . . . Her anger said, as anger is apt to say, that God was with her — that all heaven, though it were crowded with spirits watching them, must be on her side (*Middlemarch*, chapter 42).

This passage is, it seems to me, quite similar to the passage in *The Scarlet Letter* describing Hester's revulsion from her marriage, which continues:

> Such scenes had once appeared not otherwise than happy, but now, as viewed through the dismal medium of her subsequent life, they classed themselves among her ugliest remembrances. She marvelled how such

scenes could have been! She marvelled how she could ever have been wrought upon to marry him! She deemed it her crime most to be repented of, that she had ever endured, and reciprocated, the lukewarm grasp of his hand, and had suffered the smile of her lips and eyes to mingle and melt into his own. And it seemed a fouler offence committed by Roger Chillingworth, than any which she had ever done him, that, in the time when her heart knew no better, he had persuaded her to fancy herself happy by his side.

The difference is that there is in Hester's revulsion a strong element of sexual repugnance, frustration and dissatisfaction, a sense of unnatural violation by cold near-impotence. Chillingworth, in the prison interview, indeed admits " 'Mine was the first wrong, when I betrayed thy budding youth into a false and unnatural relation with my decay' " (*The Scarlet Letter*, chapter 4). And Hawthorne, after Hester's bitter reflection " 'Yes, I hate him!. . . He betrayed me! He has done me worse wrong that I did him!' ", intervenes with authorial comment: "Let men tremble to win the hand of woman, unless they win along with it the utmost passion of her heart! Else it may be their miserable fortune, as it was Roger Chillingworth's, when some mightier touch than their own may have awakened all her sensibilities, to be reproached even for the calm content, the marble image of happiness, which they will have imposed upon her as the warm reality."

George Eliot is never quite as explicit as this about the element of sexual unfulfilment in Dorothea's revulsion from Casaubon (whose sallowness and white moles Celia finds so repulsive). But already in Rome there are some pretty clear indications:

> With all her yearning to know what was afar from her and to be widely benignant, she had ardour enough for what was near, to have kissed Mr Casaubon's coat-sleeve, or to have caressed his shoe-latchet, if he would have made any other sign of acceptance than pronouncing her, with unfailing propriety, to be of a most affectionate and truly feminine nature, indicating at the same time by politely reaching a chair for her that he regarded these manifestations as rather crude and startling. Having made his clerical toilette with due care in the morning, he was prepared only for those amenities of life which were suited to the well-adjusted stiff cravat of the period, and to a mind weighted with unpublished matter (chapter 20).

And on the return of the Casaubons to Lowick, the sexual disillusionment of Dorothea (who is already in love with Will Ladislaw, though she has not admitted it to herself, and indeed is unaware of it) is subtly, and probably unconsciously, conveyed through the descriptive imagery:

> A light snow was falling as they descended at the door, and in the morning, when Dorothea passed from her dressing-room into the blue-green boudoir . . . she saw the long avenue of limes lifting their trunks from a white earth, and spreading white branches against the dim and motionless sky. The distant flat shrank in uniform whiteness and low-hanging uniformity of cloud. The very furniture in the room seemed to have shrunk since she saw it before: the stag in the tapestry looked more like a ghost in this ghostly blue-green world; the volumes of polite literature in the bookcase looked more like immovable imitations of books (chapter 28).

James McAuley, in an illuminating essay which examines similarities between the Casaubon–Dorothea–Ladislaw strand of *Middlemarch* and the Malbecco–Hellenore–Sir Paridell story in book 3 of *The Faerie Queene*, perceptively comments: "The complete passage is an extraordinary evocation of disenchantment, of a withering and shrinking world, of a chill cast upon vitality. It is enough in itself to dispose of the charge that there is no poetry in the work. Not only is this passage poetic both in method and in result: it is so in a Spenserian way, creating a psychic landscape with figures that are meaningful for the inner life of passion and desire and dread."[194]

There are important differences, but it seems to me that the characters and the developing situations — the marriage of an ardent, passionate, young woman, "glowing with girlish beauty", to a cold, self-centred, essentially misogynistic and probably impotent elderly scholar; the wife's disillusioned recognition that she has entombed herself alive; the husband's vindictive hatred of the young rival who awakens the wife's sensibilities — are so essentially similar, that George Eliot's debt to Hawthorne can hardly be doubted.

In *Daniel Deronda*, written more than a decade after the death of George Eliot's "grand favourite", I find least evidence of Hawthorne's influence. I have, however, previously quoted a paragraph from *The Hero in Eclipse* in which Mario Praz remarked, of Gwendolen Harleth, that "the consciousness of evil, of having contributed to, if not actually caused, the drowning of the odious Grandcourt, was to act in her as a leaven of redemption, in much the same way as in one of Hawthorne's characters." There is certainly some general resemblance between the situation and moral development of Gwendolen and those of characters of *The Marble Faun*.

Gwendolen, sailing in the small boat off Genoa with the husband whom she has come to loathe, and whom she has often murdered in fantasy, suffers an abeyance of will (or the momentary assertion of the will to preserve herself and destroy her enemy) which prevents her from throwing the rope which might possibly have saved the drowning Grandcourt. This is distinctly reminiscent of the moment in *The Marble Faun* when Donatello, holding Miriam's persecutor over the precipice, sees in Miriam's eyes (in Hilda's words) "a look of hatred, and triumph, vengeance, and as it were, joy at some unasked-for relief" and flings the model to his death. There is, of course, no one present to read the expression in Gwendolen's eyes, but her own broken account to Deronda (chapter 56) suggests the same mingling of emotions.

The marital situation of the Grandcourts, which culminates in Grandcourt's death, however, has little resemblance to *The Marble Faun*. It is, indeed, in some ways reminiscent rather of Dickens, especially of *Dombey and Son*. (Grandcourt's use of Lush, from whom Gwendolen has a strong aversion, as his agent and emissary in conveying to Gwendolen the provisions of his will, is very similar to Dombey's use of the hatred Carker as an intermediary to humiliate his wife.)

There is one important element, or strain of imagery, in *Daniel Deronda* which I, rather tentatively, suggest may have come from Hawthorne — not from *The Marble Faun*, but from *The House of the Seven Gables*. This is the image of the dead face. It is encountered first in the hidden picture at Offendene, from which Gwendolen recoils in dread: "The opened panel had disclosed the picture of an upturned dead face, from which an obscure figure seemed to be fleeing with outstretched arms" (chapter 3). A few months later, at the climax of the tableau from *The Winter's Tale*, the panel flies open disclosing "the picture of the dead face and the fleeing figure" (chapter 6), and reducing Gwendolen to "a statue into which a soul of Fear had entered." After her marriage to Grandcourt, this picture is assimilated into Gwendolen's sleeping and waking dreams of dread and murder and guilt — for example in chapter 54: "But in no concealment had she now any confidence: her vision of what she had to dread took more decidedly than ever the form of some fiercely impulsive deed, committed as in a dream that she would instantaneously wake from to find the effects real though the images had been false: to find death under her hands, but instead of darkness, daylight; instead of a satisfied hatred, the dismay of guilt; instead of freedom, the palsy of a new terror — a white dead face from which she was for ever trying to flee and for ever held back."

The picture and the dream are actualized in Grandcourt's death: " 'I was leaping away from myself — I would have saved him then. I was leaping from my crime, and there it was close to me as I fell — there was the dead face — dead, dead. It can never be altered' " (chapter 56).

I have suggested the possibility that the theme, in *Middlemarch*, of the dead's repressive control of the living, may have been an unconscious development of one sentence in Holgrave's fulmination against the past: " 'Whatever we seek to do of our own free motion, a Dead Man's icy hand obstructs us!' " I now suggest the possibility that the motif, in *Daniel Deronda*, of the dead face, may have been another case of unconscious lodgement, and that it derives from the immediately succeeding sentence in *The House of the Seven Gables* (chapter 12): " 'Turn our eyes to what point we may, a Dead Man's white immitigable face encounters them, and freezes our very heart!' " It seems to me that there are sufficiently strong verbal resemblance between this sentence and the quoted passages from *Daniel Deronda* to suggest that Hawthorne's (or Holgrave's) striking image lodged itself in George Eliot's mind to be developed many years later, giving an extra dimension to Gwendolen's temperament and experience.

Even if this conjecture is dismissed as fanciful, there remains, I would contend, a great deal of solid evidence of Hawthorne's influence in *Scenes of Clerical Life*, *Adam Bede*, *The Mill on the Floss*, *Silas Marner*, *Romola*, *Felix Holt* and *Middlemarch*.

Notes

General Introduction

1. Albert J. Guerard, *The Triumph of the Novel: Dickens, Dostoevsky, Faulkner* (New York, 1976), p. 5.
2. George H. Ford, *Dickens and His Readers: Aspects of Novel Criticism Since 1836* (Princeton, N.J., 1955), p. 220.
3. Ibid., p. 210.
4. Ibid., p. 224.
5. Richard Chase, *The American Novel and its Tradition* (New York, 1957).
6. Nicolaus Mills, "American Fiction and the Genre Critics", *Novel* 2, 2 (Fall, 1969): 112.
7. Northrop Frye, *Anatomy of Criticism* (Princetown, N.J., 1957), pp. 304–5. Frye's earlier version of "Specific Continuous Forms (Prose Fiction)" had appeared as "The Four Forms of Prose Fiction" in *Hudson Review* 2 (Winter 1950): 582–95.
8. Gillian Beer, *The Romance* (London, 1970), p. 10.
9. F.R. Leavis, *The Great Tradition: George Eliot, Henry James, Joseph Conrad* (London, 1948), p. 38.
10. "I am almost ready to characterize Hardy (if he must be 'placed') as an American whose ancestors failed to migrate at the proper time and who accordingly found himself stranded, a couple of centuries later, in the wrong literary climate". Donald Davidson, "The Traditional Basis of Thomas Hardy's Fiction", in *Hardy, A Collection of Critical Essays*, ed. Albert J. Guerard (Englewood Cliffs, N.J., 1963), p. 10.

Part I

1. "Dickens and Hawthorne", in *Essex Institute Historical Collections (Special Hawthorne Issue)*, 100 (Oct. 1964): 258.
2. Randall Stewart, *Nathaniel Hawthorne: A Biography* (New Haven, 1948), pp. 105, 168.
3. See Chaudhry, "Dickens and Hawthorne", p. 259.
4. Quoted by Chaudhry, "Dickens and Hawthorne", p. 260.
5. Chaudhry notes that "a letter of acceptance exists from Hawthorne to the committee in charge of the gala public dinner given . . . in Boston in 1842 to celebrate Dickens' first visit to America. But no contemporary mention is made of Hawthorne's actual attendance, nor does he himself seem ever to have referred to it . . ." ("Dickens and Hawthorne", p. 257).
6. Letter published in *The Critic*, 1885, quoted by Chaudhry, "Dickens and Hawthorne", p. 257.

7. *Heroines of Fiction* (London and New York, 1901), I, p. 161.
8. Letter in *Proceedings on the One Hundredth Anniversary of the Birth of Nathaniel Hawthorne, Essex Institute Historical Collections* 41 (Jan. 1905), p. 74.
9. In a recent article, "The House and the Railroad: *Dombey and Son* and *The House of the Seven Gables*" (*The New England Quarterly*, 51, March 1978, pp. 3-22), Jonathan Arac juxtaposes the two novels in order to "begin to elucidate much of the literary history shared by England and America in the nineteenth-century". Arac, while not going into "problems of influence", and pointing out that "only in 1850 does evidence appear for [Hawthorne's] reading *Dombey and Son*", (n3) maintains that "considered as social fables, the two novels extraordinarily resemble each other in their organization of material" (p. 3).
    Arac summarizes the resemblances in these terms:

    > Both confront a proud, established family, the Dombeys and the Pyncheons, with a society in the turmoil of transition, and both show that the family's fate is to change with society. In both novels Society and Family are symbolized by an ancestral house and the new railroad. Each ends with the last female of the old family making a mismatch, giving up her proud name to marry a man of lower social origin who has had adventures in the wide world, participated in that new mobility associated with the railroad. Acknowledging this common technical and ideological content allows us to examine English and American literature — in this case Dickens and Hawthorne — in finer comparison than is possible through nationalist approaches, whether through the American 'romance' or the English 'Great Tradition' (pp. 3-4).

    In his book *The Metaphysical Novel in England and America: Dickens, Bulwer, Hawthorne, Melville* (University of California Press, 1978), Edwin M. Eigner suggests the possible influence on *The House of the Seven Gables* of a Dickens novel that Hawthorne had certainly read:

    > Another influence can be found in *The Old Curiosity Shop*, where a similar theme pertains: bright innocence, threatened by the gloomy, grotesque, materialistic world, ultimately overthrows or redeems it, by virtue not of her actions, but of her essence. In both works a pathetic old person who makes a failure out of keeping a prosaic shop could not survive without the heroine's cheerful and responsible aid. In both works a rightful heir is locked away. And in both, a materialistic relative, Jaffrey and Fred, threatens the sympathetic, more spiritual characters because he has deluded himself into the mistaken notion that they are rich. Jaffrey has also a source in Quilp especially in the scene where the latter makes sexual advances on Nell. Each villain, moreover, is developed in terms of the worldly serpent metaphor, and each heroine is almost literally an angel (p. 150).

10. *The Life of Charles Dickens*, II (London, 1876), p. 72.
11. "Dickens and Hawthorne", n260.
12. *Life of Dickens*, II, p. 72.
13. Not, at least, in a published work. But since making this claim to priority I have seen Harry Lionel Knight's unpublished dissertation, "Dickens and American Literature" (Brown University, 1972). Knight's chapter "Dickens and Hawthorne" is concerned mainly with comparative assessment of the social and intellectual values of the two writers, as illustrated particularly in the contrast between *The Scarlet Letter* and *Edwin Drood*, and between the fire-tenders in "Ethan Brand" and *The Old Curiosity Shop*. The chapter ends, however, with three paragraphs (pp. 129-30) of which the first stresses the differences between the novelist, Dickens, and the romancer, Hawthorne; the second recognises that this contrast applies only to Dickens' earlier work, and the last tentatively suggests that Hawthorne's work may have made some contribution to the change in Dickens.

These differing world views, reflecting differing national experiences, gave rise to very different literary structures. Dickens was the great genius of the novel. His focus on society is realised by creating a paper world so real, materially and emotionally, that the reader seems to know his way about and becomes quickly committed. Hawthorne was the pioneer of the romance. His art needed a form that would free the dissected soul from the trappings of social realism.

Hawthorne's romance was a new art form in America; in England, as well, during the first half of the nineteenth century, there was nothing like Hawthorne's romance (with the possible exception of Emily Bronte's *Wuthering Heights*). Hawthorne's 'romance' cannot however, be consistently contrasted with Dickens' 'realistic didactic novel' because the later Dickens (*Bleak House, Hard Times, Little Dorrit, Great Expectations, Our Mutual Friend, Edwin Drood*) shows signs of an artistic transition. There is a heightened symbolism in these late novels and a growing moral relativism. The interest becomes ever less to show the way and ever more to illuminate the heart. This is the kind of art which Hawthorne was creating in America while Dickens was writing in England. Probably Dickens was reading Hawthorne's much-circulated novels.

Hawthorne must be seen as a major innovator in the literature of the English language, influencing not only the development of American literature but also of English literature. Could not his work have had some role in the transition from early to late Dickens as well?

14.   *A Bibliography of Nathaniel Hawthorne* (Boston and New York, 1905).

15.   *Hawthorne's Contemporaneous Reputation* (Philadelphia, 1939).

16.   "Hawthorne's Twice-Told Tales", *Arcturus a Journal of Books and Opinion* 3 (April 1842): 394.

17.   "Literary Notices and Criticism", *Boston Quarterly Review* 5 (April 1842): 251-52.

18.   "The Works of Hawthorne", *Universalist Quarterly and General Review* 8 (July 1851): 290.

19.   *Illustrations of Genius* (Boston, 1854), p. 84.

20.   "Modern Novelists — Great and Small", *Blackwood's Magazine* 77 (May 1855): 649-52.

21.   "Nathaniel Hawthorne", *Independent* 41 (26 September 1889): 1237-38; reprinted in *Adventures Among Books* (London, 1905).

22.   "Hawthorne's *Scarlet Letter*", *North American Review* 71 (July 1850): 139.

23.   "Nathaniel Hawthorne", *Southern Literary Messenger* 17 (June 1851): 347; reprinted in *Mental Portraits* (London, 1853).

24.   "*The House of the Seven Gables*", *Graham's Magazine* 38 (June 1851): 468.

25.   "Schediasns", *The Knickerbocker* 40 (November 1852): 382.

26.   "Nathaniel Hawthorne", *To-Day: A Boston Literary Journal* 2 (18 September 1852): 177.

27.   "Nathaniel Hawthorne", *Universal Review* 3 (June 1860): 761.

28.   "Hawthorne", *Christian Examiner* 78 (January 1865): 91.

29.   "Poe and Hawthorne", *The Galaxy* 6 (December 1868): 745.

30.   "American Novelists: III. Nathaniel Hawthorne", *Belgravia* 19 (November 1872): 78-79.

31.   *To-Day* 2 (18 September 1852): 178.

32.   "The Supernatural in Hawthorne", *The Overland Monthly* 2 (February 1869): 139.

33.   "The Romances of Nathaniel Hawthorne", *Westminster Review* 142 (August 1894): 211-12.

34. "The Tales of Poe and Hawthorne", *New England Magazine* 30 (August 1904): 692.
35. "The Questionable Shapes of Nathaniel Hawthorne", *Littell's Living Age* 242 (6 August 1904): 353.
36. "Poe, Irving, and Hawthorne", *Scribner's Monthly* 11 (April 1876): 802.
37. *Heroines of Fiction*, I, p. 190.
38. "Hawthorne's Place in Literature", in *Hawthorne Centenary Celebration at the Wayside* (Boston and New York, 1905), p. 58.
39. *The Life and Genius of Nathaniel Hawthorne* (Philadelphia and London, 1906), p. 124.
40. Ibid., p. 430.
41. "Studies of Prominent Novelists: No. 5 — Nathaniel Hawthorne", *Book News* 6 (February 1888): 261.
42. *Independent* 41 (26 September 1889): 1238; (*Adventures among Books*, p. 220). In *Independent* "intersect" is misprinted as "interest".
43. *Heroines of Fiction*, I, p. 162. Quoting the sentence, "Romance, as in Hawthorne . . .; romanticism as in Dickens. . . ."; Edwin M. Eigner comments: "This sounds like a meaningful distinction between the two writers , but it will not hold up for anything but the early works of Hawthorne." Quoting Howells' distinction between Dickens' "types" and Hawthorne's "persons", Eigner remarks that "one has trouble, certainly Dickens did, trying to read any of Hawthorne's allegorical figures as 'persons, rounded, whole,' and, except in, perhaps, *The Scarlet Letter* and in some of the stories the worlds of Hawthorne seem no less and no more real than those of Dickens" (*The Metaphysical Novel in England and America*, p. 149).
44. *Dickens, Money and Society* (Berkeley and Los Angeles, 1968), p. 26.
45. F.R. and Q.D. Leavis, *Dickens the Novelist* (London, 1970), p. 166.
46. Ibid., p. 292.
47. Ibid., pp. 292-93.
48. Ibid., p. 292.
49. "*Bleak House* and *The Scarlet Letter*", *AUMLA* 32 (November 1969): 177-89.
50. "Dickens and Hawthorne", 256-61.
51. Ibid., pp. 261-67.
52. Ibid., pp. 269, 271.
53. Ibid., pp. 271-72.
54. Quoted by Arlin Turner, *Nathaniel Hawthorne: An Introduction and Interpretation* (New York, 1961), p. 69.
55. *Graham's Magazine* 38 (June 1841): 468.
56. John Caldwell Stubbs, *The Pursuit of Form: a Study of Hawthorne and the Romance* (University of Illinois Press, 1970), p. 114.
57. Ibid., p. 136.
58. "Dickens and Hawthorne", p. 272.
59. *Nathaniel Hawthorne: A Reference Bibliography 1900-1971*, compiled by Beatrice Ricks, Joseph D. Adams, Jack O. Hazlerig (Boston, 1971), p. 270.
60. *English Studies* 47 (1966): 286-89.
61. *Dickens Studies* 2 (1966): 18-25.
62. "The Black Veil", *English Studies* p. 286.
63. Elizabeth Lathrop Chandler, *A Study of the Sources of the Tales and Romances written by Nathaniel Hawthorne before 1853*, Smith College Studies in Modern Languages, vol. VIII, no. 4 (July 1926), pp. 14, 28.
64. See *The Letters of Charles Dickens, Vol. I 1820-1839*, eds. Madeline House and Graham Storey (London, Mass. 1965), pp. n83, n98, 112.
65. "The Black Veil", 286-87.

66. Ibid., 288–289.
67. "Hawthornesque Dickens", p. 18.
68. Ibid., p. 18.
69. Ibid., p. 19.
70. Ibid., p. 19.
71. Ibid., pp. 20–21.
72. Ibid., p. 21.
73. Ibid., p. 23.
74. Ibid., pp. 24–25.
75. Ibid., p. 25.
76. Edwin M. Eigner, however, suggests that the quoted passage (which he accurately interprets as meaning that "romance transforms the meaningless ordinary world into cold allegory and then renders it back as palpitating and significant life") may have had a source in Dickens.

> Returning to the problem of romantic setting, I think it is possible that the two writers may have been thinking similarly when Dickens wrote *The Old Curiosity Shop* and Hawthorne, shortly before beginning *The House of the Seven Gables*, composed "The Custom House". Both works of Hawthorne speak of the power of evening and its illuminations to transfigure the actual world and make it a fit theater for romance. . . . My suggestion is that Hawthorne's idea about the power of imperfect illumination is rather like a thought developed near the beginning of *The Old Curiosity Shop* where Master Humphrey justifies his nighttime rambles. . . . The Dickensian process of spiritualizing the real world by night-light distortions may have come consciously to Hawthorne's mind while he was writing 'The Custom House', but it is certainly not necessary to insist on the specific influence (*The Metaphysical Novel in England and America*, pp. 150–51).

Even if Eigner's suggestion is correct, it seems to me likely that Hawthorne's far fuller development of the idea "of a neutral territory, somewhere between the real world and fairy-land, where the Actual and Imaginary may meet, and each imbue itself with the nature of the other," and his postulation through the metaphors of moon-light and fire-light (in Eigner's words, p. 152) "not only that the allegory must be warmed to the semblance of reality but that it should have been abstracted in the first place from the everyday world", had far more influence on Dickens' use of setting in the later novels than Dickens' rather perfunctory and conventional comment in *The Old Curiosity Shop* (". . . night is kinder in this respect than day, which too often destroys an air-built castle at the moment of its completion. . . .") had on Hawthorne.
77. *Dickens the Novelist*, p. 165.
78. *Charles Dickens, His Tragedy and Triumph*, II (London, 1953), p. 766.
79. The only attempt that I have seen to explain Tulkinghorn's name does not seem very convincing: Tulkinghorn is "the perfect emblem of impersonal devotion to family and lineage (his name suggestive of some heraldic piece of medieval weaponry) and devastatingly vicious because his devotion is so unswerving." John Lucas, *The Melancholy Man. A Study of Dickens' Novels* (London, 1970), p. 231.
80. William Bysshe Stein, *Hawthorne's Faust* (Gainesville, 1953), p. 106.
81. Hugh N. Maclean, "Hawthorne's *Scarlet Letter*: 'The Dark Problem of This Life' ", *American Literature* 27 (March 1955): 14.
82. *Hawthorne's Faust*, p. 106.
83. "The Devil in Boston", *Philological Quarterly* 32 (October 1963): 370.
84. Joseph I. Fradin, "Will and Society in *Bleak House*", *PMLA* 81 (March 1966): 103.

85. Eugene F. Quirk, "Tulkinghorn's Buried Life: A Study of Character in *Bleak House*", *JEGP* 72 (1973): 528.
86. "The Devil in Boston", p. 368.
87. "Will and Society in *Bleak House*", 103.
88. *American Renaissance* (New York, 1941), p. 276.
89. *The Dickens Theatre* (Oxford, 1965), pp. 57–58.
90. "Tulkinghorn's Buried Life", p. 534.
91. "*Bleak House* and *The Scarlet Letter*", p. 188.
92. "Esther Summerson Rehabilitated", *PMLA* 88 (May 1973): 433.
93. *Hawthorne, A Critical Study* (Cambridge, Mass., 1955), p. 138.
94. "Esther's Nicknames: A Study in Relevance", *The Dickensian* 62 (1966): 159.
95. Ibid., p. 158.
96. Osbert Sitwell, "Introduction" to *Bleak House*, New Oxford Illustrated Dickens (Oxford University Press, 1948), p. viii.
97. "The Trouble with Esther", *Modern Language Quarterly* 26 (1965): 545–46, 547.
98. Virginia Ogden Birdsall, "Hawthorne's Fair-Haired Maidens: The Fading Light", *PMLA* 75 (June 1960): 251.
99. A.E. Dyson, *The Inimitable Dickens* (London, 1970), pp. 176, 154, 175.
100. "Esther's Nicknames", p. 159.
101. *The Death of the Artist: A Study of Hawthorne's Disintegration* (The Hague, 1955), p. 66.
102. "Esther's Nicknames", p. 160.
103. Ibid., p. 161.
104. "*The House of the Seven Gables*: The Religion of Love", *Nineteenth Century Fiction* 16 (December 1961): 196–99.
105. "Modern Novelists — Great and Small", p. 563.
106. *Independent* 41 (26 September 1889): 1238; (*Adventures among Books*, p. 220).
107. "Satire and Symbolism in *Bleak House*", *Nineteenth Century Fiction* 12 (1958): 297.
108. Ibid., p. 298.
109. "Hawthorne's House of Seven Gables: a Prototype of the Human Mind", *Literature and Psychology* 17 (1967): 204.
110. *Dickens the Novelist*, p. 149.
111. Ibid., p. 152.
112. "Nathaniel Hawthorne", *The Dublin University Magazine* (October 1855): 465.
113. "Nathaniel Hawthorne", *Universal Review* 3 (June 1860): 761.
114. *Nathaniel Hawthorne* (Boston and New York, 1902), p. 214.
115. Quoted in *Hard Times*, Norton Critical Edition, eds. George Ford and Sylvere Monod (New York, 1966), p. 273.
116. Ibid., p. 239.
117. Ibid., p. 232.
118. Ibid., p. 274.
119. Ibid., p. 275.
120. *The Great Tradition* (London, 1948), p. 227. In *Dickens the Novelist*, the sentence was revised to read (p. 187): "Yet if I am right, of all Dickens's works it is the one that, having the distinctive strength that makes him a major artist, has it in so compact a way, and with a concentrated significance so immediately clear and penetrating, as, one would have thought, to preclude the reader's failing to recognize that he had before him a completely serious, and, in its originality, a triumphantly successful, work of art."
121. Ibid., pp. 227–28. In *Dickens the Novelist*, the sentence was revised to read (p. 188) ". . . free of anything that might be seen as redundance."
122. Ibid., p. 234.

123.   "The Status of *Hard Times*", *Southerly* 9 (1948): 35.
124.   Ibid., p. 39.
125.   "Charles Dickens; a Haunting", *Critical Quarterly* II (1960): 102.
126.   *Hard Times*, Norton Critical Edition, p. 277.
127.   Ibid., p. 273.
128.   *Language of Fiction* (London and New York, 1966), p. 145.
129.   *Hard Times*, Norton Critical Edition, p. 232.
130.   "Fettered Fancy in *Hard Times*", *PMLA* 84 (1969): 520.
131.   Ibid., p. 520.
132.   Ibid., p. 526.
133.   *The Great Tradition*, pp. 230–31.
134.   Ibid., p. 236; in *Dickens the Novelist* (p. 196) revised to "convincing enough as one reads."
135.   "*Hard Times*, a Further Note", *Dickens Studies* 1 (1965): 95.
136.   "*Hard Times* and F.R. Leavis", *Criticism* 6 (1964): 12.
137.   " 'Head', 'Heart', and 'Will' in Hawthorne's Psychology", *Nineteenth Century Fiction* 10 (1955): 131.
138.   "*Hard Times* and F.R. Leavis", p. 14.
139.   Quoted in *The Scarlet Letter*, Norton Critical Edition, eds. Scully Bradley, Richmond Croom Beatty, and E. Hudson Long (New York, 1961), p. 190.
140.   *American Renaissance*, p. 345.
141.   *Charles Dickens: Little Dorrit* (London, 1967), p. 28.
142.   Ibid., p. 26.
143.   "Introduction", *Charles Dickens: Little Dorrit*, ed. John Holloway (Penguin Books, Harmondsworth, 1967), p. 22.
144.   *The Melancholy Man*, p. 258.
145.   Ibid., p. 287.
146.   *A Reader's Guide to Charles Dickens* (London, 1972), p. 217.
147.   Ibid., p. 218.
148.   Ibid., see pp. 19–20.
149.   *Dickens the Novelist*, p. 292.
150.   Ibid., p. 292n.
151.   G. Robert Stange, "Expectations Well Lost: Dickens' Fable for His Time", *College English* 16 (1954): 11.
152.   *The Melancholy Man*, p. 303.
153.   See pp. 27–28.
154.   *American Renaissance*, p. 332.
155.   *Charles Dickens, A Critical Introduction*, rev. ed. (London, 1965), pp. 231–32.
156.   "*The House of the Seven Gables*: New Light on Old Problems", *PMLA*, 82 (1967): 586.
157.   "Image and Structure in *Our Mutual Friend*", *Essays and Studies* 19 (1966): 102.
158.   *American Renaissance*, pp. 332–33.
159.   "Charles Dickens", *Critical Essays* (London, 1946), p. 43.
160.   Review of *Our Mutual Friend*, *Nation* 1 (1865); rpt. in *The Dickens Critics*, eds. George H. Ford and Lauriat Lane, Jr. (Ithaca, 1961), p. 52.
161.   *A Reader's Guide to Charles Dickens*, p. 263.
162.   *Charles Dickens: Little Dorrit*, p. 16.

Part II

1.   "My Hawthorne Experience", *Critic* (July 1904): 23.
2.   *Life of Nathaniel Hawthorne* (New York, 1890), p. 194n.

3. *The Heart of Hawthorne's Journals*, ed. Newton Arvin (Boston, 1929), pp. 328–29.
4. *The George Eliot Letters*, ed. Gordon S. Haight (New Haven and London, 1954–56), II, p. 52.
5. *Letters*, II, pp. 55–56.
6. "George Eliot on the *Blithedale Romance*", *Boston Public Library Quarterly* 7 (October 1955): 207.
7. Ibid., p. 207.
8. *Review of English Studies*, N.S. 7 (April 1956): 164–72.
9. *Nathaniel Hawthorne: Man and Writer* (New York, 1961), pp. 60–61.
10. *Letters*, II, pp. 55–56n.
11. *The Victorian Newsletter* Number 10 (Autumn 1956): 1–3.
12. *PMLA* 70 (December 1955), 997–1013.
13. "George Eliot's Theory of Fiction", p. 1.
14. Ibid., p. 2.
15. *Theory of the Novel in England* 1850–1870 (New York and London, 1959), p. 176n.
16. Thomas Pinney, ed., *Essays of George Eliot* (London, 1963), pp. 457–58.
17. *Letters*, II, p. 311n.
18. *Letters*, III, p. 300, 300n.
19. "The Problem of Evil: A Correlative Study in the Novels of Nathaniel Hawthorne and George Eliot", Diss. University of Illinois 1967, p. 13. (See *Letters*, V, p. 367 and 367n. The writer could hardly have been a "schoolgirl"; she was twenty-five.)
20. Ibid., p. 1.
21. Ibid., pp. 13–14.
22. Marshall A. Ledger, "George Eliot and Nathaniel Hawthorne", *Notes and Queries* 11 (June 1964): 225. Ledger, in this brief note, was the first to point out that the *Edinburgh Review* article included the earliest comparison of Hawthorne and George Eliot.
23. *"Adam Bede"*, *Edinburgh Review* 110 (July 1859): 240–241.
24. *Letters*, III, p. 351.
25. *The North British Review* 33 (August–November 1860): 165–85.
26. *"The Scarlet Letter* and *Adam Bede"*, *Victorian Newsletter* 20 (Fall 1961): 18–19. The mistake was corrected by Marshall A. Ledger (see note 22 above).
27. "Imaginative Literature. The Author of *Adam Bede* and Nathaniel Hawthorne", p. 165.
28. Ibid., pp. 180–81.
29. Ibid., p. 183.
30. "Litterature Anglaise", *Revue des Deux Mondes* 90 (1 December 1870): 441–42.
31. "The Problem of Evil", p. 14.
32. *The Atlantic Monthly* 38 (December 1876): 684–94. Reprinted in *A Century of George Eliot Criticism*, ed. Gordon S. Haight (University Paperbacks, London, 1966), pp. 97–112.
33. "Hawthorne", *Western Monthly* 1 (January 1869): 30.
34. *American Literature* (Edinburgh, 1882), p. 339.
35. Ibid., p. 347.
36. *My Literary Passions* (New York, 1895), p. 115.
37. *Impressions and Memories* (1895), p. 74.
38. "Nathaniel Hawthorne's Romances", *Progress* (September 1887): 264.
39. Ibid., p. 265.
40. *"The Scarlet Letter* and Its Successors", *New England Magazine* n.s. 18 (August 1898): 698.

41. *Nathaniel Hawthorne* (Boston and New York, 1902), p. 201.
42. "The Work of Hawthorne", *North American Review* 179 (July 1904): 16; reprinted in *Backgrounds of Literature* (1904).
43. "A Man Under Enchantment", *The Pardoner's Wallet* (London, 1910), p. 536.
44. "Nathaniel Hawthorne's Place in Literature", *Littell's Living Age* 231 (14 December 1901): 722.
45. *The Life and Genius of Nathaniel Hawthorne* (Philadelphia and London, 1906), p. 224.
46. "An Estimate of Hawthorne", *Proceedings on the One Hundredth Anniversary of the Birth of Nathaniel Hawthorne, Essex Institute Historical Collections* 41 (January 1905): 66.
47 *Heroines of Fiction* (London and New York, 1901), II, p. 44.
48. *American Literature 1880-1930* (London, 1932), pp. 6-7.
49. Mario Praz, *The Hero in Eclipse in Victorian Fiction* (London, 1956), pp. 348-49.
50. Ibid., p. 349.
51. "*Adam Bede*", in *Anna Karenina and other Essays* (London and New York, 1967), pp. 51-52.
52. "*The Scarlet Letter* and *Adam Bede*", *The Victorian Newsletter* 20 (Fall 1961): 18-19.
53. See note 19 above.
54. *American and English Fiction in the Nineteenth Century* (Indiana University Press, 1973).
55. "When the Deity Returns: *The Marble Faun* and *Romola*", in *Studies in American Literature in Honor of Robert Dunn Faner, 1906-67, Papers on Language and Literature* 5 (Southern Illinois University, Summer 1969), ed. Robert Partlow, pp. 82-100.
56. "*Silas Marner* as Romance: The Example of Hawthorne", *Nineteenth Century Fiction* 29 (December, 1974): 287-98.
57. *Letters*, II, p. 406.
58. "George Eliot's Theory of Fiction", *University of West Virginia Philological Papers* 9 (1953): 20-32.
59. "The Art of Fiction in George Eliot's Reviews", *Review of English Studies* 7 (1956): 164-172.
60. "George Eliot and the Climate of Realism", *PMLA* 72 (March 1957): 147-64.
61. "The Literary Criticism of George Eliot", *PMLA* 72 (December 1957): 952-61; and *The Theory of the Novel in England 1850-1870* (London, 1961), pp. 40-45, 160-66 and passim.
62. "George Eliot and the Limits of Victorian Realism", *Philologica Pragensia* 6 (1963): 48-59.
63. *George Eliot's Scenes of Clerical Life* (New Haven and London, 1965), chapter 2.
64. "Ruskin and George Eliot's 'Realism' ", *Criticism* 7 (Winter, 1965): 203-16.
65. "The Natural History of German Life", *Westminster Review* 66 (July, 1856): 54; reprinted in *Essays of George Eliot*, ed. Thomas Pinney, pp. 270-71.
66. *George Eliot's Scenes of Clerical Life*, p. 30.
67. *Letters*, IV, pp. 300-301.
68 "Belles Lettres", *Westminster Review* 64 (July 1855): 289-91. Reprinted in *Essays of George Eliot*, pp. 126-29.
69. *The Theory of the Novel in England 1850-1870*, p. 43.
70. "Art and Belles Lettres", *Westminster Review* 65 (April 1856): 626.
71. *George Eliot's Scenes of Clerical Life*, p. 37.
72. "The Natural History of German Life", p. 55; *Essays*, p. 291.
73. "Hawthorne on the Romance: His Prefaces Related and Examined", *Modern Philology* 53 (August, 1955): 23.

74. "The Novels of George Meredith", *The Common Reader: Second Series* (London, 1935): pp. 233–34.

75. "Hawthorne's Theory of Art", *American Literature* 40 (November 1968): 317–18.

76. Quoted by Anthony Trollope, "The Genius of Nathaniel Hawthorne", *North American Review* 129 (September 1879): 205.

77. "Hawthorne's Theory of Art", p. 315.

78. "Hawthorne's 'Familiar Kind of Preface' ", *ELH* (September 1968): 434–35.

79. *Hawthorne* (London, 1879), p. 125.

80. See John Caldwell Stubbs, *The Pursuit of Form: a Study of Hawthorne and the Romance* (University of Illinois Press, 1970), pp. 3–5.

81. *The Anatomy of Criticism* (Princeton University Press, 1957), pp. 304–5.

82. "The Art of Fiction", *Partial Portraits* (London, 1888), p. 376.

83. Quoted by Darrel Mansell Jr., "Ruskin and George Eliot's 'Realism' ", p. 205.

84. Ibid., p. 206.

85. *Letters*, II, p. 362.

86. *The Hero in Eclipse*, p. 343.

87. "Ruskin and George Eliot's 'Realism' ", p. 209.

88. "The Problem of Evil", p. 3.

89. *George Eliot's Scenes of Clerical Life*, p. 84.

90. "Introduction", *George Eliot: Scenes of Clerical Life* (Penguin English Library, Harmondsworth, 1973), pp. 30–31.

91. *La Narrativa di George Eliot* (Bari, 1969), p. 63. More recently David Carroll, in his essay, " 'Janet's Repentance' and the Myth of the Organic", *Nineteenth Century Fiction* 35 (December 1980), has remarked (345) that "Janet's Repentance" recalls [*The Scarlet Letter*] in significant ways.

92. *George Eliot: Her Mind and Her Art* (Cambridge, 1948), p. 102.

93. *Letters*, II, pp. 502–3.

94. *American and English Fiction in the Nineteenth Century*, pp. 60–62.

95. *Hawthorne: A Critical Study* (Cambridge, Mass., 1955), p. 134.

96. "The Problem of Evil", p. 93n.

97. Mark Van Doren, *Hawthorne* (New York, 1950), pp. 147, 151.

98. D.H. Lawrence, *Studies in Classic American Literature* (1923; rpt. New York: Doubleday, 1953), pp. 104–5.

99. Lucy Lockwood Hazard, "Hawthorne: the Reluctant Puritan: the Timid Pioneer", *The Frontier in American Literature* (New York, 1927), p. 38.

100. *The Rebellious Puritan: Portrait of Mr Hawthorne* (New York, 1927), p. 229.

101. *Hawthorne's Faust: A Study of the Devil's Archetype* (Gainesville, 1953), p. 115.

102. "*Daniel Deronda*", *Edinburgh Review* 144 (October 1876): 445.

103. *A Critical Commentary on George Eliot's "Adam Bede"* (London, 1968), p. 27.

104. Ibid., p. 56.

105. "The Novels of George Eliot", *Atlantic Monthly* 18 (October 1866): 487.

106. "*The Scarlet Letter* and *Adam Bede*", p. 19.

107. "The Problem of Evil", p. 83.

108. Ibid., pp. 31–32.

109. "Dickens and Hawthorne", *Essex Institute Historical Collections* 100 (October 1964): 267.

110. "The Problem of Evil", p. 76.

111. *Nathaniel Hawthorne* (New York, 1965), p. 115.

112. Quoted in *The Scarlet Letter*, Norton Critical Edition, pp. 194–95.

113. See note 51.

114. "The Problem of Evil", p. 90.

115. "The Landscape Modes of *The Scarlet Letter*", *Nineteenth Century Fiction* 23 March 1969): 381.
116. "The Problem of Evil", p. 69.
117. "The Landscape Modes of *The Scarlet Letter*", 381.
118. "*Adam Bede* and the *Locus Amoenus*", *Studies in English Literature 1500-1900* 13 (Autumn 1973): 671.
119. See p. 13.
120. "The Problem of Evil", p. 82.
121. See note 52 above.
122. "Toward a Revaluation of George Eliot's *The Mill on the Floss*", *Nineteenth Century Fiction* 11 (June 1956): 20.
123. *Nineteenth Century Fiction* 14 (December 1959): 241–54.
124. Ibid., p. 242.
125. Ibid., p. 254.
126. Ibid., p. 242.
127. *The Great Tradition* (London, 1948), p. 32.
128. "George Eliot and the Romance", p. 243.
129. Ibid., p. 244.
130. Ibid., p. 249.
131. Ibid., p. 252.
132. Arlin Turner, *Nathaniel Hawthorne: an Introduction and Interpretation* (New York, 1961), p. 17.
133. "Hawthorne's Literary Borrowings", *PMLA* 51 (June 1936): 562. Jane Lundblad, in her book, *Nathaniel Hawthorne and the European Literary Tradition* (1947, reissued New York, 1965), devotes a chapter to "Hawthorne and Mme de Stael, in which she claims that "Mme de Stael exercised no small influence on Nathaniel Hawthorne" (p. 150), that Hawthorne's "Zenobia is partly endowed with the charms of Mme de Stael's Corinne" (p. 155), who "impressed [Hawthorne] and lent several features to Zenobia" (p. 156). The most explicit evidence of Mme de Stael's influence is in *The Marble Faun* (chapter 16), where Miriam refers to the Fountain of Trevi as the scene of the interview "between Corinne and Lord Neville, after their separation and temporary estrangement."
134. "Hawthorne's Fair-Haired Maidens: The Fading Light", *PMLA* 75 (June 1960): 254.
135. *Letters*, III, 33.
136. L. Rubin, "River Imagery as a Means of Foreshadowing in *The Mill on the Floss*", *Modern Language Notes* 71 (1956): 19.
137. *Letters*, III, p. 277.
138. See note 56 above.
139. "A Critical Edition of George Eliot's *Silas Marner*", Diss. Yale 1968, p. xxxix.
140. Ibid., pp. xcii-xciii.
141. *George Eliot* (Cambridge University Press, 1970), p. 31.
142. Ibid., p. 42.
143. "*Silas Marner* as Romance", p. 288.
144. *American Literature in Nineteenth Century England* (New York, 1944), p. 141.
145. Ibid., p. 139.
146. 24 March 1860, p. 276.
147. *American Literature in Nineteenth Century England*, p. 139.
148. "*Silas Marner* as Romance", pp. 288–89.
149. Ibid., p. 289.
150. See note 25 above.
151. "*Silas Marner* as Romance", p. 290.

152.   Ibid., p. 292.
152.   Ibid., p. 292.
153.   Ibid., p. 292.
154.   Ibid., pp. 292–93.
155.   Ibid., p. 293.
156.   Ibid., p. 295.
157.   Ibid., p. 295.
158.   *Letters*, III, p. 382.
159.   "*Silas Marner*", in *Critical Essays on George Eliot*, ed. Barbary Hardy (London, 1970), p. 66.
160.   *Letters*, III, p. 427.
161.   "The Theme of Alienation in *Silas Marner*", *Nineteenth Century Fiction* 20 (June 1965): 69.
162.   Ibid., p. 75.
163.   *Letters*, IV, p. 3.
164.   See note 18 above.
165.   See note 38 above.
166.   "When the Deity Returns", p. 98.
167.   See note 49 above.
168.   See note 19 above.
169.   *Letters*, III, p. 295.
170.   "When the Deity Returns", p. 82 n2.
171.   Van Doren, *Hawthorne*, p. 225.
172.   *The Complex Fate* (London, 1952), pp. 44–54.
173.   *The Novels of George Eliot* (New York, 1959), p. 86.
174.   "The Problem of Evil", p. 158.
175.   "When the Deity Returns", p. 88.
176.   Ibid., p. 90.
177.   See pp. 102–3.
178.   "When the Deity Returns", p. 83.
179.   "The Problem of Evil", pp. 150–51.
180.   "When the Deity Returns", p. 83.
181.   Ibid., p. 96.
182.   *La Narrativa di George Eliot*, p. 180.
183.   "George Eliot and Charles Dickens", *Notes and Queries* (6 April 1946): 143.
184.   Ibid., p. 143.
185.   "Felix Holt: Society as Protagonist", *Nineteenth Century Fiction* 17 (December 1962), p. 251.
186.   "George Eliot and Charles Dickens", p. 144.
187.   "The Problem of Evil", p. 98.
188.   Ibid., p. 112.
189.   *Hawthorne: A Critical Study*, p. 182.
190.   "The Problem of Evil", p. 106.
191.   *Letters*, V, 124.
192.   "A Probable Source for Dorothea and Casaubon: Hester and Chillingworth", *English Studies* 58 (1977): 23.
193.   Ibid., pp. 24–25.
194.   *Edmund Spenser and George Eliot: A Critical Excursion* (University of Tasmania, 1963), pp. 5–6.

Bibliography

Anonymous Articles

"Nathaniel Hawthorne." *To-Day: A Boston Literary Journal* 2 (18 September 1852): 177-81.

["Hawthorne's *The Blithedale Romance.*"] *Westminster Review* 58 (October 1852): 592-98.

"Modern Novelists — Great and Small." *Blackwood's Magazine* 77 (May 1855): 562-66.

"Nathaniel Hawthorne." *The Dublin University Magazine* (October 1855): 463-69.

"Nathaniel Hawthorne." *Universal Review* 3 (June 1860): 752-67.

"The Author of *Adam Bede* and Nathaniel Hawthorne." *The North British Review* 33 (August–november 1860): 165-85.

"*Daniel Deronda.*" *Edinburgh Review* 144 (October 1876): 442-70.

Abbott, Anne W. "Hawthorne's Scarlet Letter." *North American Review* 71 (July 1850): 135-48.

Abel, Darrel. "The Devil in Boston." *Philological Quarterly* 32 (October 1963): 366-81.

Adams, C.F. "Hawthorne's Place in Literature." In *Hawthorne Centenary Celebrations at the Wayside.* Boston and New York: 1901.

Allen, M.L. "The Black Veil: Three Versions of a Symbol." *English Studies* 2 (1966): 286-89.

Arac, Jonathan. "The House and the Railroad: *Dombey and Son* and *The House of the Seven Gables.*" *New England Quarterly* 51 (March 1978): 3-22.

Arvin, Newton, Ed. *The Heart of Hawthorne's Journals.* Boston: Houghton Mifflin, 1929.

Axton, William. "Esther's Nicknames: A Study in Relevance." *The Dickensian* 62 (1966): 158-66.

———. "The Trouble with Esther." *Modern Language Quarterley* 26 (1965): 545-57.

Battaglia, Francis Joseph. "*The House of the Seven Gables*: New Light on Old Problems." *PMLA* 82 (1967): 579-90.

Beer, Gillian. *The Romance.* London: Methuen, 1970.

Bennett, Joan. *George Eliot: Her Mind and Her Art*. Cambridge: Cambridge University Press, 1948.

Benson, Eugene. "Poe and Hawthorne." *The Galaxy* 6 (December 1868): 742-48.

Bewley, Marius. *The Complex Fate*. London: Chatto and Windus, 1952.

Bier, Jesse. "Hawthorne and the Romance: His Prefaces Related and Examined." *Modern Philology* 53 (August 1958): 17-24.

Birdsall, Virginia Ogden. "Hawthorne's Fair-Haired Maidens: The Fading Light." *PMLA* 75 (June 1960): 250-56.

Bradfield, Thomas. "The Romances of Nathaniel Hawthorne." *Westminster Review* 142 (August 1894): 203-14.

Browne, Nina E. *A Bibliography of Nathaniel Hawthorne*. Boston and New York: Houghton Mifflin, 1905.

Brownson, Orestes Augustus. "Literary Notes and Criticism." *Boston Quarterly Review* 5 (April 1842): 251-52.

Carroll, David R. "*Felix Holt*: Society as Protagonist." *Nineteenth Century Fiction* 17 (December 1962): 237-52.

_____. " 'Janet's Repentance' and the Myth of the Organic." *Nineteenth Century Fiction* 35 (December 1980): 331-48.

Casey, Weldon. "George Eliot's Theory of Fiction." *University of West Virginia Philosophical Papers* 9 (1953): 20-32.

Casson, Alan. "*The Scarlet Letter* and *Adam Bede*." *The Victorian Newsletter* 20 (Fall 1961): 18-19.

Chandler, Elizabeth Lathrop. *A Study of the Sources of the Tales and Romances written by Hawthorne before 1853*. Smith College Studies in Modern Languages 7, no. 4 (July 1926).

Chase, Richard. *The American Novel and Its Tradition*. New York: Doubleday, 1957.

Chaudhry, Ghulam Ali. "Dickens and Hawthorne." *Essex Institute Historical Collections (Special Hawthorne Issue)* 100 (October 1964): 256-73.

Coleridge, M.E. "The Questionable Shapes of Nathaniel Hawthorne." *Littel's Living Age* 242 (6 August 1904): 348-53.

Collyer, Robert. "Hawthorne." *Western Monthly* 1 (January 1869): 30-34.

Conway, Moncure D. *Life of Nathaniel Hawthorne*. London: Walter Scott, 1890.

Cook, Keningale. "American Novelists III: Nathaniel Hawthorne." *Belgravia* 19 (November 1872): 72-79.

Crompton, Louis. "Satire and Symbolism in *Bleak House*." *Nineteenth Century Fiction* 12 (1958): 284-303.

Crothers, Samuel McChord. "A Man Under Enchantment." In *The Pardoner's Wallet*. London: Constable, 1910.

Cummings, C.A. "Hawthorne." *Christian Examiner* 78 (January 1865): 89-106.

Dahl, Curtis. "When the Deity Returns: *The Marble Fawn* and *Romola*." In *Studies in American Literature in Honor of Robert Dunn Faner, 1906-67*, ed. Robert Partlow. Papers on Language and Literature 5. Southern Illinois University, 1969.

Davidson, Donald. "The Traditional Basis of Hardy's Fiction." In *Hardy: A Collection of Critical Essays*, ed. Albert J. Guerard. Englewood Cliffs, N.J.: Prentice Hall, 1963.

Di Logu, Pietro. *La Narrativa di George Eliot*. Bari: Adriatica, 1969.

Dodds, M.H. "George Eliot and Charles Dickens." *Notes and Queries* (6 April 1946): 143.

Duyckinck, Evert Augustus. "Hawthorne's Twice Told Tales." *Arcturus*, a Journal of Books and Opinion 3 (April 1842): 394.

Dyson, A.E. *The Inimitable Dickens*. London: Macmillan, 1970.

Eigner, Edwin M. *The Metaphysical Novel in England and America: Dickens, Bulwer, Hawthorne, Melville*. Berkeley: University of California Press, 1978.

Etienne, L. "Litterature Anglaise." *Revue des Deux Mondes* 90 (1 December 1870): 427-46.

Faust, Bertha. *Hawthorne's Contemporaneous Reputation*. Philadelphia: University of Pennsylvania, 1939.

Fielding, K.J. *Charles Dickens, A Critical Introduction*. London: Longmans, rev. ed. 1964.

Ford, G.H. *Dickens and His Readers: Aspects of Novel Criticism Since 1836*. Princeton, N.J.: Princeton University Press, 1955.

Ford, G.H. and Lauriatt Lane, eds. *The Dickens Critics*. Ithaca, N.Y.: Cornell University Press, 1961.

Forster, John. *The Life of Charles Dickens*. London: Chapman and Hall, 1876.

Fradin, Joseph I. "Will and Society in *Bleak House*." *PMLA* 81 (March 1966): 95-109.

Frye, Northrop. "The Four Forms of Prose Fiction." *Hudson Review* 2 (Winter 1950): 582-95.

_____. *Anatomy of Criticism: Four Essays*. Princeton, N.J.: Princeton University Press, 1957.

Garis, Robert. *The Dickens Theatre*. Oxford: Clarendon Press, 1965.

Gibson, John W. "*Hard Times*, A Further Note." *Dickens Studies* 1 (1965): 90-101.

Giles, Henry. *Illustrations of Genius*. Boston: 1854.

Gohdes, Clarence. *American Literature in Nineteenth Century England*. New York: Columbia University Press, 1944.

Guerard, Albert J. *The Triumph of the Novel: Dickens, Dostoevsky, Faulkner*. New York: Oxford University Press, 1976.

Gupta, R.K. "Hawthorne's Theory of Art." *American Literature* 40 (November 1968): 309-24.

Haddakin, Lilian. "*Silas Marner.*" In *Critical Essays on George Eliot,* ed. Barbara Hardy. London: Routledge and Kegan Paul, 1970.

Haight, Gordon S., ed. *The George Eliot Letters.* New Haven and London: Yale University Press, 1954-56.

_____. "George Eliot's Theory of Fiction." *The Victorian Newsletter* 10 (Autumn 1956): 1-3.

Hannigan, D.F. "Nathaniel Hawthorne's Place in Literature." *Littel's Living Age* 231 (14 December 1901): 720-24.

Hazard, Lucy Lockwood. *The Frontier in American Literature.* New York: Crowell, 1927.

Hirsch, David H. "*Hard Times* and F.R. Leavis." *Criticism* 6 (1964): 1-16.

Hobsbawn, Philip. *A Reader's Guide to Charles Dickens.* London: Thames and Hudson, 1972.

Holloway, John. "Introduction" *Charles Dickens: "Little Dorrit".* Harmondsworth: Penguin Books, 1967.

Howells, William Dean. *My Literary Passions.* New York: Harper, 1895.

_____. *Heroines of Fiction.* New York: Harper, 1901.

Hyde, William J. "George Eliot and the Climate of Realism." *PMLA* 72 (March 1957): 147-64.

James, Henry. "The Novels of George Eliot." *Atlantic Monthly* 18 (October 1866): 479-92.

_____. "*Daniel Deronda*: A Conversation." *Atlantic Monthly* 38 (December 1876): 684-94.

_____. *Hawthorne.* London: Macmillan, 1879.

_____. "The Art of Fiction." In *Partial Portraits.* London: Macmillan, 1888.

Johnson, Edgar. *Charles Dickens, his Tragedy and Triumph.* London: Gollancz, 1953.

Jones, Buford. *A Checklist of Hawthorne Criticism 1951.1966.* Emerson Society Quarterly 52 Supplement (III Quarter 1968).

Jones, R.T. *A Critical Commentary on George Eliot's "Adam Bede".* London: Macmillan, 1968.

_____. *George Eliot.* Cambridge: Cambridge University Press, 1970.

Junkins, David. "Hawthorne's House of Seven Gables: A Prototype of the Human Mind." *Literature and Psychology* 17 (1967): 193-218.

Kaminsky, Alice R. "George Eliot, George Henry Lewes and the Novel." *PMLA* 70 (December 1955): 997-1013.

Knight, Henry Lionel. "Dickens and American Literature." Diss. Brown University 1972.

Lang, Andrew, "Nathaniel Hawthorne." *Independent* 41 (26 September 1889): 1237-38.

———. *Adventures Among Books*. London: Longmans, 1905.

Laser, Marvin. "'Head', 'Heart', and 'Will' in Hawthorne's Psychology." *Nineteenth Century Fiction* 10 (1955): 130-40.

Lathrop, G.P. "Poe, Irving, and Hawthorne." *Scribner's Monthly* 11 (April 1876): 799-806.

Latimer, George D. "The Tales of Poe and Hawthorne." *New England Magazine* 30 (August 1904): 692-703.

Lawrence, D.H. *Studies in Classic American Literature*. 1923. Reprint. New York: Doubleday, 1953.

Lawton, William Cranston. "*The Scarlet Letter* and Its Successors." *New England Magazine* NS 18 (August 1898): 697-700.

Leavis, F.R. *The Great Tradition: George Eliot, Henry James, Joseph Conrad*. London: Chatto and Windus, 1948.

———. *Anna Karenina and Other Essays*. London: Chatto and Windus, 1967.

Leavis, F.R. and Q.D. *Dickens and Novelist*. London: Chatto and Windus, 1970.

Ledger, Marshall A. "George Eliot and Nathaniel Hawthorne." *Notes and Queries* 1 (June 1964): 225-26.

Levy, Alfred J. "*The House of the Seven Gables*: The Religion of Love." *Nineteenth Century Fiction* 16 (December 1961): 189-203.

Levy, Leo B. "The Landscape Modes of *The Scarlet Letter*." *Nineteenth Century Fiction* 23 (March 1969): 377-92.

Libby, Dorville. "The Supernatural in Hawthorne." *The Overland Monthly* 2 (February 1869): 138-43.

Lodge, David. *Language of Fiction*. London: Routledge and Kegan Paul, 1966.

———. "Introduction" *George Eliot: "Scenes of Clerical Life."* Harmondsworth: Penguin Books, 1973.

Lucas, John. *The Melancholy Man: A Study of Dickens's Novels*. London: Methuen, 1970.

Lundblad, Jane. *Nathaniel Hawthorne and the European Literary Tradition*. 1947. Reprint. New York: Russell and Russell, 1965.

Mabie, Hamilton Wright. "The Worth of Hawthorne." *North American Review* 179 (July 1904): 13-23.

McAuley, James. *Edmund Spenser and George Eliot: A Critical Excursion*. Hobart: University of Tasmania, 1963.

Maclean, Hugh W. "Hawthorne's *Scarlet Letter*: 'The Dark Problem of This Life'." *American Literature* 27 (March 1955): 12-24.

McCall, Dan. "Hawthorne's Familiar Kind of Preface." *ELH* 35 (September 1968): 422-39.

Mansell, Darrell. "Ruskin and George Eliot's 'Realism' ". *Criticism* 7 (Winter 1965): 203-16.

Martin, Terence. *Nathaniel Hawthorne.* New York: Twayne, 1965.

Matthiessen, F.O. *American Renaissance.* New York: Oxford University Press, 1941.

Mayo, A.D. "The Works of Hawthorne." *Universalist Quarterly and General Review* 9 (July 1851): 272-93.

Milner, Ian. "George Eliot and the Limits of Victorian Realism." *Philologica Pragensia* 6 (1963): 48-59.

Mills, Nicolaus. "American Fiction and the Genre Critics." *Novel* 2, no. 2 (Fall 1969): 112-22.

Morris, Lloyd. *The Rebellious Puritan: Portrait of Mr Hawthorne.* New York: Harcourt Brace and World Inc., 1927.

Muir, Kenneth. "Image and Structure in *Our Mutual Friend.*" Essays and Studies 19 (1966): 92-105.

Nicholl, J. *American Literature.* Edinburgh: 1882.

Noble, J.A. *Impressions and Memories.* London: Dent, 1895.

Noble, Thomas A. *George Eliot's Scenes of Clerical Life.* New Haven and London: Yale University Press, 1965.

Norton, Caroline E.S. "*Adam Bede.*" *Edinburgh Review* 110 (July 1859): 232-43.

Orwell, George. "Charles Dickens." In *Critical Essays.* London: Secker and Warburg, 1946.

Paris, Bernard. "Toward a Revaluation of George Eliot's *The Mill on the Floss.*" *Nineteenth Century Fiction* 11 (June 1956): 18-31.

Passerini, Edward M. "Hawthornesque Dickens." *Dickens Studies* 2 (1966): 18-25.

Pinney, Thomas, ed. *Essays of George Eliot.* London: Routledge and Kegan Paul, 1963.

Praz, Mario. *The Hero in Eclipse in Victorian Fiction.* Translated by Angus Davidson. London: Oxford University Press, 1956.

Quick, Jonathan R. "A Critical Edition of George Eliot's *Silas Marner.*" Diss. Yale, 1968.

_____. "*Silas Marner* as Romance: The Example of Hawthorne." *Nineteenth Century Fiction* 29 (December 1974): 187-98.

Quirk, Eugene F. "Tulkinghorn's Buried life: A Study of Character in *Bleak House.*" *JEGP* 72 (1973): 526-35.

Reid, J.C. *Charles Dickens: Little Dorrit.* London: Edward Arnold, 1967.

Ricks, Beatrice; Adams, Joseph D.; Hazlerig, Jack O. *Nathaniel Hawthorne: A Reference Bibliography.* Boston: G.K. Hall, 1972.

Ringler, Ellin Jane. "The Problem of Evil: A Correlative Study in the Novels of Nathaniel Hawthorne and George Eliot." Diss. University of Illinois, 1967.

Rubin, L. "River Imagery as a Means of Foreshadowing in *The Mill on the Floss*." *Modern Language Notes* 71 (1956): 18-22.

Rust, James D. "George Eliot on the *Blithedale Romance*." *Boston Public Library Quarterly* 7 (October 1955): 207-15.

——. "The Art of Fiction in George Eliot's Reviews." *Review of English Studies* NS 7 (April 1956): 164-72.

Salt, H.S. "Nathaniel Hawthorne's Romances." *Progress* (September 1887): 262-69.

Schonbach, Anton E. "An Estimate of Hawthorne." In *Proceedings on the One Hundredth Anniversary of the Birth of Nathaniel Hawthorne. Essex Institute Historical Collections* 41 (January 1905).

Siogvolk, Paul. "Schediasns." *The Knickerbocker* 40 (November 1852): 381-85.

Sitwell, Osbert. "Introduction" *Bleak House* (New Oxford Illustrated Dickens). Oxford: Oxford University Press, 1948.

Smith, Grahame. *Dickens, Money and Society*. Berkeley and Los Angeles: University of California Press, 1968.

Sonstroem, David. "Fettered Fancy in *Hard Times*." *PMLA* 84 (1969): 520-29.

Squires, Michael. "*Adam Bede* and the *Locus Amoenus*." *Studies in English Literature 1500–1900* (Autumn 1973): 670-76.

Stang, Richard. *Theory of the Novel in England 1850-70*. London: Routledge and Kegan Paul, 1959.

——. "The Literary Criticism of George Eliot." *PMLA* 72 (December 1972): 952-61.

Stange, G. Robert. "Expectations Well Lost: Dickens' Fable for his Time." *College English* 16 (1954): 9-17.

Stearns, F.P. *The Life and Genius of Nathaniel Hawthorne*. Philadelphia and London: Lippincott, 1906.

Stein, William Bysshe. *Hawthorne's Faust*. Gainesville: University of Florida Press, 1953.

Stewart, Randall. *Nathaniel Hawthorne: A Biography*. New Haven: Yale University Press, 1948.

Stokes, Edward. "*Bleak House* and *The Scarlet Letter*." *AUMLA* 32 (November 1969): 177-89.

Stubbs, John Caldwell. *The Pursuit of Form: A Study of Hawthorne and the Romance*. Urbana: University of Illinois Press, 1970.

Thale, Jerome. *The Novels of George Eliot*. New York: Columbia University Press, 1959.

Thayer, W.R. Letter. *Proceedings on the One Hundredth Anniversary of the Birth of Nathaniel Hawthorne. Essex Institute Historical Collections* 41 (January 1905).

Thompson, Fred C. "The Theme of Alienation in *Silas Marner*." *Nineteenth Century Fiction* 20 (June 1965): 69-84.

Thompson, Maurice. "Studies of Prominent Novelists: No. 5 — Nathaniel Hawthorne." *Book News* 6 (February 1888): 261-62.

Tuckerman, Henry T. "Nathaniel Hawthorne." *Southern Literary Messenger* 17 (June 1851): 344-49.

_____. *Mental Portraits*. London: Richard Bentley, 1853.

Turner, Arlin. "Hawthorne's Literary Borrowings." *PMLA* 51 (June 1936): 543-62.

Van Doren, Mark. *Nathaniel Hawthorne: A Critical Biography*. New York: William Sloane Associates, 1949.

Von Abele, Rudolph. *The Death of the Artist: A Study of Hawthorne's Disintegration*. The Hague: Martinus Nijhoff, 1955.

Wagenknecht, Edward. *Nathaniel Hawthorne: Man and Writer*. New York: Oxford University Press, 1961.

Waggoner, H.H. *Hawthorne, A Critical Study*. Cambridge, Mass.: Harvard University Press, 1955.

Waldock, A.J.A. "The Status of *Hard Times*." *Southerly* 9 (1948): 33-39.

Wallace, Robert K. "A Probable Source for Dorothea and Casaubon: Hester and Chillingworth." *English Studies* 58 (1977): 23-25.

Ward, A.C. *American Literature 1880.1930*. London: Methuen, 1932.

Welsh, Alexander. "George Eliot and the Romance." *Nineteenth Century Fiction* 14 (December 1959): 241-54.

Whipple, E.P. "*The House of the Seven Gables*." Graham's Magazine 38 (June 1851): 467-68.

Wilson, Angus. "Charles Dickens; a Haunting." *Critical Quarterly* 2 (1960): 101-8.

Woodberry, G.E. *Nathaniel Hawthorne*. Boston and New York: Houghton Mifflin, 1902.

Woolf, Virginia. "The Novels of George Meredith." *The Common Reader: Second Series*. London: Hogarth Press, 1935.

Zwerdling, Alex. "Esther Summerson Rehabilitated." *PMLA* 88 (May 1973): 429-39.

Index